Learning Latin the Ancient

What did Greek speakers in the Roman empire do when they wanted to learn Latin? They used Latin-learning materials containing authentic, enjoyable vignettes about daily life in the ancient world – shopping, banking, going to the baths, having fights, being scolded, making excuses – very much like the dialogues in some of today's foreign-language textbooks. These stories provide priceless insight into daily life in the Roman empire, as well as into how Latin was learned at that period, and they were all written by Romans in Latin that was designed to be easy for beginners to understand. Learners also used special beginners' versions of great Latin authors including Virgil and Cicero, and dictionaries, grammars, texts in Greek transliteration, etc. All these materials are now available for the first time to today's students, in a book designed to complement modern textbooks and enrich the Latin-learning experience.

ELEANOR DICKEY has taught in Canada and the United States, and is currently Professor of Classics at the University of Reading. She is a Fellow of the British Academy and of the Academia Europaea and has published widely on the Latin and Greek languages and how they were studied in antiquity, including *Greek Forms of Address* (1996), *Latin Forms of Address* (2002), *Ancient Greek Scholarship* (2007), and *The Colloquia of the Hermeneumata Pseudodositheana* (2012–15). She is a dedicated and passionate language teacher with extensive experience of teaching both Latin and Greek at all levels, in French as well as in English, and has brought this experience to bear on her adaptations of the ancient Latin-learning materials for modern students.

καλλιστα	optima	αδριανοσ, ειπεν	Adrianus dixit·
αλλα κεφαλαια	sed capitula	που θελισ	ubi uis
των ονοματων	nominum	στρατευ εσθαι	militare
και ρηματων	et uerborum	εκεινου λεγοντοσ	illo dicente
ωσ εκαστοι	unius cuiusq;	εισ το πραιτωριων	in pretorio;
ταυτα, εσονται	hae erunt	αδριανοσ σεζητασε	Adrianus interrogauit·
θεου αδριανου	diui adriani	ποιον μηκοσ εχει	qua statura habet
αποφασεισ	sententiae	πεντε, ποδεσ	quinque pedes
και επιστολασ	et epistolae	και ημισυ	et semis·
εξων μιζων	exquib; maior	αδριανοσ, ειπεν	Adrianus dixit·
ευχρηστια	utilitas	εντο σουτω	interim
ακολουθει	sequitur	εισ την πολιτικη	in urbanam
ανθρωποισ	omnibus	στρατευου	milita
αποτουτου	abeo	και εαν καλοσ	et si bonus
του αρχοντοσ	principi	στρατιωτησ εση	miles fueris
στε νετο	fuit	τριτω, οψωνιω	tertio stipendio
και αλλιοτησ	et loquella	δυνηση	poteris
διο	propter ea	εισ το πραιτωριο	in pretorium
αναγκαιωσ εισιν	necessario sunt	μεταβηναι	transire
αναγνωστα ια	legenda	δι επιστολιδιου	per libellum
και μνημη	et memoriae	λιτουντοσ, τινοσ	petente quoda
παραδοτα ια	tradenda	ινα τον ιδιον	ut suum
ευμεντοι θελωμεν·	sitani uolumus	απελευθερον	libertum
ρωμαιστι λαλειν·	latina eloquia	απολε σε	perderet
η ελληνιστι	uel grecae	ον προχρονοι	que ante tempus
χωρισ αιτιασ	sine uitio	κελευσι επαρχου	iussa praefecti
ουτωσ αρξωμεθα	sic incipiamus	γαζοφυλακιον	aerarii
αιτωντοσ τινοσ	petente quo dam	κατα νομον	secundum legem
ινα στρατευ ηται	ut militares;	αιλιου, σεντιον	aelia sententia

Frontispiece Judgements of Hadrian (see passage 2.4) in the ninth-century manuscript Vossianus Gr. Q. 7, folio 18r. Printed by kind permission of Leiden University Library.

Learning Latin the Ancient Way

Latin textbooks from the ancient world

ELEANOR DICKEY

CAMBRIDGE
UNIVERSITY PRESS

CAMBRIDGE
UNIVERSITY PRESS

University Printing House, Cambridge CB2 8BS, United Kingdom

Cambridge University Press is part of the University of Cambridge.

It furthers the University's mission by disseminating knowledge in the pursuit of
education, learning and research at the highest international levels of excellence.

www.cambridge.org
Information on this title: www.cambridge.org/9781107474574

First published 2016
Reprinted 2016
3rd printing 2016

Printed in the United States of America by Sheridan Books, Inc.

A catalogue record for this publication is available from the British Library

Library of Congress Cataloguing in Publication data
Dickey, Eleanor, author.
Learning Latin the ancient way : Latin textbooks from the ancient world / Eleanor Dickey.
    pages   cm
Includes bibliographical references and index.
ISBN 978-1-107-09360-7 (hardback)
1. Latin language – Terms and phrases – Early works to 1800.   2. Latin language – Spoken
Latin – Early works to 1800.   3. Latin language – Textbooks – Early works to 1800.
I. Title.   II. Title: Latin textbooks from the ancient world.
PA2389.D53   2015
478.2421 – dc23   2015012671

ISBN 978-1-107-09360-7 Hardback
ISBN 978-1-107-47457-4 Paperback

This book is dedicated to all the people who originally created the ancient Latin-learning materials, hundreds of individual language teachers most of whose names have long been forgotten but whose work has lasted far longer than they ever expected.

Contents

Figures

Preface

Learning Latin is one of the key experiences of the modern Classicist; nearly all of us have done it ourselves, and many of us spend much of our time helping the next generation do it. Yet most of us know almost nothing about how our experience of this crucial activity relates to the ancient one; indeed many Classicists are unaware that Latin learning was common in antiquity and that many of the materials used for that purpose have survived. This lack of awareness limits opportunities not only to compare our experience with the ancient one, but also to exploit the ancient Latin-learning materials, many of which are still useful and enjoyable today.

This book aims to show modern Latin teachers and Latin students how ancient Latin learning was conducted, by making the ancient materials accessible to modern readers in a format that allows them to be used as they were originally intended to be used. It is not a Latin textbook and cannot be used by itself to learn Latin (among other reasons, because it includes only a selection of the ancient materials and so omits a significant amount of vital information); rather it is designed to complement a textbook and/or to be used by those who have already mastered the basics. It is not cumulative: the pieces it contains can be read in any order.

Since some aspects of ancient education are alien to modern practice, teachers may actually prefer to use the ancient materials in ways that no ancient teacher ever used them, for example by asking students to translate texts that in antiquity would have been memorized rather than translated. In doing so they will have my blessing; I myself use the ancient materials inauthentically in teaching, because there are good reasons why we no longer use certain ancient methods. But inauthentic use of the ancient materials is best carried out in full awareness of how those materials were originally designed to be used, and for that reason every effort has been made to make clear what the original function of the various materials was. I hope this book will be a tool usable in a wide variety of different ways by people whose own creativity is limited neither by my intentions nor by those of the ancient authors of these texts.

Many people have helped with the creation of this book. Philomen Probert, Martin West, CUP's sharp-eyed anonymous readers, Holly Eckhardt, Mark Pitter, Cathy Bothwell, and pupils at Manchester Grammar School provided valuable feedback on a draft of the book. Rolando Ferri introduced me to these texts in the first place and helped me to understand them, Philomen Probert offered constant support and encouragement,

Maria Chiara Scappaticcio shared her forthcoming work with me, and Jane Gardner helped me understand the treatise on manumission. Generous funding from the Leverhulme Trust provided time to write the book. Iveta Adams, Christina Sarigiannidou, Fran Hiller, and Michael Sharp ran the fastest and least painful publication process I have ever experienced. Any mistakes that remain are my own.

1 | Introduction

When we think of Latin learning in antiquity, we tend to picture little Roman children learning the language from their parents (or, more likely, their nurses and *paedagogi*). Such a vision makes the gap between the ancient Latin-learning experience and the modern one seem unbridgeable, for there is bound to be a vast difference between the experience of a language's native speakers and that of people who learn it as a foreign language. But learners of Latin as a foreign language also existed in the ancient world, and their experience is in some ways very close to our own: they learned declensions and conjugations, memorized vocabulary, used dictionaries and commentaries, and read Cicero's *Catilinarians* and Virgil's *Aeneid*, for example. In other ways, however, the experience of ancient Latin students was very different from ours, and in order to understand the differences it is crucial to know who the ancient Latin learners were: for example, since many of them were native speakers of Greek, they often struggled with the Roman alphabet but had no trouble with concepts like gender and declension.

1.1 Who learned Latin in antiquity?

The Roman empire had two main parts: the Western empire, where the main language was Latin, and the Eastern empire, where the main language was Greek. In both halves numerous other languages were also spoken at the time the Romans arrived, but as the centuries passed those other languages often died out. In the West, for example, the original languages of Italy, Gaul, and Spain had largely disappeared by the end of the Roman empire, as the inhabitants of those regions shifted to using Latin; that is why people in those countries now speak Romance languages descended from Latin. Such a language shift implies some foreign-language learning, but not necessarily sustained foreign-language learning: as soon as the inhabitants of the Western empire started speaking to their children in Latin rather than (or even in addition to) Gaulish, Etruscan, etc., those children grew up as native speakers of Latin and had no need to learn it as a foreign language. The fact that we have no Latin-learning materials from the West could be due to a relatively short period of foreign-language Latin learning, but it could also be an accident of preservation, since comparatively few non-literary texts survive from the ancient West in any case.

In the East the situation was different: although the native languages had a tendency to die out there too, their speakers shifted to Greek rather than to Latin. Indeed, although Westerners living temporarily in the East no doubt taught their children Latin, we have no evidence that native speakers of Greek or other Eastern languages ever thought it sensible to raise their children as Latin speakers. The result was that whenever Easterners learned Latin, they learned it as a foreign language.

Much of the Greek-speaking world was under the domination of Latin speakers from the second century BC until the late sixth century AD, when contact with the West was largely cut off and the highest levels of administration in the East shifted completely to Greek. That is a very long period of contact, and the relationship between Latin and Greek changed considerably during those centuries. In the early centuries of this period the linguistic relationship was also different in different parts of the East, some of which were conquered by the Romans earlier than others. Greeks, that is people who lived in Greece itself and whose ancestors had lived there during the Classical period, were confident in their linguistic and cultural superiority and remained uninterested in learning Latin for several centuries after the Roman conquest. Greek speakers in other parts of the East, however, had a different attitude: often their ancestors had learned Greek relatively recently because of the social and economic benefits attached to doing so, and they in turn were perfectly happy to learn Latin if it would benefit them. As time went on and the position of the Greek language was strengthened in the East, these Greek speakers outside Greece came to greatly outnumber the Greek speakers in Greece, and their attitudes predominated; eventually even the Greek speakers in Greece wanted to learn Latin when it was in their interests to do so.

One of the benefits of learning Latin was improved interaction with the Roman army. Officially the language of the army was Latin; though in practice members of Eastern units normally spoke Greek to one another, knowledge of Latin was still useful in the army. Latin was also useful for people who had dealings with the army, for example merchants wanting to sell produce to an army base: such transactions could be performed in Greek and no doubt often were, but knowledge of Latin could give a merchant a valuable competitive edge. We have some Latin-learning materials clearly connected with the army (e.g. passage 7.3) and others, such as manuals designed to impart basic Latin conversation skills (e.g. 8.10), that may have been intended for dealing with the army but would also have been useful for interacting with other Latin-speaking travelers in the East.

Another reason for learning Latin was a desire to practice Roman law. In theory all aspects of Roman law were conducted entirely in Latin, both in writing (the will of a Roman citizen was not valid unless it was written in Latin) and in speech (court cases were supposed to be conducted in Latin). In practice the adherence to Latin was less rigid in parts of the empire where the main language was Greek; we have transcripts of court proceedings in which Latin was used only for set procedural formulae and Greek was used for the actual arguments, and the wills of Greek-speaking Roman citizens might be written in Greek and then provided with a Latin translation (which might never be used by anyone, if neither the testator nor the heirs knew Latin) to make them valid. Even taking this flexibility into account, however, knowledge of Latin was highly desirable for aspiring lawyers, and law schools were obliged to provide instruction in it if they wanted to keep their students; we have a lament of Libanius complaining that people were no longer interested in studying traditional rhetoric at his school because they wanted to learn Latin.[1] Some Latin-learning texts are likely to have been designed specifically for law students (see passages 2.1.14–15).

Travel to the West must have been another reason for learning Latin, but we have surprisingly little hard evidence of this motivation. The surviving Latin-learning materials offer very little in the way of targeted help for the traveler. Staying in inns, eating out, and seafaring (or indeed any type of travel more complicated than riding a horse) are all conspicuously absent from the extant materials. Since many Westerners knew Greek, Greek speakers may have felt that there was no need to learn Latin before traveling to the West.

Greek speakers' Latin learning was largely a utilitarian enterprise; there is little evidence of Latin learning for the sake of experiencing Latin literature at first hand, and (until a very late period) knowledge of Latin conveyed no social cachet in the East. For this reason Greek speakers who learned Latin did not do so as schoolchildren, the way Latin speakers learned Greek. The parents of Roman children could be confident that knowing Greek would be beneficial to them whatever their future professions, because knowledge of Greek was part of the definition of an educated, civilized Roman; therefore it made sense for Roman parents to ensure that their children learned Greek at the earliest opportunity. But since the parents of Greek-speaking children had no such assurances about the value of learning Latin, Greek speakers who learned Latin normally did so as young adults, when they were training for specific professions and recognized that they needed the language.

At the very end of antiquity Latin lost its utility in Byzantium; with the fall of the Western empire the Latin-speaking army ceased to exist and the flow of merchants and travelers between East and West largely dried up. In the sixth century the immensely complex body of texts on which Roman law was based were codified into finite works on which Greek commentaries (and, in some cases, translations) were immediately produced, and knowledge of Latin became less useful for lawyers. Ultimately, of course, this loss of utility meant the loss of the language; the Byzantine court was entirely Greek-speaking, and none of the Latin-learning texts that must have existed in sixth-century Byzantium were copied enough to survive via the Byzantine manuscript tradition. But at the same time Latin suddenly developed the social cachet that it had lacked for so many centuries, and the imperial court used fossilized Latin phrases (often written

---

[1] *Oration* 43.4–5; cf. Rochette (1997: 133–4).

out in Greek script, as knowledge of the Latin alphabet had been lost) for its grand ceremonials.[2]

1.2   How did ancient students learn Latin?

The educational environment in which Latin learning took place is difficult to recover, because most Latin learning did not take place in the one educational setting about which we are reasonably well informed, the ancient school.[3] Some evidently took place in law schools and some in army camps, but almost certainly some Latin learning occurred outside any formal educational context. What we know, therefore, comes from the materials themselves. Most Latin learners started by learning the alphabet (see section 6), with which they appear to have had considerable difficulty. They then read easy-reader texts designed for beginners (see section 2), in which the Latin was divided into narrow columns one to three words wide and accompanied by a Greek translation that matched line for line.[4] Such a translation enabled the ancient learner to understand both what the individual words meant (as with our interlinear translations) and what the sentence as a whole meant (as with our facing-page translations). Of course, once such a translation was provided the students could not be asked to engage with the Latin by translating it; rather they memorized the Latin, using the translation to make sure they understood it. This procedure is not dissimilar to that sometimes used in modern-language teaching today, where students memorize a dialogue concerning some activity that they are likely to participate in once they start using the language. Thus a modern student learning French might memorize a dialogue in which a character goes to a café in Paris and orders a sandwich, and the ancient student learning Latin would memorize one in which a character goes to the baths in Rome and gets someone to watch his clothes while he swims. Many bilingual texts were written specifically for language learners; these are known as "colloquia," because much of their content (though not all of it) is in dialogue form (see sections 2.1, 7.1, 8.1–2, and 8.10).

   This bilingual format was used not only for the colloquia, but also for any other works that students read early in their studies. These included stories about the Trojan War (passages 2.2, 8.3, and 9.2), Aesop's fables (2.3 and 8.4), philosophical maxims,[5]

---

[2]   For more information on the knowlege and use of Latin in the Eastern empire see Rochette (1997), Adams (2003a), and Dickey (2012–15: I.4–15).

[3]   For ancient education see e.g. Cribiore (1996, 2001), Morgan (1998), Bonner (1977), Russell (2001), Joyal *et al.* (2009), Derda *et al.* (2007), and Bloomer (2011).

[4]   For more information on this translation system and its history, see Dickey (2015b).

[5]   These are not included in this book because they are now too mutilated to make good reading material; for an overview of what survives see Dickey (2012–15: I.25–7).

mythography (9.1), legal texts (2.4, 2.5, 8.5, 8.6), early books of Virgil's *Aeneid* (2.6 and 8.8) and Cicero's *Catilinarians* (8.7).

Latin students also learned grammatical paradigms and read explanations of syntax (see sections 3, 7.2, 8.11–13, and 9.3). The ancient world had a convention that grammatical works were composed in the language under discussion; therefore grammars of Greek were written in Greek and grammars of Latin in Latin, regardless of who the intended audience was. Some Latin grammatical texts, such as that of Charisius, were clearly aimed at learners with little knowledge of Latin, and yet it would have required considerable knowledge of Latin to read them. Exactly how Charisius expected his work to be used is a debated point, but I think it likely that teachers provided an oral Greek translation for their students (who probably also memorized Charisius' original Latin). One grammarian, Dositheus, appears to have become exasperated by the inevitable failure of students to understand the Latin grammars, for he provided part of his work with a running Greek translation in the same format as the colloquia.

Once students had learned enough Latin to read texts without a translation, they were presented with monolingual Latin texts and a dictionary; sometimes they also had a commentary and/or a running word-list in the order of the text. Students prepared their texts by writing translations of the hard words in the margins or over the words concerned, by adding word dividers and/or punctuation, and by adding macrons to long vowels, particularly *e* and *o*. The addition of macrons shows that students were expected to read the Latin aloud with correct pronunciation, and the presence of the glosses on the hard words indicates that they were expected to translate and/or paraphrase it. Literature read at this level included Sallust's *Bellum Catilinae*, Terence's *Andria*, and Seneca's *Medea* as well as works by Cicero, Virgil, and Juvenal.

The dictionaries used by these Latin students were varied (see sections 4, 7.3–4, and 8.14–16). Some were general collections of words in alphabetical order, like modern dictionaries; these ranged from the really very small up to about 30,000 entries (i.e. about the size of an intermediate dictionary today; there was no ancient equivalent of the *Oxford Latin Dictionary* or Lewis and Short). Often, however, learners' dictionaries were arranged by topic; they were what is now known as classified glossaries, with a list of words on a topic such as parts of the body followed by a list of words on a different topic such as kinship terms. Such dictionaries are very space-efficient, for whereas an alphabetically arranged dictionary for learners who need both active and passive competence in a language needs to list every pair of words twice, once alphabetized in each language, a classified dictionary need list each pair only once. But classified glossaries are difficult to use if you are faced with an unknown word in a foreign language and do not know which section to look it up in, so they were not the dictionary form of choice when reading texts; for that the ideal work was a running word-list in the order of the text. One of the main uses of the classified dictionaries was vocabulary learning:

students went through them one section at a time and learned by heart the words they contained.

We also have some evidence for prose composition, in the form of a set of Greek fables that have been translated into Latin by someone who was clearly an advanced learner (see passage 5). Interestingly we have no evidence for the translation of individual sentences into Latin; perhaps all the evidence has been lost, but perhaps that skill was not practiced in antiquity.

There was also a group of ancient Latin learners who did not start with the alphabet and therefore learned Latin in transliteration. Clearly these people were aiming only for oral proficiency and did not feel a need to read and write Latin, but nevertheless the skills they aimed for were not negligible. A considerable quantity of transliterated material survives and includes not only glossaries but also colloquia and grammatical paradigms (see section 7). The use of transliterated materials seems to have declined over time, for they make up the majority of Latin-learning papyri in the early centuries of the empire but are outnumbered by other materials in the third century and become rare from the fourth century onwards.

1.3   How do their textbooks survive?

The ancient Latin-learning materials have reached us in two different ways. Many are preserved on papyri found in Egypt; these texts have the advantage of being securely datable to antiquity and do not contain post-antique corruptions (though they may contain corruptions that arose in antiquity). Most of the papyri are too fragmentary to be individually usable today, but collectively they allow us to build up a picture of what ancient students did and how common each type of language-learning activity was in comparison to others. The papyri also provide evidence of some types of activity, such as alphabet learning and the use of transliterated texts, that are not attested in other sources. For reasons of climate papyri survive primarily from Egypt, and therefore our knowledge of certain aspects of ancient Latin learning is heavily biased toward what took place in Egypt. A few papyri are well enough preserved to be usable by modern students; these have been included in this volume whenever possible,[6] and a complete list of all Latin-learning papyri known to me is given in section 10.1.

Despite the large number of surviving papyri the number of actual words on each is small, and therefore the bulk of extant Latin-learning materials comes to us in the same way that most ancient texts have come: via the medieval manuscript tradition. The tradition concerned is strictly the Western one, as no Latin-learning materials were preserved in Byzantium. The conventional wisdom is that medieval Westerners knew

---

[6]   The texts in sections 2.6–8, 3.3, 4.4, 5, 6, 7, 8.7–10, 8.13, and 8.15–16 come from papyri.

no Greek, so it is somewhat surprising to find that the bilingual materials were copied by Latin speakers who wanted to learn Greek. The reason seems to be that although actual knowledge of Greek was indeed rare in the medieval West, attempts to learn it were considerably more common.[7] These learners were responsible for the preservation of the bilingual materials – which were, of course, just as useful for learning Greek as for learning Latin.[8] Generally speaking the only adjustment made to change the texts from Latin-learning to Greek-learning materials was reversing the order of the columns so that the Greek rather than the Latin appeared on the left. But other changes could be made, and sometimes were made: classified glossaries and even texts could be rearranged into alphabetical order, Greek could be transliterated, pagan references could be replaced by Christian ones, etc. Some of these changes render surviving materials difficult or even impossible to use, but mercifully many of the texts seem to have escaped them.[9]

The main collection of bilingual materials that survives via this route is known by the unfortunate name of Hermeneumata Pseudodositheana (*hermeneumata* "translations" is the title given to several of these works in the manuscripts, and *pseudo-Dositheana* indicates that they were once thought to have been written by Dositheus but are now believed to have no connection with him). The Hermeneumata consist of nine different versions of a language textbook containing an alphabetical glossary, a classified glossary, a colloquium, and some other bilingual texts; one of their distinctive features is that everything they contain is bilingual. Originally the Hermeneumata did not include any grammatical material, and perhaps for this reason they were grouped with Dositheus' grammar in some manuscripts, leading to the modern name Pseudodositheana. The main Hermeneumata versions from which material in this book has been drawn are the Hermeneumata Leidensia, Hermeneumata Monacensia, Hermeneumata Montepessulana, Hermeneumata Stephani, and Hermeneumata Celtis.[10]

The survival of the monolingual Latin grammars had a different cause: they too come via the Western manuscript tradition, but because of their value for

---

[7]   For the learning of Greek in the medieval West see Herren (1988), Kaczynski (1988), Berschin (1988), Dionisotti (1982b), and Bischoff (1951).

[8]   How important these medieval copyists considered their Greek studies can be gauged by the way the monks of Heiligenkreuz Abbey in Austria valued their Greek-learning materials. In AD 1133 these monks came from Morimond in Burgundy to the remote Austrian mountains, carrying with them everything they would need to found a new monastery: those essentials included a copy of a long, difficult, and highly corrupt set of bilingual language-learning materials (the Hermeneumata Monacensia), and there is evidence that within five years, long before they had finished building their monastery, the monks of Heiligenkreuz had made a complete copy of those materials. (See Dickey: 2012–15: 1.60 and Rössl 1974: 49–51, 96–8.)

[9]   The texts in sections 2.1–5, 3.1–2, 4.1–3, 8.1–6, 8.11–12, 8.14, and 9 come from medieval manuscripts.

[10] For more information on the Hermeneumata and their different versions see Dickey (2012–15: 1.16–44) and Dionisotti (1982a).

understanding Latin, for in the Middle Ages Westerners had to learn Latin as a foreign language. Works about Latin designed for native speakers also existed (for example Varro's *De lingua Latina*), but because non-native speakers have different needs from those of native speakers the Latin grammars designed for Greek speakers were actually more useful in the Middle Ages. Dositheus' grammar could in theory have been useful both for Latin (the language it describes) and for Greek (the language into which part of it was translated), but in practice it seems to have been copied only by people interested in Greek. In fact they appear to have wanted to use it as a grammar of Greek, a purpose for which it is woefully unsuited – but mercifully the copyists did not realize that unsuitability.

1.4   What is in this book?

This book contains examples of all the main types of ancient Latin-learning materials, in order to give readers an overview of what the range of materials was, and multiple examples of the materials most usable today. The goal is to make it possible for those who wish to do so to recreate the ancient Latin-learning experience, by presenting the ancient materials in a format that enables modern students to use them as the ancient students did. This goal does not, however, result in simply presenting the ancient materials exactly as they appeared in antiquity, for modern students have very different backgrounds from their predecessors. Most significantly, the ancient learners for whom the surviving texts were designed knew Greek, whereas modern learners very often do not. The provision of a running Greek translation would therefore not have the same effect for a modern student as it had for an ancient one, and as a result I have usually replaced the Greek translation with an English one. Of course, provision of an English translation renders the texts difficult to use in the way that modern students most often use Latin texts, namely translating them. This barrier could act as a salutary reminder that the authentic way to use these texts is to memorize and recite them, not to translate them – but those whose affection for authenticity has limits will find a selection of texts without English translation in section 8, where the original Greek has been retained.

Another major change is the presentation of the texts in modern format, with word division, capitalization, punctuation, standardized spelling, supplements of missing words, and correction of corruptions. This is justified on the grounds that modern students need to be given reading material in the format they are used to, just as ancient students were given reading material in the format they were used to; a modern student faced with an original papyrus roll would have an experience completely different from that of an ancient student. At the same time the fact that the modern format makes texts vastly easier to read than they were in antiquity does raise issues of authenticity; in my view the main reason why ancient language students were given translations is that without modern aids such as word division beginners would have found a Latin text simply impossible to translate (see section 9). For this reason a selection of texts is given without word division in section 9, and photographs of manuscripts are also provided to enable students to experience this aspect of ancient reading.

What is not provided is a scholarly framework: there are no brackets, no dotted letters, no *apparatus criticus*, and in general no specific information on how the texts presented here have been reconstructed from manuscripts and papyri. Likewise there are no alternatives in the presentation of individual texts: either the original Greek is preserved or it is replaced by a translation, so there is never a translation in addition to both the original languages. Provision of such information would have been authentic in one way but inauthentic in another and arguably more important way: the trappings of modern scholarship would have obscured the simplicity and immediacy of the originals. The ancient student was faced simply with a text, and his or her interaction with that text was not mediated by brackets, dots, apparatus, or any such details; I believe that the simplicity and immediacy of that interaction was a key part of the ancient experience and needs to be preserved here. Therefore I have included only what a modern student absolutely needs, and that around the text rather than in it: introductions explaining essential background and notes to clarify things that will not be understood without clarification.

For those who want proper scholarly editions the notes explain where these can be found; about half the passages included come from works of which I myself have recently produced a scholarly edition, and many of the other half come from works of which someone else has produced one. Unfortunately, a few texts worth including have never received real editions; in those cases the text presented here is my own silent correction of a manuscript, but reference is given to published transcripts of the manuscript that can be consulted to determine what the original readings were. I have attempted to make clear in the introductions to the individual passages what the situation is with each so that at least the overall level of editorial interference can be determined.

2 | Texts

2.1 Colloquia

Colloquia are bilingual dialogues and narratives designed to be used at an early stage of language learning. The text is arranged in two narrow columns, with the language the students already know on the right and the one they are learning on the left; the two languages match line for line, so that whenever students get stuck they can easily find the translation of the word or phrase that confuses them. This line-for-line or "columnar" translation system is more flexible than a word-for-word interlinear translation, and therefore it allows the creation of a text in which both languages are idiomatic – that is, as long as the text is bilingual from the start and so can be composed with the restrictions of both languages in mind. Columnar translation is more awkward when English, a language with fairly rigid word order rules, is fitted to a pre-existing Latin text – and yet it is possible to make an English translation work in this system more often than one might expect. The English translation that replaces the original Greek in the extracts below, therefore, adheres to the original columnar system most of the time but cannot be relied upon to do so with complete consistency.

Many colloquia passages are vignettes about daily life in the Roman world; like their modern equivalents in French and German textbooks today, they contain cultural as well as linguistic information. The numerous scenes in which characters eat, bathe, shop, or engage in other daily activities were written in the Eastern empire but are set in Rome and have characters with Latin names – just as French textbooks used in England today typically depict characters with French names and are set in France. These passages were probably composed by a variety of authors (most of them no doubt Latin teachers) in the second, third, and fourth centuries AD.

The most famous portions of the colloquia, however, come from the West rather than the East and were originally designed to teach Greek to Roman children. These are the "schoolbooks," which depict the day of a Roman child from dawn until lunchtime. They are older than the Eastern material, dating back at least as far as the first century AD and perhaps considerably earlier; it is possible that Cicero and Atticus used a version of these texts as children. We do not, however, have these schoolbooks in their original Western version, but rather in a set of revised versions made in the Greek East after the Western materials were borrowed by Easterners and adapted for learning Latin (probably in the second century AD). In theory such adaptation need not have involved significant alteration; it was only necessary to move the Greek from the left-hand column to the right-hand one and change the language mentioned as being learned from Greek to Latin. In practice, however, teachers must have made more extensive changes and gone on reworking these scenes well into the imperial period, for the language of the school scenes as they have come down to us is clearly post-classical in many places. Of the passages from colloquia included in this book, therefore, only the ones about adults are certain to have been originally written as Latin-learning texts; those about children are likely to be adapted versions of texts originally written for learning Greek.[1]

The colloquia survive primarily in medieval manuscripts, where they are preserved in six different versions; ancient papyri contain fragments both of the colloquia known from these manuscripts and of other colloquia, indicating that more than six versions originally existed. The manuscript colloquia are known as "Colloquia of the Hermeneu-mata Pseudodositheana" because they are part of the Hermeneumata collections of glossaries and other language-learning materials (see section 1.3 above). The six col-loquia versions are in theory named after the Hermeneumata versions in which they are found, which are themselves named after the most famous manuscript of each ver-sion. Re-evaluation of the relationships between different versions has, however, led to the colloquia not always having the same names as the Hermeneumata; the names of the six surviving colloquia are Monacensia–Einsidlensia (from manuscripts in Munich and in Einsiedeln Abbey in Switzerland); Leidense–Stephani (from a manuscript in Lei-den and a Renaissance edition by Henricus Stephanus or Henri Estienne), Stephani (from another edition by Stephanus), Harleianum (from a manuscript in the Harley collection in the British Library), Montepessulanum (from a manuscript in Mont-pellier), and Celtis (from a manuscript copied by the Renaissance scholar Conrad Celtes).

The language in which the colloquia are written is not Classical literary Latin, but a mixture of the conversational language of the writers' own time (a period that stretches from the first century AD or earlier to the fourth century AD or later) with occasional elements taken from earlier periods. Much of it is in kinds of Latin that used to be called "vulgar" and are now often called "non-standard" by scholars looking at ancient texts – but the usual term for them is "wrong" when detected in the compositions of modern students. Deponent verbs often appear in active forms, *domus* is regularly used with prepositions such as *ad*, *ubi* is used where *quo* might be expected, etc. Modern students whose feel for correct Latin risks being damaged by access to such writing can protect themselves from harm by watching out for these non-standard features and identifying them when found.

---

[1] Thus the material originally written for Latin learners is passages 2.1.11–27, 7.1, and 8.10, while that probably first written for Greek learners is passages 2.1.1–10 and 8.1–2.

In addition to the colloquia extracts given below, further extracts can be found in passages 7.1, 8.1, 8.2, and 8.10.

2.1.1 The preface

The preface to the colloquia is valuable in telling us who the original writers thought their audience was. The exact description of that audience varies from version to version; this one comes from the Colloquium Celtis.[2]

1a	Conversatio,	Conversation,
	usus cottidianus,	everyday usage,
	debet dari	ought to be given
	omnibus pueris	to all boys
	et puellis,	and girls,
1b	quoniam necessaria sunt	since they are necessary
	minoribus	for both younger
	et maioribus,	and older (children),
	propter antiquam	on account of ancient
	consuetudinem	custom
	et disciplinam.	and learning.
2	sic incipiam scribere,	Thus let me begin to write,
	ab exordio lucis	from the beginning of daylight
	usque ad vesperum.	until evening.

2.1.2 A child gets up in the morning

The Western portions of the colloquia, most famous for their school scenes, depict a day in the life of a child. The day starts at dawn, when the child gets up and prepares to go to school. Surprisingly, the child never eats breakfast or even a snack before setting out for school, and he usually puts on his shoes before any other garments (presumably because the floor was too cold for bare feet). Dressing scenes were often used as opportunities to teach a wide range of clothing vocabulary, leading to absurdities such as the one in this passage, where the boy ends up wearing three large, bulky garments (the mantle, outer garment, and cape), none of which could realistically have been worn underneath any of the others. This morning scene comes from the Colloquia Monacensia–Einsidlensia;[3]

---

[2] Additional information on this text and a scholarly edition of it can be found in Dickey (2012–15: II.141–266).

[3] Additional information on this text and a scholarly edition of it can be found in Dickey (2012–15: I.59–184).

watch for non-standard syntax with *domus*, *sic* meaning "then," and purpose expressed with an infinitive rather than an *ut*-clause.

2a	Ante lucem	Before daylight
	vigilavi	I awoke
	de somno;	from sleep;
	surrexi	I got up
	de lecto,	from the bed,
	sedi,	I sat down,
	accepi	I took
	pedules,	gaiters,
	caligas;	boots;
	calciavi me.	I put on my boots.
2b	poposci	I asked for
	aquam	water
	ad faciem;	for my face;
	lavo	I wash
	primo manus,	my hands first,
	deinde faciem	then my face
	lavi;	I washed;
	extersi.	I dried myself.
2c	deposui dormitoriam;	I took off my night-clothes;
	accepi tunicam	I took a tunic
	ad corpus;	for my body;
	praecinxi me;	I put on my belt;
	unxi caput meum	I anointed my head
	et pectinavi;	and combed (my hair);
2d	feci circa collum	I put around my neck
	pallam;	a mantle;
	indui me	I put on
	superariam	an outer garment,
	albam, supra	a white one, (and) on top
	induo paenulam.	I put on a hooded cape.
2e	processi	I went out
	de cubiculo	of the bedroom
	cum paedagogo	with my *paedagogus*
	et cum nutrice	and with my nurse,
	salutare	to greet
	patrem	my father

	et matrem.	and mother.
2f	ambos salutavi	I greeted them both
	et osculatus sum,	and I kissed them,
	et sic descendi de domo.	and then I came down from the house.

2.1.3 A good child goes to school

Ancient education was full of moral *exempla*, illustrations of good and bad conduct that were thought to help children form their own standards of behavior. This emphasis on moral *exempla* was a long-standing part of the educational tradition by the time the colloquia were written, as it is satirized already in Terence.[4] *Exempla* are not common in the portions of the colloquia originating in the East (which were not written for children and therefore did not address the people that the ancients believed would most profit from *exempla*) or in the versions of the Western schoolbook that were adapted for use in the East, but they are very common in the one version of the Western schoolbook that shows no clear evidence of ever having been to the East, the Colloquium Stephani.[5]

In this extract from the Colloquium Stephani[6] the writer explains the best way to go to school: taking a direct route with no detours, politely greeting each acquaintance that one sees, never running up the stairs, and making sure one looks neat and tidy before entering the classroom. The children of the colloquia are typically assisted by a *paedagogus*, an adult whose job it was to accompany them whenever they left the house to keep them safe. They often had a slave boy as well; he carried the schoolboy's books and school equipment.

7a	Post haec	After this
	graphium	I asked for a stylus
	requisivi,	
	et membranam;	and a book;
7b	et haec tradidi	and I handed over these things
	meo puero.	to my (slave) boy.
8a	paratus ergo	So having been prepared
	in omnia,	for everything,
	processi	I went forth
	bono auspicio,	with a good omen,
	sequente me	with my *paedagogus* following me,
	paedagogo,	

---

[4] *Adelphoe* 413–31.

[5] For the evidence that the other schoolbooks moved from the West to the East and the possibility that the Colloquium Stephani did not do so, see Dickey (2012–15: I.46–7).

[6] Additional information on this text and a scholarly edition of it can be found in Dickey (2012–15: I.219–45).

8b	recte	straight
	per porticum	through the colonnade
	quae ducebat	that led
	ad scholam.	to the school.
8c	sicubi mihi noti occurrerunt,	If acquaintances met me anywhere,
	salutavi eos;	I greeted them;
	et illi me	and they
	resalutaverunt.	greeted me in return.
9a	ut ergo veni	So when I came
	ad scalam,	to the staircase,
	ascendi	I went up
	per gradus,	step by step,
	otio,	unhurriedly,
	ut oportebat.	as was proper.
9b	et in proscholio	And in the school vestibule
	deposui birrum;	I deposited my cloak;
	et demulsi	and I smoothed down
	capillos.	my hair.
10a	et sic	And thus
	elevato centrone	lifting the curtain
	introivi,	I entered,
	et primum	and first
	salutavi	I greeted
	praeceptores,	the teachers (and my)
	condiscipulos.	fellow students.

2.1.4 The start of school

When the child arrives at school he finds it already in session, but there is never any suggestion that he is late. Greetings are exchanged (presumably interrupting the work that was in progress when the child arrived), and then he quickly gets down to work. This extract comes from the Colloquium Harleianum;[7] note the non-standard conditional clause.

---

[7] Additional information on this text and a scholarly edition of it can be found in Dickey (2012–15: II.3–80). The British Library has generously posted photographs of the manuscript (Harley 5642) at www.bl.uk/manuscripts/Viewer.aspx?ref=harley_ms_5642_fs001v; this passage is on folio 29v.

4a	"Ave,	"Hello,
	domine	sir
	praeceptor;	teacher;
	bene tibi	may it be well for you.
	sit.	
4b	ab hodie	From today
	studere	I want to work hard.
	volo.	
4c	rogo te ergo,	So please
	doce me Latine	teach me to speak Latin."
	loqui."	
4d	"Doceo te,	"I (shall) teach you,
	si me attendas."	if you pay attention to me."
	"Ecce, attendo."	"Look, I'm paying attention."
4e	"Bene dixisti,	"You have spoken well,
	ut decet	as befits
	ingenuitatem tuam.	your free birth.
5a	porrige mihi, puer,	Hand me, boy,
	manuale.	the book-stand.
5b	cito ergo	So, quickly
	porrige	hand (me)
	librum,	the book,
	revolve,	turn (to the right place),
5c	lege	read
	cum voce,	aloud,
	aperi	open
	os,	your mouth,
	computa.	count.
5d	modo bene	Now mark well
	fac	
	locum,	the place,
	ut scribas	so that you may write
	dictatum."	an exercise."

2.1.5 Doing schoolwork

Most of the school scenes describe the different kinds of learning activities that an ancient child engaged in; this makes them invaluable as sources of information on ancient educational practice. It is, however, very difficult to be sure that material describing the university-level classrooms in which Greek speakers learned Latin has not been mixed with the material describing the schools in which Latin speakers learned Greek. This extract comes from the Colloquia Monacensia–Einsidlensia;[8] note the use of *ars* "art" to mean "grammar" (i.e. the art of grammar; compare the English word "arti-grapher" meaning "writer of a grammatical treatise") and of *artificia* to mean "grammatical questions" (i.e. ones about language and literature; note that while both the examples of such questions fall under the ancient definition of grammar, a modern classification of subjects would put the first question in the field of literary interpretation and consider only the second one to be grammatical). "Hermeneumata" refers to bilingual language-learning materials, both colloquia such as this one and various types of lexica (see section 1.3 above). *Reddo*, translated here as "produce," is a technical term for handing in schoolwork in whatever form is appropriate to the assignment concerned: here *reddo* means reciting the material from memory to demonstrate that it has been learned, but for written work *reddo* means handing over a tablet or other written document. *Personae*, here translated "persons," refers to indications of who speaks which lines of a dramatic text: ancient copies of tragedies and comedies frequently did not specify speakers, putting a considerable burden of interpretation on the reader. The meaning of *praeductorium* is uncertain; the translation "ruler" given here is only one of a number of possibilities. The reference to "declining the genders of nouns" indicates use of a list of noun declensions classified by gender as well as ending, like that in passage 3.3; "parsing" refers to giving a systematic explanation of the grammatical forms of the different words in a sentence and how they relate syntactically. Note the non-standard declension of *alius*.

2h	Porrexit mihi	He handed to me,
	puer meus	my (slave) boy
	scriniarius	who carries the case of books:
	tabulas,	writing-tablets,
	thecam graphiariam,	a stylus-case,
	praeductorium.	a ruler.
2i	loco meo	In my place
	sedens	sitting
	deleo.	I rub out (the previous writing on the tablets).
	praeduco	I rule lines
	ad praescriptum;	following the model;
	ut scripsi,	when I have written
	ostendo	I show (my work)

---

[8] Additional information on this text and a scholarly edition of it can be found in Dickey (2012–15: I.59–184).

	magistro;	to the teacher;
	emendavit,	he corrected it,
	induxit.	he crossed it out.
2j	iubet me	He orders me
	legere.	to read.
	iussus	When asked to do so,
	alio dedi.	I gave (the book) to another (pupil).
	edisco	I learn thoroughly
	interpretamenta,	the Hermeneumata,
	reddidi.	I produced them.
	. . .	. . .
2o	deinde	Then,
	ut sedimus,	as we were seated,
	pertranseo	I go through
	commentarium,	the commentary,
	linguas,	word-lists,
	artem.	grammar.
2p	clamatus ad lectionem	When called to (do) a reading,
	audio expositiones,	I listen to explanations,
	sensus,	meanings,
	personas.	persons.
2q	interrogatus	When asked,
	artificia	grammatical questions
	respondi:	I answered:
	"Ad quem dicit?"	"To whom is he speaking?"
	"Quae pars orationis?"	"What part of speech (is that)?"
2r	declinavi	I declined
	genera nominum,	the genders of nouns,
	partivi versum.	I parsed a verse.

2.1.6 A model schoolboy in a model school

Like passage 2.1.3 above, this extract comes from the Colloquium Stephani[9] and therefore provides moral *exempla* of desirable conduct for children to imitate. Surprisingly,
it concludes with *exempla* for a teacher to imitate: indications of how a model school
should be run. This last is interesting not only for the principles it espouses – ones

---

[9] Additional information on this text and a scholarly edition of it can be found in Dickey (2012–15: 1.219–45).

very different from the ones used in most schools today – but also for the implication it carries that its writer expected the text to be used by other teachers. This passage is not something composed for the writer's own students that was accidentally passed down to us; it was deliberately composed for publication and for use by other teachers.

Note the reference to pronouncing *h* where it should be: this was a challenge in the Roman empire. Already in the Classical period some Latin speakers had not pronounced *h* and/or pronounced it where it did not belong (cf. Catullus 84.1–2: *Chommoda dicebat, si quando commoda vellet | dicere, et insidias Arrius hinsidias...* "Arrius used to say *chommoda* when he meant *commoda*, and *hinsidias* for *insidias...*"), and later this problem became more widespread. *Cottidiana* "everyday idioms" refers to the colloquia; as ancient books could only be produced by copying them individually by hand, a common way for a students to obtain their own copies of textbooks was to copy the books themselves – a process that was not only much cheaper than paying someone else to make the copy but also helped the students become familiar with the contents of the book. Note also the technical terms *reddo* and *persona* (see introduction to passage 2.1.5) and the very non-standard use of *ubi*.

11a	Scripsi ergo	So I wrote
	meum nomen;	my name;
11n	et ita steti,	and I stood like that
	donec antecedentes	until those ahead of me
	reddiderunt,	produced (their work),
11c	et attendi	and I paid attention to
	pronuntiationes	the pronunciations
	praeceptoris	of the teacher
	et condiscipuli.	and of my fellow-student.
11d	etenim inde	For it is from this
	proficimus,	that we progress,
	attendentes aliis,	from paying attention to others,
	siquid ipsi	if they are advised of something.
	monentur.	
11e	audacia hinc	From this self-confidence
	fit,	arises,
	et profectus.	as does progress.
12a	ut ergo	So when
	meo loco	my place
	accessi,	I reached,

	sedi,	I sat down,
12b	protuli	I extended
	manum dextram,	my right hand,
	sinistram	the left one
	perpressi	I pressed
	ad vestimenta.	against my clothing.
13a	et sic coepi	And thus I began
	reddere	to produce (my work),
13b	quomodo acceperam	just as I had received it
	ediscenda:	to be learned:
13c	versus	(reciting) verses
	ad numerum	rhythmically
	et distinctum	and with proper pauses for punctuation
	et clausulam,	and ends of sentences,
13d	cum aspiratione	with the sound *h* pronounced
	ubi oportebat,	where it should be,
	et metaphrasin.	and (giving) a paraphrase.
14a	dum reddo	While I was reciting
	emendatus sum	I was corrected
	a praeceptore,	by the teacher,
14b	ut et vocem	so that I would also develop a faculty of
	praeparem	speaking
	propiorem.	closer (to the standard).
15a	accessi,	I came forward,
	et posita manu	and having put down my hand
	tabulam	I handed over the tablet (with my lesson on
	reddidi,	it),
15b	et reddidi	and I produced
	memoria	from memory
	subscriptionem	an outline
	eorum ubi egeram.	of the things I had done.
16a	post haec	Afterwards,
	dimissus	having been dismissed,
	consedi	I settled down
	meo loco.	in my seat.
16b	librum accepi,	I took the book,
	scripsi	I wrote out
	cottidiana.	everyday idioms.

17a	interrogavi,	I asked questions,
	et emendatus	and having been corrected
	legi	I read
	lectionem meam,	my reading,
17b	quam mihi	which (the teacher)
	exposuit	explained
	diligenter,	carefully,
17c	donec intelligerem	until I understood
	et personas	both the characters
	et sensum	and the meaning
	verborum	of the words
	auctoris.	of the poet.
17d	deinde	Then (I read)
	ab oculo	at sight,
	citatim	quickly,
	ignotum	an unknown (work)
	et quod	and (one) that is
	rare	rarely
	legitur.	read.
18a	haec acta sunt	These things were done
	per singulos	individually
	et universos,	and for everyone,
18b	iuxta unius cuiusque	according to each individual's
	vires	abilities
	et profectum,	and progress,
	et tempora,	and the appropriate times,
	et aetatem	and the age(s)
	condiscipulorum.	of my fellow-students.
19a	sunt enim	For there are
	et naturae variae	also different natures
	studentium,	of those studying,
19b	et difficiles	and difficult
	voluntates	dispositions
	ad laborem	with regard to the hard work
	literarum,	of literary study,
19c	in quibus	in which
	cum multum proficias,	even when you make great progress,
19d	plus superest	there is still more remaining

	ut ad summum	in order for you to arrive at the summit of
	venias	progress.
	profectum.	

2.1.7 The children argue

Several colloquia depict squabbles at school. The first of these passages comes from the Colloquia Monacensia–Einsidlensia[10] and the second from the Colloquium Leidense–Stephani.[11] Note the use of *non* for *nonne*, the shifting meanings of *dicto*, and the non-standard sequence of tenses.

2k	Sed statim	But at once
	dictavit mihi	a fellow-student dictated to me.
	condiscipulus.	
	"Et tu," inquit,	"You too," he said,
	"dicta mihi."	"recite for me."
	dixi ei:	I said to him,
	"Redde primo."	"You produce (your work) first!"
2l	et dixit mihi:	And he said to me,
	"Non vidisti,	"Didn't you see,
	cum redderem	when I produced (my work)
	prior te?"	before you (did)?"
	et dixi:	And I said,
	"Mentiris,	"You're lying;
	non reddidisti."	you didn't."
	"Non mentior."	"I'm not lying!"
3c	"Condiscipuli,	"Fellow-students,
	locum	give me my place!
	mihi	
	date	
	meum.	
3d	densa te."	Move over!"

---

[10] Additional information on this text and a scholarly edition of it can be found in Dickey (2012–15: I.59–184).

[11] Additional information on this text and a scholarly edition of it can be found in Dickey (2012–15: I.187–215). In the original this passage contains some extra vocabulary words; they have been removed in this version to produce a coherent text.

4a	"Illuc accedite:	"Go over there:
	meus locus est,	(this) is my place,
	ego	I
	occupavi."	got it first."

2.1.8 Tuition payments

The school scenes also show us the practicalities of school management. Tuition was paid in installments, usually at the end of the term being paid for, and the child could be asked to take the money with him to school. Parents did not always pay the fees they owed, either because they did not have the money or because they were unhappy with their child's progress. Since teaching certification, like professional certifications of all kinds, was unknown in the ancient world, parents could legitimately be worried about the validity of a teacher's claims to knowledge and instructional skill; the usual method of finding out whether a child was learning successfully was for a parent to go along to school and ask the teacher to put the child through his paces. In this scene, from the Colloquium Harleianum,[12] the teacher appears nervous at the prospect of such an examination, but the child assures him that all will be well, since he has studied after dark. Artificial light was both expensive and of poor quality in antiquity, and papyri were hard to read at the best of times, so schoolwork tended to be confined to daylight hours; studying after dark was the mark of an exceptionally diligent pupil. Watch for non-standard use of *ibi* and *non* for *nonne*.

6a	"Mercedem	"The tuition money,
	non attulisti?"	didn't you bring it?"
	"Petivi	"I asked
	patrem,	my father,
	et dixit,	and he said,
6b	'Ego ipse	'I myself
	veniam	will go
	ibi	there
	noviter.	at once.
6c	volo enim	For I want to get
	et experimentum	a demonstration (of your progress) too.'"
	accipere.'"	

---

[12] Additional information on this text and a scholarly edition of it can be found in Dickey (2012–15: 11.3–80). The British Library has generously posted photographs of the manuscript (Harley 5642) at www.bl.uk/manuscripts/Viewer.aspx?ref=harley_ms_5642_fs001v; this passage is on folio 30r.

6d	"Age ergo	"So behave
	diligenter,	carefully,
	ut paratus sis."	so that you will be ready."
	"Paratus sum;	"I am ready;
6e	incendi enim	for I lit
	lucernam	the lamp,
	et nocte	and at night
	meditatus sum."	did I study."
6f	"Bene fecisti;	"You have done well;
	modo te laudo."	now I praise you."

2.1.9 An accusation of truancy

In this scene a child is faced with the serious accusation of not having turned up when he should have; the penalty for such offences would usually have been a beating, so the original readers of this passage must have expected such punishment. Instead the child silences criticism by producing an excellent excuse that allows him, the son of a very important father, to pull rank over the teacher. The writer of this scene, who must have been a teacher himself, shows a keen awareness of what sort of story the students would enjoy and what would keep them working on their language texts.

The father's legal duties begin unusually early in the day, for the first hour was the hour that began at sunrise. The Roman day started at sunrise, regardless of the time of year, and counted twelve hours from then until sunset, with the sixth hour being our noon; the night then had its own twelve hours, with the sixth being our midnight. In summer the daytime hours were longer than the nighttime ones, particularly in the more northerly sections of the empire, and in winter the reverse was true. Legal business normally started at the third hour (around 9 a.m. in our terms), as in passage 2.1.14. This passage is from the Colloquium Harleianum;[13] it is tempting to date it to the fourth century or later because of the mention of "emperors" in the plural, but in fact joint rule by two or more emperors occurred sporadically from the later second century onwards. Watch for extremely non-standard syntax with *domus* and a peculiar meaning of *alumnus*.

8a	"Heri	"Yesterday
	cessabas	you slacked off
	et meridie	and at midday

---

[13] Additional information on this text and a scholarly edition of it can be found in Dickey (2012–15: II.3–80). The British Library has generously posted photographs of the manuscript (Harley 5642) at www.bl.uk/manuscripts/Viewer.aspx?ref=harley_ms_5642_fs001v; this passage is on folios 30r and 30v.

	in domum non eras.	you were not at home.
8b	ego te quaesivi	I looked for you,
	et audivi omnia ab alumno tuo, quae fecisti."	and I heard everything that you did from your nurse."
8c	"Mentitur qui tibi dixit;	"He's lying, the person who spoke to you;
9a	duxit enim me pater meus	for my father took me
	in praetorium secum.	to the praetorium with him.
9b	salutatus est a magistratibus	He was greeted by the magistrates,
	et epistulas accepit	and he received letters
	a dominis meis	from my masters
	imperatoribus;	the emperors;
9c	et continuo ascendit	and immediately he went up
	in templum	to the temple
9d	et immolavit	and made a sacrifice
	pro aeterno	for the eternity
	et victoria	and victory
	imperatorum,	of the emperors,
	et descendit.	and (then) he came down.
9e	hodie autem	But today
	condictiones audit	he is hearing disputes
	ab hora prima."	from the first hour."

2.1.10 The child goes home

The school sections of the colloquia normally end with the child going home to lunch (in this passage lunchtime is around 1 p.m. by our time reckoning: see 2.1.9 for Roman hours). This lunchtime dismissal was the normal practice in antiquity; sometimes the students might return to the same school in the afternoon, but often they did not, since the afternoon might be needed for other kinds of training: perhaps wrestling and other athletic activities, but perhaps also another school. Since different teachers often had expertise in different areas, a child old enough to be studying a range of subjects might well attend several schools. Because of this range of afternoon engagements and the impracticality of studying after dark (see 2.1.8), as well as the fact that much of the child's time in school was taken up in individual study, homework was rarely set.

This description of lunch comes from the Colloquium Celtis,[14] where it originally contained numerous alternative vocabulary items that have been removed here for the sake of coherence. In one place the list of alternatives is interesting: the child's drink was originally said to be wine, beer, spiced wine, wormwood-flavored wine, or milk. None of these is likely to have been a schoolboy's usual lunchtime beverage, for in another version of the lunch scene the only beverage is chilled water. The list was probably added for vocabulary-learning purposes at a stage when this text was no longer being used by children (i.e. once it had moved from the West to the East). Watch for non-standard syntax in indirect statements and with *domus*.[15]

39e	fit dimissio:	The dismissal happens:
	dimittimur	we are dismissed
	circiter horam	around the seventh hour.
	septimam.	
	. . .	. . .
43a	Intro	I enter
	domum patris,	my father's house,
	exuo vestimenta,	I take off my clothes,
	habitum mundiorem;	my finer clothing;
	induo cottidianum.	I put on my ordinary (clothing).
43b	posco	I call for
	aquam ad manus.	water for (washing) my hands.
	quoniam esurio,	Since I am hungry,
44a	dico meo puero,	I say to my (slave) boy,
	"Pone mensam	"Set out the table
	et mantele	and tablecloth
	et mappam;	and napkin;

---

[14]   Additional information on this text and a scholarly edition of it can be found in Dickey (2012–15: II.141–266).
[15]   The expression *habeo reverti*, though it looks unusual, is probably Classical.

44b	et vade	and go
	ad tuam dominam,	to your mistress,
	et affer panem	and bring bread
	et pulmentarium	and relish
44c	et potionem lactis.	and a drink of milk.
45a	dic meae matri	Say to my mother
	quod iterum	that again
	habeo reverti	I have to return
	ad domum	to the house
	magistri.	of the teacher.
45b	ideo ergo	For this reason, therefore,
	festina	hasten
	nobis afferre	to bring us
	prandium."	lunch."

2.1.11   A trip to the bank

At lunchtime the child seems to turn into an adult, for the second half of the colloquia describes adult activities. This half was composed in the Eastern empire, independently of the schoolbook sections, and was later attached to them. The activities are arranged roughly in the order of a Roman day: first business of various sorts, then an afternoon at the public baths, then dinner and bedtime. This scene describes the process of borrowing money; in the immediately following scene the money is returned, perhaps to make the point that borrowing must be followed by repayment. Note the polite question about the interest rate (in reality a standard rate was known to both parties, and they simply confirm here that they will use it) and the care that was needed to avoid problems with debased coinage. The banker wanted borrowers to check for bad coins before leaving the bank, because the borrower who acknowledged having checked his coins in the presence of the banker could not later return with a valueless coin and claim that the banker had given it to him. The passage comes from the Colloquia Monacensia–Einsidlensia;[16] note the use of *numquid* for *num*.

5a	"Domine,	"Sir,
	quid imperasti?"	what did you order?"
	"Numquid habes	"Do you perhaps have
	pecuniam	any money

---

[16]   Additional information on this text and a scholarly edition of it can be found in Dickey (2012–15: I.59–184).

	vacuam?"	available?"
	"Quid opus habes	"What do you need
	mutuari?"	to borrow?"
5b	"Si habes,	"If you have it,
	commoda mihi	lend me
	quinque sestertia."	five thousand sesterces."
	"Etsi non habuissem,	"Even if I hadn't had it,
	undecumque	from somewhere
	explicassem."	I would have sorted it out."
5c	"Pignus vis?"	"Do you want some security?"
	"Absit,	"Heaven forbid!
	non opus habeo.	I have no need (of one).
	cave mihi	Certify for me that
	te accepisse."	you have taken (the money)."
	"Quibus usuris?"	"At what rate of interest?"
	"Quibus vis."	"At the rate you want."
5d	"Cavi."	"I have certified it."
	"Gratias tibi ago;	"Thank you;
	signa."	(now) put your seal on it."
	"Signavi."	"I have put my seal on it."
	"Numero	"By number
	numera."	count (the money) out."
	"Numeravi."	"I have counted it."
	"Proba."	"Examine it."
	"Probavi."	"I have examined it."
5e	"Sicut accepisti,	"Just as you took it,
	probum reddas."	return it in good coin."
	"Cum tibi	"When I return (it) to you
	reddidero,	
	et satisfaciam."	I shall also give satisfaction."

2.1.12 A trip to the clothes market

This passage has been damaged; some material is missing in the middle. Nevertheless it is interesting as a rare account of clothes-buying in a second-century marketplace. The buyer is evidently accompanied by a slave who carries his purse and does some of the bargaining. Of the items mentioned the *paenula* (a hooded cape) and *lintea* (linen towels) are well known, but the identification of *amicula* is doubtful (the translation "underwear" is based, not at all securely, on the Greek) and *pareclum* "pair" has not been identified; it probably refers to a specific garment. The prices suggest that this passage was composed in the second century AD, for in later centuries such garments would have cost much more owing to inflation. The passage comes from the Colloquium Montepessulanum.[17]

13b	Ego duco me	I am going
	ad vestiarium.	to a garment-seller.
	"Quanti pareclum?"	"How much is the pair?"
	"Centum denariis."	"A hundred denarii."
	"Quanti paenula?"	"How much is the cape?"
	"Ducentis denariis."	"Two hundred denarii."
13c	"Multum dicis;	"You're asking a lot;
	accipe centum denarios."	accept a hundred denarii."
	"Non potest tanti.	"It's not possible at that price.
13d	tanti constat	That's what it costs (us to get it)
	de infertoribus."	from the importers."
	. . .	. . .
13e	"Eamus	"Let's go
	et ad lintearium.	to the linen-seller too.
	confer et illi."	Deal with him too."
13f	"Da nobis amicula	"Give us underwear
	et quattuor lintea.	and four linen towels.
	quanti omnia?"	How much (for them) all?"
	"Trecentis denariis."	"Three hundred denarii."

2.1.13 A visit to a sick friend

Two friends set out to console a third, whom they believe to be ill in bed. He lives in an *insula* or multi-level apartment building, so this scene gives us a rare glimpse into the practicalities of finding someone in such a building: negotiating with the doorman at the bottom, getting directions to the right apartment, and then negotiating with its individual doorman on arrival. This passage is from the Colloquia Monacensia–Einsidlensia.[18] Watch for non-standard use of *ubi*, *ipse*, and *ad*, an indirect question with *si* + indicative verb, an infinitive of purpose, the future indicative used to give a command, *maneo* in its post-classical meaning "live," and *a quando* "from when." The use of *sis* "please"

[17] Additional information on this text and a scholarly edition of it can be found in Dickey (2012–15: II.83–137).
[18] Additional information on this text and a scholarly edition of it can be found in Dickey (2012–15: I.59–184).

is surprising because that term is a literary archaism that had vanished from ordinary speech centuries before this passage was written: literary archaisms are rare in the colloquia.

6b	"Si vis,	"If you want,
	veni mecum."	come with me."
	"Ubi?"	"Where?"
	"Ad amicum	"To our friend Lucius:
	nostrum Lucium:	
	visitemus eum."	let's go see him."
6c	"Quid enim habet?"	"What's wrong with him?"
	"Aegrotat."	"He's sick."
	"A quando?"	"Since when?"
	"Intra paucos dies	"A few days ago
	incurrit."	he fell ill."
	"Ubi manet?"	"Where does he live?"
	"Non longe.	"Not far off.
6d	sis ambula."	Please walk (there with me)."
	"Haec est, puto,	"This, I think, is
	domus eius.	his house.
	haec est.	This is it.
6e	ecce ostiarius.	Here's the doorman.
	interroga illum,	Ask him
	si possumus intrare	if we can enter
	et videre dominum eius."	and see his master."
6f	et ille dixit,	And he said,
	"Quem quaeritis?"	"Who are you looking for?"
	"Dominum tuum.	"Your master.
	de salute eius	About his health
	venimus."	have we come."
6g	"Ascendite."	"Go on up."
	"Quot scalas?" "Duas.	"How many flights of stairs?" "Two.
	ad dexteram pulsate,	Knock (on the door) to the right,
	si tamen venit;	that is, if he has come (back);
	processerat enim."	for he had gone out."
6h	"Pulsemus."	"Let's knock."
	"Vide; quis est?"	"(Go and) see: who is it?"
	"Avete omnes!"	"Hello, all of you!"

	"Dominum tuum volumus	"It's your master we want
	visitare. si vigilat,	to visit. If he is awake,
	nuntia me."	announce me."
6i	et ille dixit, "Non est hic."	And he said, "He's not here."
	"Quid narras?	"What are you saying?
	sed ubi est?"	But where is he?"
	"Illuc descendit	"He went down there
	ad lauretum	to the laurel grove
	deambulare."	to take a walk."
6j	"Gratulamur illi!	"We congratulate him!
	cum venerit, dices illi	When he comes back, tell him
	nos ad ipsum gratulantes	that we came to him rejoicing about his health,
	venisse ad salutem eius,	
	quia omnia recte habet."	because he's entirely recovered."
	"Sic faciam."	"I shall do that."

2.1.14 Two criminal trials

One of the main reasons for learning Latin during the Roman empire was to enter the legal profession. Some writers of colloquia must have been teachers of aspiring lawyers (perhaps at the school in Berytus, modern Beirut), for they make an effort to keep the students engaged by describing in alluring terms the life of a legal professional. In the colloquia lawyers always win their cases, apparently without effort, and are well paid by their grateful clients; it is their "literary skills" (i.e. their performance in law school) that determines how much business they have. This passage comes from the Colloquium Celtis;[19] the view it provides of Roman justice is an unattractive one and not completely in accord with Roman law (a defendant who did not confess should have been allowed an appeal if convicted), but the writer probably intended the reader to assume that the first defendant is actually guilty. The fact that the witnesses were not tortured is not to be taken for granted: witnesses were often tortured during the empire. The start time of the third hour (*ca.* 9 a.m. in our terms: see passage 2.1.9) is corroborated by the poet Martial (4.8.2). Note the non-standard use of *suus*, and *idoneus* in its rare sense "lavish"; the last clause might mean either that everyone believed the verdict (leaving the acquitted man without a stain on his reputation) or that everyone signed the official record of the trial (certifying that it was a correct account of the proceedings).

---

[19] Additional information on this text and a scholarly edition of it can be found in Dickey (2012–15: II.141–266). Some alternative phrases have been removed for coherence.

73a	Fit hora tertia.	The third hour arrives.
	ingrediuntur advocati,	The advocates enter,
	causidici,	the pleaders,
	scholastici,	the legal advisers,
	evocati	those called
	in secretarium	into the private court
	iudicis sui.	of their own judge.
73b	agunt	They conduct
	plures causas,	many cases,
	quisque ut potest	each as he is able
	secundum	according to
	litterarum	his literary
	facundiam.	skills.
74a	sunt et causae	There are also cases
	in temporum	at their time
	finem,	limit,
	quas hodie	which today
	credo terminandas.	I believe have to be finished.
74b	exinde	Then
	descendit praeses	the provincial governor comes down
	ad tribunal	to the speaker's platform
	sessurus.	to take his seat.
74c	sternitur tribunal,	The speaker's platform is laid out,
	conscendit iudex	the judge mounts
	tribunal,	the speaker's platform,
74d	et sic voce	and thus by the voice
	praeconis	of the herald
	iubet	he orders
	sisti personas.	the persons (on trial) to be made to stand up.
75a	reus sistitur	The defendant is made to stand up,
	latro.	a robber.
	interrogatur	He is interrogated
	secundum merita:	according to his deserts:
75b	torquetur,	he is tortured,
75c	flagellatur,	he is whipped,
	fustibus vapulat,	he is beaten with cudgels,
	et adhuc negat.	and still he denies (that he is guilty).
75d	puniendus est:	He must be punished:
	ducitur ad gladium.	he is led off to execution.

76a	deinde alter	Then another (accused person)
	sistitur,	is made to stand up,
	innocens,	an innocent one,
	cui adest	for whom there is
	grande patrocinium,	a great pleading,
76b	et viri diserti	and learned men
	adsunt illi.	are supporting him.
	hic etenim habebit	And indeed this man will have
	bonum eventum:	a good outcome:
	absolvitur.	he is acquitted.
77a	testes	The witnesses
	bene venerunt	came off well
	in sua causa;	in his case;
	sine iniuria	without injury
	absoluti sunt.	they were released.
77b	haec causa habuit	This case had
	idoneam	a lavish
	defensionem,	defense,
77c	et fidem	and the faith
	veritatis	of truth
	apud acta	in the result (the official record?)
	deposuit	placed
	unus quisque.	each and every one.

2.1.15 A lawsuit

Much of a lawyer's business, of course, comes from civil rather than criminal cases, and therefore lawsuits are more common than criminal trials in the colloquia. This passage about a lawsuit comes from the Colloquia Monacensia–Einsidlensia.[20] Note the unusual vocative forms *Gaie* and *Lucie*, the non-standard use of *ibi*, and the indirect statement with *quia* + indicative.

4a	Et paterfamilias	And the master of the house
	procedens	going forth
	occurrit	met
	amico suo	his friend
	et dixit, "Ave, Gaie!"	and said, "Hello, Gaius!"

[20] Additional information on this text and a scholarly edition of it can be found in Dickey (2012–15: I.59–184).

	et osculatus est eum.	and he kissed him.
4b	et resalutavit dicens,	And (Gaius) returned the greeting, saying,
	"Bene valeas, Lucie;	"May you be well, Lucius;
	est te videre?"	do I really see you?"
	"Quid agis?"	"How are you doing?"
4c	"Omnia recte.	"Everything's going well.
	quomodo habes?"	How are you?"
	"Gratulor tibi	"I rejoice for you
	sic quomodo mihi.	in the same way as for myself.
4d	est mihi	I have
	iudicium."	a court case."
	"Ad quem?	"Before whom?
	ad quaestorem?"	Before the quaestor?"
	"Non ibi."	"Not there."
4e	"Sed ubi?	"But where?
	ad proconsulem?"	Before the proconsul?"
	"Nec ibi,	"Not there either,
	sed ad magistratus	but before the magistrates
	ex subscriptione praesidis	(established) out of the response of the governor
	provinciae."	of the province."
4f	"Quale autem est	"But what sort of thing is
	ipsa res?"	the case itself?"
	"Non valde magnum;	"Not a very big thing;
	est enim pecuniarium,	for it's a financial matter,
	ut omne videas.	so that you may see it all.
4g	si vacat tibi,	If you're at leisure,
	adesto nobis;	join us;
	iudices enim	for the judges
	diem nobis dederunt	have given us as a (court) date
	hodiernam:	today:
	sententia dicitur.	the verdict (will) be declared.
4h	quare volo te praesente	Therefore I want, in your presence,
	de causa	to discuss the case
	cum advocatis	with my advocates."
	tractare."	
	"Adhibuisti?"	"Did you call in (advocates)?"
	"Adhibui."	"I did."
	"Quos?" "Tuos amicos."	"Whom?" "Your friends."

	"Bene fecisti."	"You did well."
4i	"Constituisti?	"Have you fixed a meeting?
	circa quam horam?	Around what hour?
	in quo loco?"	In what place?"
	"In foro,	"In the forum,
	in porticu,	in the portico,
	iuxta stoam	near the stoa
	Victoriae."	of Victory."
4j	"Post modicum ibi venio."	"I (shall) come there after a little while."
	"Sed rogo, in mente habeas."	"But please, keep it in mind."
	"Securus esto;	"Be without worry;
	mihi pertinet."	it is a concern to me."
4k	"Eamus nos	"Let's go
	ad nummularium;	to the banker;
	accipiamus ab eo	let's get from him
	denarios centum.	a hundred denarii.
	demus causidico	Let's give them to the pleader
	honorarium	as an honorarium,
	et advocatis	and to the advocates
	et iuris peritis,	and the legal experts,
	ut incessanter	so that unflaggingly
	defendant nos."	they may defend us."
4l	"Iste est.	"This is he.
	accipe ab eo nummos	Take the coins from him
	et sequere."	and follow (me)."
4m	"Sicut constituimus,	"As we agreed,
	adest Gaius.	Gaius is here.
	convocemus eum	Let's call him
	in consilium.	into our discussion.
	hic habemus	Here we have
	instrumenta."	the evidence."
4n	"Denuntiasti illi?"	"Did you serve him a summons?"
	"Denuntiavi."	"I did."
	"Testatus es?"	"Did you produce evidence?"
	"Testatus sum."	"I did."
	"Paratus esto."	"Be ready."
	"Paratus sum."	"I am ready."
4o	"Et adversarius	"And (your) opponent
	interpellare vult."	wants to interrupt."

Cecodespotas	Et pater.
Perchomenos	Pcedens
Apuntises	Occurristi
Apuntisen	Occurrit
Tufiliu auttu	Amico suo
Ceapen chere gaie	Et dixit Aue gaie
Cecatese nauton	Et osculatus est eu.
Ccantespasatolegon	Et resaluauit dies.
Calohesef Lucie	Bene ualeas Lucie
Cstinse ydin	Este uidere
Typratus	Quid agis
Panthaortus	Omnia recte
Possechis	Quom habes
Synchoromesin	Gratulor tibi
Ifrosofemy	Si quom in.
Cruyrion	Iudicium
Prostina	AD QVEM
Pstomamian	Ad questorem
Veei	Hon ibi
Allarpv.	Seu ibi
Pthonanthyparos	Adpconsulem
Ifdeei	Nec ibi
Allapstu farcontas	S; admagistratos
Cxypogafiftu die	Cx subseptione pfi
Tyne parnon	Puirie
Potapondestin	Quale aute est
Auiotopragma	Ipsa res
Ypanumega	Non ualde magnu
Cstingarethrimatieo	Est eni pecuniaru
Inaolonydis	Vt omne uides
Yscola hyffu	Si uacat tibi
Paredriusummin	A desto nobis.
Ifuttegar	Iudices enim
Ymerani mynorisa	Diem nobis dederit.
Tynsemeron	Hodiernam
Apofasireumeni	Sententia dicit
Diabulome separon	Quare uolo te pfiitie
Pentisdicis	De causa
Synuffynigoris	Cum aduocatis
Scepfaste	Tractare
Parelabes	Adhibuisti
Parelabon	Adhibui

Figure 1 First part of colloquium lawsuit scene in the twelfth-century manuscript Zwettl 1, folio 11r (bottom of columns 1 and 2); the Greek is transliterated in this medieval copy. Printed by kind permission of Zisterzienerstift Zwettl.

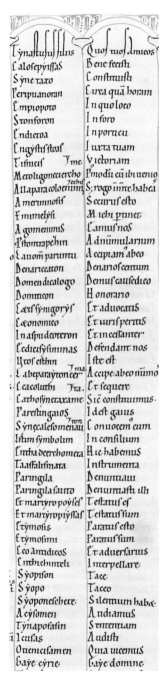

Figure 2 Second part of colloquium lawsuit scene in manuscript Zwettl 1, folio 11r (top of columns 3 and 4). Printed by kind permission of Zisterzienerstift Zwettl.

"Tace!"	"Be quiet!"
"Taceo."	"I am being quiet!"
"Silentium habete,	"Keep silence,
audiamus	let's hear
sententiam."	the verdict."
4p "Audisti	"Did you hear
quia vicimus,	that we have won,
Gaie?"	Gaius?"

2.1.16 A dispute resolution procedure

This scene depicts an alternative dispute resolution procedure: taking an oath by the gods. In order to be usable by a wide range of people the words provided here are very generic: it is not specified what the dispute is or even which god is being asked to witness the oath. In real life oaths would no doubt have been far more specific. The outcome, in which the speaker's opponent believes him as a result of the oath, is well paralleled in antiquity, where the gods were supposed to punish those who invoked them falsely and where it was consequently considered dangerous to lie in an oath. This passage is from the Colloquium Leidense–Stephani.[21]

10a	"Si non periurus,	"If you (are) not an oath-breaker,
	iura mihi."	swear for me."
10b	et ego	And I
	iuravi	swore
	simpliciter,	frankly,
	et non	and I did not
	periuravi:	swear falsely:
10c	"Per deum	"By the god,
	optimum,	the best,
	maximum,	the greatest (god),
	sic mihi	so to me
	deus propitius,	(may) the god (be) propitious,
	per salutem	by the health
	cuiuslibet:	of anyone you please:
10d	quod periurus	that I shall not be found false
	in hoc	in this

---

[21] Additional information on this text and a scholarly edition of it can be found in Dickey (2012–15: I.187–215).

	sacramento	oath."
	non inveniar."	
10e	tunc mihi	Then me
	credidit.	he believed.

2.1.17 An attempt at debt recovery

One of the purposes for which the ancients might resort to taking oaths was disputed debts. In this scene a character named Lucius is accosted by someone who claims to have lent him money; he denies that he is the person who took out the loan in the first place, and the dispute is resolved by his taking an oath on this point. This scene comes from the Colloquium Harleianum;[22] note the non-standard use of cases in expressions of time as well as *non* for *nonne*.

23a	"Non est iste	"Isn't this fellow
	Lucius,	Lucius,
	qui meum	who has my
	aes	money?
	habet?	
23b	hic est.	This is he.
	accedens ergo	So, approaching him
	salutabo eum."	I shall greet him."
	"Ave,	"Hello,
	paterfamilias.	master of a household.
23c	nondum	Can't I yet
	possum	
	accipere	have back
	meum	my (money)
	quod mihi	that you (have been) owing me
	debes	
	tanto tempore?"	for such a long time?"
23d	"Quid dicis?	"What are you saying?
	insanis!"	You're insane!"
23e	"Faeneravi tibi	"I lent you
	aes	money,

---

[22] Additional information on this text and a scholarly edition of it can be found in Dickey (2012–15: II.3–80); alternatives have been removed for coherence. The British Library has generously posted photographs of the manuscript (Harley 5642) at www.bl.uk/manuscripts/Viewer.aspx?ref=harley_ms_5642_fs001v; this passage is on folio 32v.

	et dicis,	and you say,
	'Insanis'?	'You're insane'?
	fraudator,	Swindler,
	non cognoscis me?"	don't you know me?"
23f	"Duc te,	"Take yourself off,
	quaere	look for
	cui	(the person) to whom
	faenerasti;	you lent it,
	ego enim	for I
	nihil tuum	don't have anything of yours."
	habeo."	
23g	"Iura mihi."	"Swear for me."
	"Iuro	"I (shall) swear
	ubi velis."	where(ver) you want."
	"Eamus.	"Let's go.
	iura	Swear
	in templo."	in the temple."
23h	"Per deum hunc,	"By this god,
	nihil mihi	nothing to me
	dedisti."	have you given."
23i	"Modo bene;	"Very well;
	rixam	to have a fight
	et controversiam	and argument
	facere	
	non est	is not
	bonum	good
	libero	for a free
	homini	man
	et patrifamilias."	and the master of a household."

2.1.18 A message from a friend in need

This passage is interesting because of its emphatically Roman orientation: not only do the characters have Roman names, but formal wear involves a toga and nobility consists of being able to trace one's ancestry back to Romulus and Aeneas. Since the passage was composed in the East, this evocation of a Roman atmosphere was probably part of a strategy of evoking the culture that went with the language being learned. The passage comes from the Colloquium Montepessulanum;[23] note the non-standard indirect statement.

---

[23] Additional information on this text and a scholarly edition of it can be found in Dickey (2012–15: II.83–137).

4a	"Quis pulsat ostium?"	"Who is knocking at the door?"
	"A Gaio	"(A messenger) from Gaius
	ad Lucium.	to Lucius.
	si hic est,	If he is here,
	nuntia."	announce (me)."
4b	"Venit a Gaio."	"(Someone) has come from Gaius."
	"Roga illum."	"Ask him (in)."
	"Quid est, puer?	"What is it, boy?
	omnia recte?"	Is everything all right?"
4c	"Etiam, domine.	"Yes, sir.
	misit tibi	He sent you
	epistulam	a letter,
	signatam."	sealed."
4d	"Da, legam.	"Give (it to me), let me read it.
	scripsit mihi	He has written to me
	de negotio.	about business.
	vade, puer,	Go, boy,
	et nuntia	and tell (him)
	quoniam venio.	that I'm coming.
4e	date mihi calciamenta.	Give me my shoes.
	affer aquam	Bring water
	ad faciem.	for my face.
	da subarmale,	Give (me) the belted garment;
	cinge me.	put on my belt.
	da togam,	Give (me my) toga;
	operi me.	drape it on me.
	da paenulam	Give (me my) hooded cape
	et anulos.	and rings.
4f	quid stas, sodalis?	Why are you standing there, comrade?
	tolle quae opus sunt	Pick up the things that are necessary
	et veni mecum.	and come with me.
4g	festino	I am hastening
	ad amicum	to (the aid of) an old friend,
	antiquum,	
	senatorem	a senator
	populi Romani,	of the Roman people,
	qui a Romulo	who traces his lineage from Romulus,
	deducit genus,	
	a Troianis	from the Trojan
	Aeneadis."	descendants of Aeneas."

2.1.19 Preparations for having a guest to lunch

The main character invites his friend Gaius to lunch and then sets off to buy food for the meal, accompanied by multiple slaves. Whenever something is purchased he hands it to a slave to take home; then at the end of the trip he returns home himself to instruct the cook in the preparation of the meal. Rather than agreeing a fixed time with Gaius in advance of the meal, he sends slaves periodically to update his friend on the state of the preparations, so that Gaius turns up exactly when the meal is ready.

Some of the food may be unfamiliar. Azaroles are exotic fruits that resemble cherries but have multiple stones (the Latin resembles the term for "truffle" but has a different gender and a different nominative singular, *tubur* as opposed to *tuber*). *Pulmentarium*, here translated "relish," refers to tasty food eaten with bread and here may encompass everything that has been purchased or a subset of it. *Liquamen*, here translated "fish-sauce" and often known as "garum," was a salty liquid made by leaving fish entrails in the sun; despite sounding revolting by modern standards it was ubiquitous in Roman cuisine. "Black" wine is a common ancient term for what we would call red wine. The axe mentioned was used for cutting firewood and the ember for lighting a fire in the dining room; the fire might have been used for warming the diners but could also have been used for heating wine and food that was served hot. The purpose of throwing water outside was probably to dampen the dust in front of the house.

The passage is from the Colloquia Monacensia–Einsidlensia;[24] note the non-standard use of *ubi, hic, foras, domus,* and *prae* as well as the use of the present tense for the future and the accusative of price.

7a	"Tu ubi vadis?"	"You, where are you going?"
	"Ad domum festino.	"I'm hurrying home.
	quare inquisisti?"	Why did you ask?"
7b	"Si tibi suave est,	"If it appeals to you,
	hodie prae me prande	have a modest lunch with me today.
	frugaliter.	
	vino bono	Good wine
	domestico	from our own estate
	utimur."	we have."
	"Sic fiat."	"So be it."
7c	"Temperius ergo	"So at the right time
	veni ad nos." "Quando vis,	come to us." "When you want (me there),

[24] Additional information on this text and a scholarly edition of it can be found in Dickey (2012–15: I.59–184).

	mitte ad nos;	send (a slave) to us;
	domi sum."	I (shall) be at home."
	"Sic fiat nobis."	"Agreed."
8a	"Tu, puer,	"You, boy,
	sequere me	follow me
	ad macellum;	to the butcher's shop;
	aliquid emamus	let's buy something
	ad prandium.	for lunch.
8b	interroga,	Ask (him)
	quantum piscis."	how much the fish (is)."
	"Denarios decem."	"Ten denarii."
8c	"Tu, puer,	"You, boy,
	refer ad domum,	take it home,
	ut possimus ire	so that we can go
	ad holerarium	to the greengrocer's shop
	et emere holera,	and buy vegetables,
	quae necessaria sunt,	which are needed,
	et poma:	and fruit:
	mora,	mulberries,
	ficus,	figs,
	persos,	peaches,
	piras,	pears,
	tuberes.	azaroles.
8d	ecce habes omnia	There you have everything
	quae emimus.	that we bought.
	refer ad domum."	Take it home."
9a	"Clamet aliquis coquum;	"Someone call the cook;
	ubi est?"	where is he?"
	"Sursum ascendit."	"He went upstairs."
	"Et quid vult?	"And what does he want (up there)?
	descendat hic."	Let him come down here."
9b	"Tolle, coque diligenter	"Take (this food), carefully cook
	pulmentaria;	the relish;
	conditura	let it become good sauce."
	bona fiat."	
9c	"Affer clavem.	"Bring the key.
	aperi loculum	Open the casket
	et eice clavem cellarii.	and take out the key of the cellar.
	profer quae necessaria sunt:	Bring out the things that are necessary:

9d	sale,		salt,
	oleum Spanum,		Spanish oil,
	et apparatum		and provision (i.e. oil)
	ad lucernas,		for the lamps,
	liquamen		fish-sauce (that is, both the)
	primum		first
	et secundum,		and second (grade),
	acetum acrum,		sharp vinegar,
9e	vinum album		white wine
	et nigrum,		and black (wine),
	mustum,		new (wine),
	vetus,		old (wine),
	ligna sicca,		dry firewood,
	carbones,		coals,
	prunam,		a burning ember,
	securim,		an axe,
9f	vasa,		vessels,
	catina,		dishes,
	caccabum,		a cooking-pot,
	ollam,		a pot,
	craticulam,		a grid-iron,
	coopertorium,		a cover,
	mortarium,		a mortar,
	pistillum,		a pestle,
	cultellum."		a little knife."
9g	"Quid aliud vis?"		"What else do you want?"
	"Haec tantum, puer:		"Only this, boy:
	vade ad Gaium		go to Gaius
	et dic illi,		and say to him,
	'Veni, inde		'Come, from there
	lavemus.'		let's go to the baths.'
	vade, curre,		Go, run,
	cito fac;		do it quickly,
	nihil tardius,		not at all slower,
	sed velocius."		but faster."
9h	"Fuisti ad ipsum?"		"Have you been to him?"
	"Fui." "Ubi erat?"		"I have." "Where was he?"
	"Ad domum sedebat."		"He was sitting at home."

9i	"Et quid faciebat?"	"And what was he doing?"
	"Studebat."	"He was studying."
	"Et quid dixit?" "Meos	"And what did he say?" "(He said,) 'For my (friends)
	exspecto;	I am waiting;
	veniunt	they are coming
	et sequor."	and I (shall) follow.'"
9j	"Vade iterum et dic illi,	"Go again and say to him,
	'Omnes hic sunt.'	'Everyone is here.'
	cum illo veni."	Come (back) with him."
9k	"Vos interim componite	"You (slaves), meanwhile, set out
	diligenter	carefully
	vitreamina	the glassware
	et aeramenta.	and the bronze vessels.
9l	sternite cenationem	Arrange the dining room
	et proicite foras	and throw water outside.
	aquam.	
	volo videre	I want to see (you hurrying)
	quasi iuvenes."	like young men."
9m	"Iam stravimus.	"Now we have arranged it.
	omnia parata sunt."	Everything is ready."
9n	"Nondum venit?	"Hasn't he come yet?
	vade, dic illi,	Go, say to him,
	'Sero nos facis	'You're making us late
	prandere.'"	to eat lunch.'"
9o	"Ecce venit;	"There, he has come;
	hic veniebat."	he was on his way here."
	"Occurre ei;	"Go meet him;
	roga illum."	invite him (in)."
	"Quid foras stas?"	"Why are you standing outside?"

2.1.20 A visit to the baths

Many Romans went to the public baths after lunch every day; like a modern trip to the beach, this expedition involved not only immersion in water but also other activities. Most ancient bathing complexes had an open area for exercising, a toilet block (usually a single long seat with a row of holes in it), a room for undressing and leaving one's clothes, a warm room in which bathers would be rubbed with olive oil, one or more hot rooms in which they would sweat and perhaps bathe in a hot tub, and one or more pools of cold water. The *thermae* or state-owned baths were the largest and had the most amenities; privately owned bath complexes were usually smaller. Both types were open to the public on payment of a small fee. The writer of this passage has taken care to mention all the rooms of a large bath complex in the order that a bather would use them, to give readers the necessary vocabulary; when he comes to the hot rooms, only one of which would be visited on each trip to the baths, he gets the words for both rooms in by including a discussion about which one to use.

The main character issues a number of orders; many of these, such as the commands to carry things, are clearly directed at slaves, but some (the orders to undress and to swim, for example) are difficult to explain in that fashion. Perhaps the group of bathers includes a child who is instructed by a parent in how to behave at the baths.

The procedure at the end of the visit is interesting: between bathing and drying themselves with a towel, the characters pour water over themselves (like a shower) and apply the strigil, a metal scraper that was normally used for removing dust, grime, and oil after an activity like wrestling. Although the characters have indeed oiled themselves and wrestled, one would expect the resultant grime to have been removed in the course of washing in the hot tub and then swimming in the pool. The only plausible explanation for the shower and scraping is that the bathers are still grimy after swimming; the baths were only cleaned once a month, and there is no evidence about how often the water was changed between cleanings, so it is distinctly possible that a Roman was dirtier upon emerging from a swimming pool than he had been on entering it.[25]

This passage is from the Colloquia Monacensia–Einsidlensia.[26] Note the references to slaves being sent ahead to hold places for their masters in crowded baths, so that high-status visitors would not have to wait on arrival, and to the perennial danger of thieves stealing bathers' clothes. Note also the indirect questions using *si* and the indicative, non-deponent use of *luctor*, non-standard use of cases for time expressions and with *in*, *non scio* for *nescio*, *numquid* for *num*, and the unclarity over who speaks which lines in 10b–d.

10a	"Deferte sabana	"Take the towels down
	ad balneum,	to the bath,
	strigilem,	the strigil,
	faciale,	face-cloth,
	pedale,	foot-cloth,

[25] See Fagan (1999: 181–5).
[26] Additional information on this text and a scholarly edition of it can be found in Dickey (2012–15: I.59–184).

	ampulam,	flask (of oil),
	aphronitrum.	soap.
10b	antecedite,	Go ahead (of us),
	occupate locum."	get a place."
	"Ubi iubes?	"Where do you direct (it to be)?
	ad thermas	At the public baths,
	aut in privato?"	or in a privately-owned one?"
10c	"Ubi iubetis."	"Wherever *you* order."
	"Antecedite tantum;	"Just go ahead;
	vobis dico, qui hic estis."	I'm talking to you, the ones who are here."
10d	"Calida fiat nobis;	"Let there be hot water for us;
	quando imus,	I'll tell you when we're coming.
	narrabo tibi.	
	surge, eamus."	Get up, let's go."
10e	"Hinc vis per porticum,	"Do you want (to go) from here through the portico
	propter lumen?	on account of the light?
	Numquid vis venire	Do you perhaps want to come
	ad secessum?"	to the toilet?"
10f	"Bene me admonuisti,	"You reminded me well;
	venter me cogit.	my belly compels me (to go).
	eamus iam."	Let's go now."
10g	"Exspolia te."	"Take off your clothes."
	"Discalcia me,	"Take off my shoes,
	compone vestimenta,	put the clothes together,
	cooperi, serva bene;	cover (them), watch (them) well;
	ne obdormias,	don't doze off,
	propter fures."	on account of the thieves."
10h	"Rape nobis pilam;	"Grab a ball for us;
	ludamus in sphaeristerio."	let's play in the ball-court."
10i	"Exerceri volo	"I want to practice
	in ceromate.	on the wrestling-ground.
	veni, luctemus	Come, let's wrestle
	post tempus	after a while
	uno momento."	for a moment."
10j	"Non scio, si possum;	"I don't know if I can;
	olim enim cessavi	for a long time ago I stopped
	luctare.	wrestling.

	tamen tempto	Nevertheless I (shall) try
	si possum."	if I can."
10k	"Leviter	"Easily
	fatigatus sum."	have I been tired out."
	"Introeamus in cellam	"Let's go into the first room,
	primam	
	tepidaria.	the tepidarium.
10l	da balnitori nummos;	Give the bath-keeper coins;
	recipe reliquum.	get the change.
10m	unge."	Anoint (me)."
	"Unxi."	"I have anointed (you)."
	"Ungo me."	"I anoint myself."
	"Frica."	"Rub (me)."
	"Veni ad sudatorium."	"Come to the sweat-room."
	"Sudas?"	"Are you sweating?"
	"Sudo;	"I am sweating;
	lassus sum."	I am exhausted."
10n	"Introeamus ad solium;	"Let's go in to the hot pool;
	descende."	go down."
	"Utamur assa	"Let's use the dry heat room
	et sic descendamus	and go down that way
	ad solium."	to the hot pool."
10o	"Descende,	"Go down,
	fomenta me.	pour hot water over me.
	exi iam.	Now get out.
	mitte te ipsum	Throw yourself
	ad piscinam	into the pool
	subdivalem.	in the open air.
	nata."	Swim!"
	"Natavi."	"I have swum."
10p	"Accede ad luterem;	"Go over to the basin;
	perfunde te."	pour (water) over yourself."
	"Perfudi;	"I have poured (it);
	resumpsi."	I have put (the basin) up again."
	"Porrige strigilem;	"Hand me the strigil;
	deterge me.	rub me down.
10q	cinge sabana.	Wrap the towels around (me).
	terge mihi caput	Dry my head
	et pedes.	and feet.

10r	da caligulas,	Give (me my) shoes,
	calcia me.	put on my shoes.
	porrige amiclum,	Hand (me my) underwear,
	pallam, dalmaticam.	mantle, Dalmatian tunic.
10s	colligite vestimenta	Gather up the clothes
	et omnia nostra.	and all our things.
	sequimini ad domum,	Follow (me) home,
10t	et emite nobis	and buy for us,
	a balneo minutalia	from the bath-shop, chopped food
	et lupinos	and lupins
	et fabas acetatas."	and beans in vinegar."
10u	"Bene lavasti,	"You bathed well;
	bene tibi sit."	may it be well for you."

2.1.21 A dinner party

Dining in a group was an activity requiring good linguistic skills; not only did one need to know how to talk to the other diners, but in order to get any food one had to be able to communicate with the servants. Most colloquia have dinner scenes, and this is one of the most elaborate. It is emphatically Roman rather than Greek in the conventions pre-supposed: the diners first meet for drinks in a separate room where they sit on chairs, then go into the dining room and recline on couches for the meal itself. After eating the diners wash their hands (they have eaten with their fingers) and have a second drinking session. Drinks are mixed individually to the taste of each diner, using a variety of different kinds of wine and both hot and cold water to provide a wide range of options. The seating at dinner is hierarchically arranged, so that a guest is honored by being invited to recline in the first place. The wide variety of food on offer could reflect an elaborate meal, as some Roman banquets were very impressive, but it might simply be the result of an attempt on the part of the writer to squeeze in as much food vocabulary as possible. This passage comes from the Colloquia Monacensia–Einsidlensia;[27] note the non-standard usage of *ad* and *hic* as well as *cum* with the accusative case.

11a	"Date hic cathedras,	"Give here chairs,
	sellas, scamnum,	seats, a bench,
	bisellium,	a double seat,
	cervicale.	a pillow.

[27] Additional information on this text and a scholarly edition of it can be found in Dickey (2012–15: I.59–184).

	sede."	Sit."
	"Sedeo."	"I am sitting."
	"Quid stas?"	"Why are you standing up?"
11b	"Lava calicem,	"Wash out a cup (to warm it),
	aqua calida	with hot water
	tempera;	mix (a drink);
	valde enim sitio.	for I'm very thirsty.
	misce omnibus.	Mix (some) for everyone.
11c	quis quid vult?	Who wants what?
	aut conditum	Spiced wine
	aut caroenum?	or sweet boiled wine?
	ipsum illi misce.	Mix it for him.
	tu quid vis?	You, what do you want?
	lava calicem."	Wash out a cup."
11d	"Misce mihi	"Mix me
	calidum,	a hot drink,
	noli ferventem	don't (make it) boiling
	neque tepidum,	nor lukewarm,
	sed temperatum,	but tempered,
	et effunde deinde modicum.	and then pour out a little.
	mitte recentem.	Put in fresh water.
	adice merum."	Add wine."
11e	"Quid statis?	"Why are you standing up?
	sedete, si vultis."	Sit down, if you want."
	"Discumbamus."	"Let's recline."
	"Ubi iubes?"	"Where do you direct (us to recline)?"
	"In primo loco	"In the first place
	discumbe."	recline."
11f	"Date nobis hydrogaron.	"Give us fish-sauce prepared with water.
	da nobis gustare	Give us a taste of
	malvas ferventes.	boiled mallows.
	porrige mihi mappam.	Hand me a napkin.
	afferte.	Bring (it).
11g	mitte impensam	Put some fish-oil sauce
	ad acetabulum.	into the vinegar-cup.
	divide ungellas.	Divide up the pigs' trotters.
	concide aqualiculum,	Cut up the paunch,
	chordam ex aqua.	the boiled tripe.

11h	vide si habes piperatum.	See if you have a pepper dressing.
	intinge.”	Dip it in.”
	“Utor.”	“I use it.”
	“Utere!”	“Use it!”
	“Da ficatum tenerum,	“Give (us) some tender fig-fattened liver,
	turdos,	thrushes,
	glandulas,	sweetbreads,
	lactucas.	lettuces.
11i	unus de vobis panem frangat	Let one of you (slaves) break the bread
	et in canistellum inferat.	and put it in a basket.
	ad ordinem trade.	Pass it around in order.
	frange quadras.	Break the loaves.
11j	cenate!	Eat!
	utique ille	He is certainly
	dignus est apud nos	worthy among us
	cenare.	to dine.
11k	da salsum,	Give us salted fish,
	sardinas,	pilchards,
	suriacas,	beans,
	cyma	a sprout
	cum liquamine	with fish-sauce
	et oleum Spanum,	and Spanish oil,
	rapatum,	meat in grated turnip,
	gallinam assam,	a roast chicken,
	ofellas	pieces of meat
	iuscellatas,	in sauce,
	copadia,	slices of meat,
	porcellum assum.	roast suckling pig.
11l	pone discum	Put out the platter
	cum scarias,	with endives,
	radices,	radishes,
	mentam,	mint,
	olivas albas	white olives
	et caseum	and cheese
	prosalsum,	(that is) freshly salted,
	tubera,	truffles,
	fungos.	mushrooms.

11m	ministrantibus	To the servants
	date cenare	give dinner
	et coquo;	and to the cook;
	et bellaria,	and (give him) dessert,
	quia bene	because well
	ministravit.	has he served.
11n	date aquam manibus.	Give (us) water (to wash our) hands.
	terge mensam.	Wipe the table.
	da phialam,	Give (us) a cup,
	da merum.	give (us) undiluted wine.
	bibamus recentem de gillone."	Let's drink fresh water from the cooler."
11o	"Misce calidum."	"Mix some hot (wine)."
	"In maiore?"	"In the bigger (cup)?"
	"In minore."	"In the smaller one."
	"Libenter."	"Gladly."
	"Spero enim et aliam bibere."	"For I hope to drink another one too."
11p	"Si permittis,	"If you allow it,
	propino tibi;	I drink to you;
	bene accipis?"	do you take this well?"
	"A te, libenter!"	"From *you*, gladly!"
11q	"Quare non bibis?	"Why aren't you drinking?
	bibe, domine!"	Drink, sir!"
	"Postulavi et nemo mihi dedit."	"I asked (for wine) and no-one gave me (any)."
11r	"Date nobis dulcia placenta."	"Give us sweet cakes."
11s	"Sufficit nobis;	"It is enough for us.
	eamus iam.	Let's go now.
	accende lampadam."	Light the torch."
	"Accipe."	"Take it."
	"Bene nos accepisti."	"You have entertained us well."

2.1.22 Getting a scolding

Roman dinner parties were not always decorous affairs; participants might drink more than was sensible and while under the influence might do things that they would later regret. The colloquia do not describe any of these scenes, but they do include a scene in which a character is rebuked for his (unspecified) behavior while drunk. It is unclear what the relationship between the scolder and the miscreant is, though some type of family connection seems likely. This passage comes from the Colloquium Celtis; watch for non-standard indirect statement and *numquid* for *num*.[28]

66a	"Quis sic facit,	"Who acts like this,
	domine,	sir,
	quomodo tu,	as you do,
	ut tantum bibis?	that you drink so much?
66b	quid dicent	What will they say,
	qui te viderunt talem?	the people who saw you in such a condition?
	quod numquam	That you never
	foris cenasti	dined out
	tam aviditer?	so greedily?
66c	ita hoc decet	Is this a fitting way for a
	sapientem	prudent
	patrem familias	master of a household
	qui aliis consilia dat	who gives advice to others
	semet ipsum regere?	to conduct himself?
67a	non potest	It is not possible (for things)
	turpius	more shamefully
	nec ignominiosius	nor more ignominiously
	evenire	to happen
	quam heri gessisti."	than you acted yesterday."
67b	"Me certe valde	"I certainly am very much
	pudet."	ashamed."
	"Quid dicunt alii	"What do others say
	in absentia tua?	in your absence?
67c	infamiam maximam	Great infamy
	tibi cumulasti.	have you accumulated for yourself.
	accidit ad haec	In addition to this,
	grandis denotatio	great censure (of you) has occurred
	de tali intemperantia.	as a result of such intemperance.
67d	rogo te	Please,
	ne postea	in the future don't
	tale facias.	do such a thing.

[28] Additional information on this text and a scholarly edition of it can be found in Dickey (2012–15: II.141–266). Alternatives have been deleted for coherence.

| 68a | sed modo numquid vomere vis? et miror quae passus es." | But now you don't want to vomit, do you? And I'm amazed at what has become of you." |
| 68b | "Nescio quid dicam, ita enim perturbatus sum ut rationem nulli possim reddere." | "I don't know what to say, for so upset have I been that no explanation to anyone can I give." |

2.1.23 Bedtime

These words about the end of the day come from the Colloquium Celtis, where they are found in two separate places in the text.[29]

65	Extinguite luminaria et focum diligenter cooperite. ite pausatum.	Put out the lamps, and cover the fireplace carefully. Go to sleep.
	. . .	. . .
69a	Claudite, pueri, ostia et fenestras, imponite seras,	(Slave) boys, close the doors and windows, put up the bars,
69b	adponite necessarium. ite, pausate.	set out the chamber pot. Go, get some rest.

2.1.24 A phrasebook section on insults

Some portions of the colloquia consist of sets of disconnected phrases, rather like a modern Berlitz phrasebook. These are arranged by topic, again like a modern phrasebook, but they were probably not used quite like their modern equivalents. One of the longest and most detailed phrasebook sections is a set of insults, and it is difficult to imagine that such a section could have been used like a modern phrasebook, which is essentially a reference work and is deployed in the course of a conversation. Such use

---

[29] Additional information on this text and a scholarly edition of it can be found in Dickey (2012–15: ii.141–266).

of a phrasebook requires considerable patience and often active co-operation on the part of the addressees, who may be asked to read off the phrase in their own language. This co-operative usage works in situations where both parties have something to gain from successful communication – for example if the language learner is a potential customer of the person helping with the phrasebook – but could not be successful in the type of interaction where insults are deployed. The inclusion of an insults section, therefore, tells us that ancient phrasebooks were probably not reference works designed to be used during a conversation, but rather collections of material that would be memorized before the user needed it.

Note the frequent references to slavery; many of the insults that seem to be designed for slaves were probably really intended to be used for free men, since pretending to mistake a free man for a slave would have been an enormous insult in antiquity. The animal-fighter was someone who fought wild beasts in the arena, a very low-status occupation. This passage comes from the Colloquium Harleianum;[30] as the insults section is long and some portions are not coherent, only selections are given here.

16a	"Duc te ergo.	"So take yourself off.
	quid stas?"	Why are you standing around?"
	"Quid tibi pertinet?	"What business is it of yours?
	procurator meus es?"	Are you my overseer?"
16b	"Duc te,	"Take yourself off,
	recede,	withdraw,
	impostor."	impostor."
16c	"Maledicis me,	"Do you revile me,
	maligne	baleful
	et odiose?"	and hateful man?"
	. . .	. . .
16e	"Tace!"	"Shut up!"
	. . .	. . .
16g	"Ista audiet	"He will hear about this,
	dominus tuus,	your master,
	si obviat mihi."	if he encounters me."
	. . .	. . .
17b	"Non curo	"I don't care about
	minationes."	your threats."

---

30 Additional information on this text and a scholarly edition of it can be found in Dickey (2012–15: II.3–80). The British Library has generously posted photographs of the manuscript (Harley 5642) at www.bl.uk/manuscripts/Viewer.aspx?ref=harley_ms_5642_fs001v; these extracts begin on folio 31v.

17c	"Multa vindico, desperate."	"I avenge a lot of things, you no-hoper."
17d	"Ibi manus habe!"	"Keep your hands over there!"
	. . .	. . .
18a	"Maledicis me, malum caput? crucifigaris!"	"Do you revile me, villain? May you be crucified!"
	. . .	. . .
18c	"Qua re? quoniam ego ingenuus homo sum, tu autem nequam servus."	"Why? Because myself a freeborn man I am, but you are a useless slave."
18d	"Silentium habe!"	"Be quiet!"
	. . .	. . .
18f	"Volo discere utrum servus es aut libertus."	"I want to find out whether you are a slave or a freedman."
18g	"Non do tibi rationem." "Qua re?" "Quoniam non es dignus."	"I'm not giving you an explanation." "Why?" "Because you aren't worthy."
18h	"Eamus ad dominum tuum."	"Let's go to your master."
	. . .	. . .
24a	"Et maledicit bestiarius? dimitte me et dentes eius excutio."	"And does he revile (me), that animal-fighter? Let me go, and I shall shake out his teeth."
24b	"Ego te excaeco."	"I (shall) blind you."
	. . .	. . .
24c	"Ego te faciam in carcerem ire,	"I shall make you go to prison,

ubi dignus es	where you deserve
senescere."	to grow old."

2.1.25 A phrasebook section on excuses

Another phrasebook section provides a list of excuses that, to a modern eye, look pretty feeble. The fact that the ancient writer clearly thought these were the excuses his readers might find useful gives us fascinating insight into a respect in which ancient culture was very different from our own. This passage comes from the Colloquium Harleianum.[31]

15e	"Sed cito	"But immediately
	fecisti	you did
	quod tibi dixi?"	what I told you (to do)?"
	"Nondum."	"Not yet."
15f	"Qua re?"	"Why?"
	"Modo facio;	"I (shall) do it soon,
	propero enim foras,	for I'm in a hurry to go out,
15g	esurio,	I'm hungry,
	in nuptias,	(I'm hurrying) to a wedding,
	ad amicum,	(I'm hurrying) to a friend,
	expectant me,	they're waiting for me,
	ut lavem."	(I'm hurrying) to take a bath."

2.1.26 A phrasebook section on complaints about absence

This set of complaints comes from the Colloquium Harleianum.[32] Note the preposition with *domus*, the use of *civitas* for "town," and the term "brother," which was widespread during the empire (in both Latin and Greek) for friends and even casual acquaintances.

26a	Quid est,	What is it,
	frater?	brother?
	quare non	Why didn't

---

[31] Additional information on this text and a scholarly edition of it can be found in Dickey (2012–15: II.3–80). The British Library has generously posted photographs of the manuscript (Harley 5642) at www.bl.uk/ manuscripts/Viewer.aspx?ref=harley_ms_5642_fs001v; this passage is on folios 31r and 31v.

[32] Additional information on this text and a scholarly edition of it can be found in Dickey (2012–15: II.3–80). The British Library has generously posted photographs of the manuscript (Harley 5642) at www.bl.uk/ manuscripts/Viewer.aspx?ref=harley_ms_5642_fs001v; this passage is on folios 33r and 33v.

	venisti ad templum?	you come to the temple?
26b	ad domum?	to our house?
	ad forum?	to the forum?
	ad auditorium?	to the lecture hall?
	ad iudicem?	to the judge?
	ad consularem?	to the ex-consul?
26c	in civitatem?	to town?
	ad villam?	to the country estate?
	ad fratrem nostrum?	to our brother?
26d	ego te sustinui	I waited for you
	et propter te tarde prandidi.	and because of you I ate lunch late.

2.1.27 The conclusion

This conclusion to the colloquia comes from the Colloquium Harleianum.[33]

25e	Feliciter scripsi de sermone cottidiano.	With good fortune have I written about daily speech.

2.2 Stories about the Trojan War

The Homeric poems, and particularly the *Iliad*, held a pre-eminent position in ancient literature; their status as the greatest works of classical literature went virtually unchallenged for more than a thousand years. Over that period, however, the Greek language changed considerably; as all languages change over time, to get a sense of the scale of changes in a thousand years an English speaker can consider the difference between our English and that of Shakespeare, who wrote about 400 years ago, or Chaucer, who wrote about 600 years ago. As a result, by the time Latin-learning texts were

---

[33] Additional information on this text and a scholarly edition of it can be found in Dickey (2012–15: II.3–80). The British Library has generously posted photographs of the manuscript (Harley 5642) at www.bl.uk/manuscripts/Viewer.aspx?ref=harley_ms_5642_fs001v; this passage is on folio 33r.

developed during the Roman empire, many Greek speakers had considerable diffi-culty reading the *Iliad* itself; they often experienced Homer not directly but through summaries and paraphrases. Book-by-book summaries of the *Iliad* were common, and one of these sets of summaries was turned into a bilingual work and used for learning Latin.

This work survives (or rather part of it survives; the summaries of the poem's early books are missing, as is the very end of the text) in the Hermeneumata Leidensia.[34] The extracts given here cover books 8–10; in the manuscript the numbers of the books are given only in Greek, so they are reproduced here only in English. The summaries do not always contain what a modern Classical scholar would include if he or she were to summarize the same book at the same length; for example in book 9 Agamemnon's offer of reconciliation to Achilles, which is the point of the embassy, is not mentioned, nor are Achilles' grounds for rejecting it, though many modern scholars would say that the speeches made by the embassy and by Achilles are absolutely pivotal for the plot of the *Iliad*. On the other hand Diomedes' words when the embassy returns, which we would consider less important, do get mentioned in the summary. Such differences could be attributed to varying perspectives, but other points in the summary of book 9 can only be described as outright errors. In the *Iliad* itself Diomedes does not terrify the army with threats, and the role of Nestor is to agree with Diomedes' speech to Agamemnon, not to be its addressee. It seems likely that the author of these summaries either did not base them on the *Iliad* itself (he or she may have read a paraphrase instead, and the paraphrase may have contained errors) or read the *Iliad* but did not entirely understand it.

Note the non-standard sequence of tenses *suadet . . . ut mitteret*, the use of an infini-tive instead of an *ut*-clause for an indirect command, and the way that *autem* can mean both "and" and "but" (probably because it was considered the equivalent of Greek δέ, which has both those meanings). In addition to the extracts given below, portions of this text can be found in passages 8.3 and 9.2.

Book 8

61.8	Pugna autem commissa periclitantem	And when battle was joined Nestor, who was in danger from Hector,
61.10	ab Hectore Nestorem vix Diomedes rapuit; eum	Diomedes just barely saved; him (Nestor)

---

[34] Additional information on this text can be found in Dickey (2012–15: I.27–8). The text given here is a slightly emended version of the scholarly edition of Flammini (2004: 110–11), but the layout follows that of the Leiden manuscript, Vossianus Gr. Q. 7, and the numbering refers to Goetz's transcription of that manuscript (Goetz 1892: 61–2).

	curro imposuit	he (Diomedes) put in a chariot
	et ad naves	and to the ships
61.15	perduxit.	brought him back.
	Teucrum autem multos	But Teucer, (who was) killing many of the
	occidentem Troianorum	Trojans,
	Agamemnon laudavit,	Agamemnon praised,
	quem postea Hector magno	(Teucer) whom afterwards Hector
61.20	saxo exterminavit.	removed from the scene with a great stone.
	et Iuppiter tunc Iunonem	And Zeus then ordered Hera and Athena to
	et Minervam	depart
	ab exercitu Graecorum	from the army of the Greeks,
	discedere iussit,	
61.25	et sic victoria	and thus the victory
	Troianorum fuit.	was the Trojans'.

Book 9

	Cum videret Agamemnon	When Agamemnon saw
	in victoria Hectorem	that in victory Hector
	superiorem esse,	was superior,
61.30	suadebat fugere Graecos,	he advised the Greeks to flee,
	sed Diomedes,	but Diomedes,
	ut vidit hoc fieri,	when he saw that happen,
	pavoravit eos,	terrified them,
	ut fugientes interficeret;	(acting as if) he would kill the men fleeing;
61.35	vitium autem et Nestori	and also to Nestor that there was a flaw
	dixit consilio huius.	in his (Agamemnon's) plan he (Diomedes)
		said.
	convocavit ergo Graecos	So he called together the Greeks
	ad componendas eorum	to settle their
	animas,	spirits,
61.40	et tunc Nestor	and then Nestor
	suadet Agamemnonem	advises Agamemnon
	ut mitteret legatos	to send envoys
	ad Achillem,	to Achilles,
	Phoenicem et Aiacem	Phoenix and Ajax
61.45	et Ulixem,	and Odysseus,
	ut indignantem eum	so that him, who was angry,
	placarent.	they might appease.

	revertentes ergo sine effectu	So when they came back without success
	contristati sunt,	they were saddened,
61.50	quos Diomedes sua voce	and Diomedes consoled them with his words.
	consolatus est.	

Book 10

62.1	Postea autem	And afterwards
	Agamemnon	Agamemnon
	et Menelaus	and Menelaus
	excitant Nestorem	wake up Nestor
62.5	et ceteros	and others
	Graecorum,	of the Greeks,
	et Nestor	and Nestor
	impetrat ad Ulixem,	asks Odysseus
	ut iret cum Diomede	to go with Diomedes
62.10	Troianorum speculator;	as a spy on the Trojans;
	quibus oblatus Dolo	(and) Dolon meeting them
	occiditur ab eis,	is killed by them,
	sed et Rhesum	but also Rhesus,
	Thracorum regem	the king of the Thracians,
62.15	interfecerunt,	they killed,
	et continuo iussu	and immediately by order
	Minervae,	of Athena,
	antequam luceret,	before it grew light,
	ad naves redierunt.	they returned to the ships.

2.3   Aesop's fables

Aesop's fables were popular easy readers for children learning to read for the first time, not only because they are short and relatively easy but also because their explicitly drawn morals fitted in with ancient educational theories. These same characteristics made them useful for foreign-language reading practice as well: fables were read, translated both into and out of the foreign language, and memorized. These bilingual versions from the Hermeneumata Leidensia[35] were probably intended to be memorized. Note

---

[35]   Additional information on this text can be found in Dickey (2012–15: 1.24–5); for general background on the Aesop corpus see Perry (1952). The fables reproduced here are known by the following references: *De infirmo* is number 7 in the Hermeneumata Leidensia, 134 Ch. in Aesop, and 75 in Babrius; *De corvo* is number 9 in the Hermeneumata Leidensia, 126 H. in Aesop, 77 in Babrius, and 1.13 in Phaedrus; *De culice* is number 16 in the

how the writer loses track of sequence of tenses in 43.17, an indirect command with the infinitive, an indirect question introduced by *si*, the non-standard negative command construction *non timeas*, and the use of *post tempus* for *postea*. "Orcus" is a god of the underworld; the Greek has "Charon" as its equivalent, but Charon's usual mythological role fits poorly with the next sentence. In addition to the extracts given below, portions of this text can be found in passage 8.4.

42.56	**De infirmo**	**About the sick man**
	Quidam infirmus	A certain sick man,
	ab indocto medico	who by an ignorant doctor
	desperatus	had been given up for lost,
43.1	convaluit,	recovered;
	et obviatus ei	and when the doctor encountered him
	medicus	
	post tempus	later
43.5	interrogavit,	he (the doctor) asked
	si ipse sit,	if he (the recovered man) was the person
	quem desperavit.	whom he had given up on.
	is respondit	He answered that
	Orci gratia	by the grace of Orcus
43.10	remissum se esse	he had been sent back
	ab inferis,	from the underworld,
	praeterea autem	and that besides,
	Orcum statuisse	Orcus had decided
	omnes medicos	that all doctors
43.15	intra paucos dies	in the next few days
	apud se duci,	should be brought to him,
	ut eos torqueat,	so that he could torture them,
	quoniam eorum neglegentia	since by their negligence
	multi moriuntur.	many people are dying.
43.20	"Sed tu	"But as for you,
	non timeas;	don't be afraid;
	ego enim dixi ei	for I told him
	te medicum	that you had never been a doctor;
	numquam fuisse;	

Hermeneumata Leidensia, 140 H. in Aesop, and 84 in Babrius. The text given here is a slightly emended version of that of Flammini (2004: 84, 85, 90), but the layout follows that of the Leiden manuscript, Vossianus Gr. Q. 7, and the numbering follows Goetz's transcript of that manuscript (Goetz 1892: 42–7).

43.25	primum enim te adduci adnotaverat."	for he had written down to have you brought first."
	haec fabula potest	This fable can
43.30	ad eum pertinere, qui quod nescit promittit.	apply to him who promises what he knows nothing about.
	…	…

De corvo — **About the crow**

43.52	**De corvo**	**About the crow**
	Corvus caseum rapuit et super arborem	A crow snatched a piece of cheese and flying up into a tree
43.55	volans sedit. speculata ergo eum vulpis accessit et laudare coepit	sat there. So having caught sight of him a vixen approached and began to praise
44.1	eius virtutem; arguebat autem quod tale animal vocem non haberet.	his abilities; but she asserted that such an animal could not have a voice.
44.5	fallacia ergo corvus aperuit rostrum, cui caseum cadentem vulpis raptum comedit.	So by this trick the crow opened his beak (to show off his voice), whose falling cheese the vixen snatched and ate.
44.10	sic complures, quod virtutibus non possunt, sapientia explicant.	Thus very many people, what they cannot do by strength, they manage by brains.
	…	…
46.43	**De culice**	**About the gnat**
	Culex sedit adveniens	A gnat came and sat
46.45	cornuo curvo tauri, et post paululum dixit haec fritinniens,	on the curved horn of a bull, and after a little while said this, twittering,

	"Si te gravo	"If I weigh down
	cervicem et campso,	your neck and bend it,
46.50	discedam dormiturus	I shall go off to sleep
	in fluminalibus populis."	in the poplar-trees by the river."
46.51a	ille autem,	But he (the bull)
47.1	"Non ad nos pertinet,"	said, "It makes no difference to us,"
	inquit,	
	"nec si maneas,	"neither if you stay,
	nec si te ducas,	nor if you depart,
	nec quando veneris, ego	nor did I notice when you came."
	scivi."	

2.4 Judgements of Hadrian

Faced with classes made up largely of future lawyers (see section 1.1 above), many Latin teachers may have found it difficult to arouse interest in topics like Aesop's fables or the Trojan War. They therefore sometimes taught from legal texts, which for the early stages of teaching had to be provided with running translations like the colloquia. Here is an extract from one of the bilingual texts that was used this way, the judgements of Hadrian. The emperor Hadrian was revered after his death, especially in the Greek-speaking portions of the empire, for his wisdom and understanding; he held a position analogous to that of the wise king Solomon in Judaeo-Christian popular imagination. It is that aspect of him that is emphasized in these short vignettes, each of which is suitable for memorizing in a short session, even by a beginner. They depict Hadrian giving public judgements in person; the extent to which these depictions are historically valid can be debated, but it is by no means certain that they are inaccurate, as other evidence for imperial judgements of this sort exists. This text, which comes from the Hermeneumata Leidensia, is valuable in part because, unlike other texts pertaining to Roman law, it has not been preserved through other channels: only the bilingual version used for learning Latin is known today.[36]

The Praetorian Guard was the emperor's personal guard and the most prestigious unit; only particularly tall soldiers were allowed to serve in it. The point of the first story is that Hadrian did not let people into this guard, even if they met the height requirement, without making sure they were of good character. The *congiarium* was a periodic

---

[36] Additional information on this text can be found in Dickey (2012–15: I.28) and Schiller (1971a, 1971b). The text given here is a slightly emended version of the scholarly edition of Flammini (2004: 68–9, 71, 74), but the layout follows that of the Leiden manuscript, Vossianus Gr. Q. 7, and the numbering follows Goetz's transcript of that manuscript (Goetz 1892: 31–6).

distribution of public funds; evidently it was possible under certain circumstances for one person to claim another's share of this money, and such claims gave rise to legal disputes. The point of the second story is that Hadrian realized that the petitioner's only reason for wanting to kill the freedman was a desire to take his share of the *congiarium* (to which he would not be entitled if the man was still alive) and rebuked him for his greedy cruelty, thereby protecting the weaker members of society from the stronger ones. The point of the third story is that Hadrian upheld the traditional social order and protected the weak by ensuring that children looked after their parents. The point of the fourth story is that Hadrian did not make hasty decisions without examining the evidence (he wanted to know why the petitioner's father had been exiled before determining whether to recall him) but at the same time did not use the resulting delay as an excuse for inaction: his request that the petitioner return shows that he intended to find the information and make a decision. The final story concerns a guardian, an adult male legally responsible for managing property owned by a fatherless child; such a guardian could receive income such as the *congiarium* on behalf of the child and was supposed to make sure that income from the property was given to the household where the child lived as needed. The guardian in this story came under suspicion of embezzlement by claiming the *congiarium* when he had not distributed any funds to the child's household, and Hadrian again protected the weak by insisting that he fill his role as guardian properly in the future.

The writer begins with a bold assertion of the high quality of the language of this text, but within a few lines we find both the accusative *in urbanam* where Classical Latin would require an ablative, and the ablative *in praetorio* where the Classical language would require an accusative. Note also the non-standard indirect statement, indirect commands using the infinitive, the use of cases with *in*, non-reflexive possessives where Cicero would have employed *se* or *suus*, and *ante tempus* for *antea*.

Another set of extracts from this text can be found in passage 8.5.

31.2	Haec erunt	These will be
	divi Adriani	the divine Hadrian's
	sententiae	judgements
31.5	et epistulae,	and letters,
	ex quibus maior	from which rather great
	utilitas	usefulness
	sequitur	follows
	hominibus;	for people;
31.10	ab eo	from that
	principe	ruler
	fuit	came

	et loquella,	also (correct) language,
	propterea	and for that reason
31.15	necessario sunt	they are necessarily
	legenda	to be read
	et memoriae	and memorized,
	tradenda,	
	si tamen volumus	at least if we want
31.20	Latine loqui	to speak in Latin
	vel Graece	or in Greek
	sine vitio.	flawlessly.
	sic incipiamus.	Then let us begin.
	Petente quodam	When someone asked
31.25	ut militaret,	to serve in the army,
	Adrianus dixit,	Hadrian said,
	"Ubi vis	"Where do you want
	militare?"	to serve?"
	illo dicente,	When he said,
31.30	"In praetorio,"	"In the Praetorian Guard,"
	Adrianus interrogavit,	Hadrian asked,
	"Quam staturam habes?"	"How tall are you?"
	dicente illo,	When he said,
	"Quinque pedes	"Five feet
	et semis,"	and a half,"
31.35	Adrianus dixit,	Hadrian said,
	"Interim	"For the time being
	in urbanam	serve in the city guard,
	milita,	
	et si bonus	and if a good
31.40	miles fueris,	soldier you are,
	tertio stipendio	in your third year of service
	poteris	you will be able
	in praetorio	to transfer to the Praetorian Guard."
	transire."	
31.45	Per libellum	Via a petition
	petente quodam,	when someone asked
	ut suum	to have his own freedman killed,
	libertum	
	perderet,	

31.50	quem ante tempus	(a freedman) whom previously
	iussu praefecti	by order of the prefect
	aerari,	of the treasury,
	secundum legem	according to the Lex
	Aeliam Sentiam,	Aelia Sentia,
31.55	in lautumias	he had sent to the quarries (as punishment),
32.1	miserat,	
	et modo cum	and when (the petitioner)
	congiarium	sought the (freedman's) share of public funds,
	huius peteret,	
32.5	Adrianus dixit,	Hadrian said,
	"Quid quaeris perdere	"Why do you seek to destroy
	hominem	a man
	et congiarium	and take his share of public funds,
	auferre,	
32.10	ex quo iam	(a man) on whom already
	vindicatus es?	you have taken vengeance?
	improbus es."	You are wicked!"
	Petente quodam	When someone made a request
	de suo filio,	about his own son,
32.15	quoniam eum	(alleging) that (the son) neglected him (his
	neglegeret	father)
	valetudinarium	who was afflicted by ill health
	et pauperem,	and poor,
	et pascere nollet,	and did not want to look after him,
32.20	in quo omnes	(the son) on whom he had spent all
	facultates suas	his resources,
	expenderat,	
	Adrianus dixit	Hadrian said
	iuveni,	to the young man,
32.25	"Custodi patrem tuum,	"Take care of your father,
	ideo enim te	for that is why he
	genuit;	fathered you;
	cura ergo	so make sure
	ne iterum	that he does not again complain
32.30	de te	about you
	apud me	to me."
	queratur."	...
	...	

33.26	Petente quodam	When someone asked
	permitti sibi	for it to be granted to him
	patrem suum	that his father
	ab exilio	be recalled from exile,
33.30	revocari,	
	Adrianus dixit,	Hadrian said,
	"Sine videam	"Let me look
	commentarios;	at the records;
	tu tamen cura	but you, take care
33.35	reverti	to come back
	ad me."	to me."
	. . .	. . .
35.41	Petente quadam	When a certain woman made a request about
	muliere de curatore	the guardian
	filii sui,	of her son,
	qui ei	(a guardian) who had not provided food for him
35.45	triennium	for three years,
	non praestiterat	
	alimenta,	
	et hodie	and today
	congiarium	had taken away his share of public funds,
35.50	eius	
	abstulit,	
	Adrianus	Hadrian
	curatorem	asked the guardian
	interrogavit,	
35.55	quando esset	when he had been
	procurator	appointed guardian,
	datus,	
	et si quid	and whether he had done anything
	praestitisset	
35.60	pupillo.	for the ward.
	curator dixit,	The guardian said
	quoniam socius	that his colleague
	eius	
36.1	absens esset	was absent
	et non potuisset	and that he had not been able

	aliquid solus	to do anything by himself.
	praestare.	
36.5	Adrianus dixit	Hadrian said
	curatori,	to the guardian,
	"Propter hoc ergo	"So were you for this purpose
	datus es,	appointed (guardian),
	ut fame neces	to kill by starvation
36.10	pupillum?	your ward?
	pro modo ergo	Therefore to the best
	facultatis	of your ability
	alimenta ei	provide food for him!"
	praesta."	

2.5   Treatise on manumission

This difficult technical treatise on Roman law seems at first sight like peculiar reading material for language learners, but its bilingual transmission in the Hermeneumata Leidensia tells us that it was indeed so used.[37] Probably the demand for it came from law students who wanted to start practicing on a real legal manual at an early stage of their Latin learning, but owing to its difficulty the treatise is not completely suitable for beginners.

Manumission, the procedures by which a slave could be freed, was a complex subject in Roman law because there were numerous different types of manumission with different restrictions on their use and different outcomes for the new freedman. The extract quoted here discusses one type, "Latin" manumission. The distinction between the status it conveyed and full citizenship has to do with the fact that during the Republic Roman colonies were autonomous rather than being part of Rome; therefore a Roman citizen who joined such a colony ceased to be a full Roman citizen. Watch for indirect questions with the indicative, the unusual meaning "citizenship" for *administratio*, and the surprising phrase *hoc tamen sic habens* for what Cicero would have expressed with *quae cum ita sunt*; this last may be a calque of the Greek τοῦτο δὴ οὕτως ἔχον. For further extracts from this treatise see passage 8.6.

---

[37] The text is known to lawyers as the *Fragmentum Dositheanum*; additional information on it can be found in Dickey (2012–15: I.28–30) and Honoré (1965). The text given here is a slightly emended version of that of Flammini (2004: 95–7), but the layout follows that of the Leiden manuscript, Vossianus Gr. Q. 7, and the numbering refers to Goetz's transcript of that manuscript (Goetz 1892: 49–51). In line 51.11 *liberi* "free" is an emendation of the manuscript's *liberti* "freed."

49.62	Omnes enim	For all (free) men
	vel ingenui sunt	are either free-born
	vel liberti.	or freedmen.
49.65	sed ut magis	But so that
	possint	the individual points can better be made,
	singula declarari,	
	melius videtur	it seems better
	incipere	to begin to introduce them
49.70	a libertis	starting with the freedmen,
	adferre,	
	et primum	and to write first
	de Latinis	about the Latins,
50.1	scribere,	
	ne saepius	lest we should be compelled to explain rather often
	eadem	the same things.
	interpretari	
50.5	cogamur.	
	primum ergo	So first
	videamus,	let us see
	quale est	what sort of thing is
	quod dicitur	that which is said,
50.9a	eos qui inter amicos veteres	that those of former times who among friends
50.9b	manumittebantur	were manumitted
50.10	non esse liberos,	were not free,
	sed domini	but by their master's
	voluntate	wish
	in libertatem	at liberty
	morari,	remained,
50.15	et tantum	and only
	servitutis	from slavery's
	timore	burden
	dimitti.	were they released.
	ante enim	For previously
50.20	una libertas erat,	there was (only) one (kind of) freedom,
	et libertas	and freedom
	fiebat	was created
	ex vindictis,	from *vindicta* (manumission),

	vel ex testamento,	or from (manumission by) will,
50.25	vel in censu,	or from (manumission by) census,
	et administratio	and the citizenship
	Romana	of Rome
	competebat	protected (the freedom of)
	manumissis;	manumitted people;
50.30	quae appellatur	which (kind of freedom) was called
	iusta	proper
	libertas.	freedom.
	hi tamen,	But those
	qui domini	who by their master's
50.35	voluntate	wish
	in libertate erant,	were in freedom
	manebant servi,	remained slaves,
	et manumissores	and their manumitters
	ausi erant	dared
50.40	in servitutem	to reduce them again to slavery by force.
	denuo eos	
	per vim	
	perducere.	
	interveniebat praetor	(By contrast), a praetor used to intervene
50.45	et non patiebatur	and not allow
	manumissum	a man who had been (properly) freed
	servire.	to be enslaved.
	omnia tamen	But (a person freed among friends)
	quasi servus	just like a slave
50.50	adquirebat	used to get everything
	manumissori;	for the benefit of his manumitter;
	vel si quid stipulabatur	whether if he made a covenant about something
	vel mancupatione	or by purchase
	accipiebat, vel si	he acquired (something), or whether
50.55	ex quibuscumque	from any
	causis aliis	other legal channels
	adquisierat,	he had obtained (something),
	domini	(the possession) of his master
	hoc fiebat;	it became;
50.60	id est	that is,

	manumissi	the manumitted man's
	omnia bona	entire property
	ad patronum	to his patron
	pertinebant.	belonged.
50.65	sed nunc	But now
	habent propriam	they have their own
	libertatem	freedom,
	inter amicos	the men who among friends
	manumissi,	are freed,
50.70	et fiunt	and they become
	Latini	Junian Latins,
	Iuniani,	
51.1	quoniam	since
	lex Iunia,	the *lex Junia*,
	quae	which
	libertatem	gave them freedom,
51.5	eis dedit,	
	exaequavit eos	equated them
	Latinis	to Latin
	colonariis,	colonists,
	qui cum essent	who although they were
51.10	cives Romani	Roman citizens
	liberi,	and free,
	nomen suum	their names
	in coloniam	in the colony
	dedissent.	they had registered.
51.15	in eis	In the case of those
	qui inter	who among
	amicos	friends
	manumittuntur,	are freed,
	voluntatem	the wish
51.20	domini	of the master
	spectant;	they (the judges) consider;
	lex enim	for the *lex*
	Iunia	*Junia*
	eos fieri	orders them to become
51.25	Latinos	Latins,
	iubet,	

	quos dominus	(those) whom the master
	liberos	wanted to be free.
	esse voluit.	
51.30	hoc tamen	But under these circumstances,
	sic habens,	
	debet voluntatem	the master must have the wish
	manumittentis	of manumitting (his slave),
	habere	
51.35	dominus,	
	unde si	whence (it follows that) if
	per vim	having been compelled by force,
	coactus,	
	verbi gratia	for example
51.40	ab aliquo populo	by some group
	vel a singulis	or by individual
	hominibus,	men,
	manumiserit,	he manumits (the slave),
	non perveniet	the slave will not arrive
51.45	servus	
	ad libertatem,	at freedom,
	quia non intellegitur	because he is not understood
	voluisse	to have wanted (to free the slave),
	qui coactus est.	(he) who was forced.
51.50	similiter,	Similarly,
	ut possit	in order that a slave may be able
	habere	to have
	servus	
	libertatem,	freedom,
51.55	talis esse	such a type (of freedman)
	debet,	he ought to be,
51.57	ut praetor	that a praetor
51.59	sive proconsul	or proconsul
51.60	libertatem	his freedom
51.58	eius	
51.61	tueatur.	can protect.
	nam et hoc	For this too
	lege Iunia	by the *lex Junia*
	tutatum est.	was protected.

51.65	sunt autem	There are, however,
	plures causae	more cases
	in quibus non tueatur	in which a proconsul would not protect
	proconsul	
	manumissionem,	the manumission,
51.70	de quibus	concerning which
	procedentes	as we proceed
	ostendemus.	we shall explain.

2.6 Virgil's *Aeneid*

The first Latin poetry read by ancient Latin students was often a selection from one of the early books of Virgil's *Aeneid*; these were presented in a bilingual format like the other elementary texts, though that format required the lines of verse to be broken up into smaller units. The extract below, from a fourth-century papyrus,[38] covers lines 247–60 of book 1, the end of Venus' complaint to Jupiter about the poor treatment of Aeneas and the beginning of Jupiter's reply. In several places the word order has been rearranged to make the meaning clearer;[39] such rearrangement would have been helpful for student comprehension and probably did not cause problems with scansion, since there is no evidence that Greek-speaking Latin learners ever scanned Virgil or read the poems aloud metrically. There are also a few mistakes, both in the Latin itself and in the Greek translation.[40]

247	"Hic tamen ille	Here, nevertheless, that man
	urbem Patavi	established the city of Padua, and a home
	sedesque locavit	
248	Teucrorum, et genti	for the Trojans, and to the people
	nomen dedit	he gave a name,
	armaque fixit	and he hung up the arms
249	Troia, nunc	of Troy, (and) now

[38] *P.Ryl.* III.478 + *P.Cairo* inv. 85644, which is number 5 in Scappaticcio (2013a), number 2940 in the Mertens–Pack database (http://promethee.philo.ulg.ac.be/cedopal/indexsimple.asp), and number 4146 in the Leuven Database of Ancient Books (www.trismegistos.org/ldab/). The text given here is based on that of Scappaticcio but with spelling corrected. For more information on this text and the Virgil papyri in general see Scappaticcio (2013a), Fressura (2013), Gaebel (1970), and Rochette (1990).

[39] In Virgil's version line 251 runs *navibus (infandum!) amissis unius ob iram*, and 252 runs *prodimur atque Italis longe disiungimur oris.*

[40] In 256 the Greek translation has φιλήματα ἐθέσπισεν "he prophesied a kiss," perhaps owing to a misunderstanding of *libavit*, which can mean "dedicate, consecrate." In 258 *tibi* was probably omitted by the writer of the papyrus. I have corrected both these errors to avoid misleading anyone.

	placida compostus	settled in tranquil
	pace quiescit:	peace he rests;
250	nos, tua progenies,	(but) we, your children,
	caeli quibus	to whom of heaven
	adnuis arcem,	you allocate the citadel,
251	navibus amissis	with our ships lost
	(infandum!) unius	(unspeakable!) on account of one individual's
252	ob iram prodimur	anger we are forsaken,
	atque Italis oris	and from the shores of Italy
	longe disiungimur.	we are separated by a long distance.
253	hic pietatis honos?	Is this the reward of piety?
	sic nos in sceptra	Is this the way that us to power
	reponis?"	you restore?"
254	Olli subridens	Smiling on her,
	hominum sator	the father of men
	atque deorum	and gods,
255	vultu, quo caelum	with the face with which the heavens
	tempestatesque	and storms
	serenat,	he calms,
256	oscula libavit	he tasted a kiss
	natae,	from his daughter,
	dehinc talia fatur:	and then spoke as follows,
257	"Parce metu, Cytherea:	"Spare yourself from fear, Cytherea:
	manent immota	they remain unchanged,
258	tuorum fata tibi;	the destinies of your offspring;
	cernes urbem	you will see the city
	et promissa Lavini	and Lavinium's promised
259	moenia	walls,
	sublimemque feres	and you will take up
	ad sidera caeli	to the stars of heaven
260	magnanimum Aenean;	great-souled Aeneas;
	neque me sententia	nor has an opinion
	vertit . . . "	changed me . . . "

2.7   Model letters

Many of the things one might want to express in a Latin letter were predictable: people wrote thank-you notes, letters of reference, consolations, congratulations, requests, etc., often in standardized formats. Sets of model letters therefore existed, giving ready-made letters in Latin with their Greek translations; today's foreign-language dictionaries often contain similar model letters, though the letters' topics may be different. It is unclear whether such letters should really count as Latin-learning texts, since the people who used a collection of model letters may have done so instead of, rather than in the course of, learning how to write their own Latin letters; the letters have been given the benefit of the doubt for inclusion here because they are interesting, but the Latin is fairly difficult. The letters quoted here, a set of ways to congratulate someone on receiving an inheritance, come from a papyrus of the third or fourth century AD.[41]

Inheritance was far more important in the Roman world than it is today, as there were comparatively few other methods of acquiring substantial property. If a man had children, they might remain financially dependent on him until he died and they inherited his estate. If he had no children, or chose not to leave them his whole estate, an opportunity for social mobility was created for his friends, for poor people could become rich overnight by an opportune inheritance. Under these circumstances "legacy hunters" assiduously courted rich, childless old men and women; sometimes the old people encouraged this behavior, played their various pursuers off against one another, and managed to rake in endless favors from legacy hunters whom they knew to be trying to exploit them. The letters here are not intended for people who simply inherited their parents' property: friends are explicitly mentioned as the testators in letter after letter, showing that the expected addressees were people who suddenly became rich at the death of someone outside their family. Since the friend who received the largest legacy from a deceased person was often the one who felt or pretended to feel the greatest affection for him, the sorrow felt (or assumed) by the addressees at the death of their friends was part of their credentials for receiving the inheritance and as such was acknowledged by the writer. The third letter is for someone who has managed to snare a legacy from a friend who had plenty of relatives to leave his money to; such successes were harder to pull off than receiving legacies from friends without family members, and the addressee's exceptional devotion to his friends is therefore signaled as having been the cause of this success.

Each line that projects to the left marks the start of a new letter; none of the letters begins with the greetings that were standard in ancient letters, because those had to be

---

[41]   *P.Bon.* 5. Additional information on this text, which is number 2117 in the Mertens–Pack database (http://promethee.philo.ulg.ac.be/cedopal/indexsimple.asp) and number 5498 in the Leuven Database of Ancient Books (www.trismegistos.org/ldab/), can be found in Kramer (1983: no. 16), whose text is reproduced here in a slightly emended version. A photograph of the complete papyrus can be found at http://amshistorica.unibo.it/247; the extract quoted here comes from columns V–XII.

personalized with the names of writer and addressee. Note the use of *frater* for friends and acquaintances, the use of *domine* as a term of general affection and respect without implying servility, and a concessive *cum* clause with indicative instead of subjunctive. In line 111 the papyrus is damaged and the restoration uncertain; *memorem* is my own supplement and probably not exactly correct, but it gives the sense of what must have stood here. In 124 the Latin does not entirely make sense; perhaps the writer originally intended *per processuum tuorum fructus* "through the benefits of your advancements" or *per processus tuos* "through your advancements." Other extracts from the same papyrus can be found in passage 8.9.

65 **Gratulatoriae hereditatum acceptarum**
   Congratulatory letters on the receipt of
   inheritances

	Meritissimo tibi,	You who are most worthy,
	frater,	brother,
70	hereditatem	I congratulate on having accepted an inheritance
	cum summo honore	with highest honor;
	accessisse gratulor;	
	et iudicium	and that the judgement
	amicorum tuorum,	of your friends,
75	usque ad supremam	right up to the final
	suimet memoriam,	remembrance of themselves,
	obsequiis tuis	responds favorably to your attentions,
	grate respondere	
	laetor.	I rejoice.
80	Quamquam tibi	Although
	hereditate accepta	on the acceptance of an inheritance
	gratulari fas,	it is proper to congratulate you,
	tamen uni tibi	nevertheless in your case alone
	non audeo;	I do not dare (to do so);
85	novi enim	for I know
	animi tui propositum.	the intention of your mind.
	cum numquam par est	Although it is never equal to (bearing)
	desiderio amici,	the longing for (a departed) friend,
	ex iudicio eius	from his judgement (in making you his heir)

90	solacium fit.	consolation arises.

	Multum tibi, frater,	That to you, brother,
	proficere reverentiam	your reverence is a great advantage,
	qua semper amicos	(the reverence) with which you always
	intueris	regard your friends,
95	et plenissima	and you keep (them) in the greatest
	veneratione	veneration –
	conservas,	
	memoria	by the memory (in making his will)
	Rutili amici,	of your friend Rutilius,
100	aliquando communis	I too have jointly
	sum expertus;	experienced (this fact);
	qui etiam si videbatur	(Rutilius) who even if he seemed to have died
	non exiguo numero	with not a small number
	propinquorum relicto	of relatives left behind,
105	processisse,	
	parte tamen te	nevertheless judged you worthy of a part,
	non minima	and not the smallest one,
	hereditatis	of the inheritance
	una cum suis	together with his family.
110	dignum iudicavit.	

	Memorem, domine,	Sir, that Licinnius in his last hours was mindful
	tuorum obsequiorum	of your attentions
	fuisse	
	in supremis suis	
115	Licinnium	
	gratulor tibi,	I congratulate you,
	sed et eis pariter	but also (I congratulate) equally those
	quos amas,	whom you love,
	id est nobis.	that is us.
120	quando enim	For since
	obsequia tua	everyone rewards your attentions,
	remunerantur	
	omnes,	
	per processorum tuorum	through your advancement

125	clientes tui	your clients
	augentur.	are advanced.
	Memoria Sulpici	That by the memory of Sulpicius
	auctum te,	you are enriched,
	pauperis quidem	(Sulpicius who was) indeed poor
130	sed amici tui,	but your friend,
	gaudeo,	I rejoice,
	quod voluntas eius	because his decision
	praestantiam tuam	has so rewarded your excellence
	sic remuneravit	
135	ut intellegi possit	that it is possible to perceive
	eum tibi	that he left you
	non tantum quod voluit,	not as much as he wanted,
	sed quod potuit	but as much as he could.
	reliquisse.	
140	diuturnus enim languor	For a long illness
	et senecta,	and old age,
	quae saepe etiam	which often even
	languore deterior est,	worse than illness is,
	universam	had consumed all
145	substantiam eius	his property.
	absumpserat.	
	Honesto titulo te	That by the honorable writing
	Fabiani amici tui	of your friend Fabianus,
	obiti honoratum,	deceased, you have been honored,
150	quamquam tu	although you
	moleste feras,	may be unhappy about it,
	ego tamen	I nevertheless
	dupliciter gaudeo:	doubly rejoice:
	quod et iudicia eius	both because his decisions reveal
155	qualis in eum fueris	what you meant to him,
	ostendunt	
	et quod candori	and because to the nobility
	animi tui	of your mind
	ampliamentum	a (possibility of) increase
160	liberalitatis	of generosity

	accessit.	has arrived.
	suadeo ergo	Therefore I suggest
	dolore desinas;	that you cease from grief;
	amicus enim	for a friend
165	qui ita testatur	who makes a will like that –
	non lacrimis	not with tears
	sed animo	but with the soul
	desiderandus est.	should he be mourned.

2.8   A marked copy of Sallust

The bilingual texts are easy to identify as works designed for learners, but once students progressed to the stage of reading monolingual Latin texts the identification of their materials becomes more difficult. Any monolingual Latin text could have been used for reading practice by a Greek speaker, but as there were also native Latin speakers in all parts of the empire there is no guarantee that they were not the owners and users of such materials. A Latin papyrus recovered from Egypt is like a copy of Racine's plays in French found in a used book store in England: one strongly suspects its owner was a language learner, but one can never exclude the possibility that he or she was simply a visitor from France.[42] The exceptions to this generalization are texts that have been annotated by Greek speakers. Like modern students, ancient Latin students often wrote translations of difficult words into their texts; they also had a tendency to mark word divisions, but as such marking could also be done by Latin speakers it does not uniquely identify language learners.

One such papyrus (*PSI* I.110, from the fourth or fifth century AD)[43] is a learner's copy of Sallust's *Bellum Catilinae*; in the extract reproduced below (from the recto, i.e. the front side of the papyrus, containing sections 10.4–5) a Greek speaker has written translations over some difficult words. The learner has also added macrons, but not consistently: only long *e* is marked, and not all instances of long *e* are marked. (In general Greek speakers were much more interested in the lengths of *e* and *o* than of other Latin vowels, because the Greek alphabet had separate letters for long and short versions of these vowels.) Usually, but not always, the vowels marked long in this papyrus are important for determining the position of the accent. It is likely that the annotations

---

[42]   For more information on Latin speakers in Egypt see Thomas (2007).

[43]   Additional information on this text, which is number 2932 in the Mertens–Pack database (http://promethee. philo.ulg.ac.be/cedopal/indexsimple.asp) and number 3877 in the Leuven Database of Ancient Books (www. trismegistos.org/ldab/), can be found in Funari (2008). There is a photograph online at www.psi-online.it/ documents/psi;1;110.

were made by a student preparing to read the passage aloud in Latin and translate it. Note the incorrect addition of *in* before *promptum* in the Latin and, in the Greek, the omission of final iota in τω and the confusion of iota and epsilon iota in προχιρωι; both of these types of mistake are extremely common in Roman-period papyri.

πρα]σιμα
ve]nalia, habēre edocuit· am[bitio]
κατηναγκασεν
[multos mortales falsos fie]ri subēgit· aliud clausu[m in]
εν τω προχιρωι
[pectore, aliud in lingua i]n promptum habēre· [ami-]
[citias inimicitiasque] non ex rē, sed ex com[modo]
[aestumare, magisqu]e voltum quam in[genium]

3 | Grammatical works

Ancient grammatical works were always written in the language being discussed, regardless of their intended audience: grammars of Greek were composed in Greek and grammars of Latin in Latin, even when they were intended to be used by language learners. This rule applied not only to grammars proper, that is to explanatory works in continuous prose, but also to paradigm tables, whose headings and labels were always in Latin if the paradigms themselves were Latin. This convention persisted through the Middle Ages and into the early modern period;[1] our idea that one language can be effectively explained in another language is a relatively recent one.

This language barrier naturally made grammatical texts difficult for beginners to use. That fact, coupled with the relatively small number of surviving grammatical papyri compared to other surviving language-learning papyri, has led some scholars to believe that grammatical instruction was not a part of elementary language learning at all and that formal language analysis was introduced only at a comparatively advanced level.[2] There is, however, considerable counter-evidence to this view. The schoolbook sections of the colloquia, which describe children in the process of language learning, frequently mention grammatical instruction.[3] Some grammatical materials survive in transliteration (e.g. passage 7.2), suggesting that they were used even by learners who had not yet invested the time needed to learn the Roman alphabet. The way that Dositheus translated his grammar (see below) indicates that he intended it to be used by students at the very beginning of their Latin studies. And the rarity of Latin grammatical papyri may be illusory, not a feature of what has actually survived but a feature of what has been published. Sets of paradigms are, for good reason, relatively far down the priority list of most papyrological collections, and recent investigations have revealed a number of unpublished and partially published Latin grammatical papyri.[4]

It is therefore likely that ancient Latin students used grammatical materials early in their studies: how exactly did they do that, if the materials were entirely in Latin? A theoretical possibility is a sort of "immersion course" conducted entirely in Latin, but this can be ruled out on the basis of the large number of translated texts evidently used by beginners: clearly elementary students operated primarily in Greek during their Latin

---

[1] Cf. Shakespeare, *Merry Wives of Windsor* Act 4 scene 1, where a boy asked a grammatical question in English says "singulariter, nominativo, hic, haec, hoc."

[2] See Morgan (1998: 162–9).   [3] For example, passages 2.1.5 and 8.2 in this volume.

[4] Cf. the recent publications of *P.Oxy.* LXXVIII.5161 and Scappaticcio (2013b), both of which texts had been known for some time before being published.

classes. For paradigm tables it is likely that students were simply taught the Latin gram-matical terminology needed to understand the framework. A similar phenomenon sometimes occurs today in the teaching of modern foreign languages, for example when tense labels like "passé composé" and "passé simple" are used in English-language dis-cussions in a French class; those labels can be used as headings for paradigms and cause students very little trouble. Since many of the Latin words used as the framework for paradigms reflected concepts such as "singular" and "plural" or "masculine" and "femi-nine" that would have been familiar to Greek-speaking learners on the basis of their own language, learning this new terminology would probably not have been very difficult.

The grammars proper, however, would have posed a challenge of a different order: it is very hard to imagine that a beginning Latin student could have read and understood the grammar of Charisius. That this problem was a real one is shown by the fact that Dositheus translated his grammar into Greek, but at the same time it cannot have been an insuperable problem since Charisius and other grammarians did not translate their works. The question remains open, but in my view the most likely answer is that stu-dents memorized sections of the grammars, in Latin, and had them paraphrased and explained orally in Greek by the teacher.

3.1   Dositheus' grammar

The grammar of Dositheus is generally ignored today on the grounds that it is unorig-inal, apparently deriving most of its doctrine from sources that have better-preserved descendants elsewhere in the grammatical tradition. It is also less coherent and less detailed than the more famous grammatical treatises; from reading it one can get the impression that Dositheus had not always understood the material he repeated and was not always thinking very hard about it. Nevertheless Dositheus' work is uniquely orig-inal and creative in one very important respect: he provided a translation of parts of the grammar into the language its readers already knew. We know that the translation was done by Dositheus himself, rather than a later user of the work, because it uses the narrow-column bilingual format, which imposes restrictions on the Latin: in the translated sections Dositheus' Latin shows characteristics distinctive of texts bilingually composed for this format, but in the monolingual sections it does not.[5] The translation was clearly intended as an aid to reading the original, not a substitute for it, for it covers only portions of the work and does not always include all the words in the sections it does translate.

The portions of the work that Dositheus decided to translate are likely to have been the ones he expected students to read first; there are signs of progression from full

---

[5]   See Dickey (forthcoming a).

translation in sections intended to be read by absolute beginners through partial translation in sections read slightly later to no translation at all in sections read by more advanced students. This evidence allows us to observe that Dositheus expected his students to use the work in a different order from the one in which it was written. The grammar follows a common organizational principle for ancient grammars, arrangement by parts of speech: first introductory material, then nouns, pronouns, verbs, participles, adverbs, prepositions, conjunctions, and interjections. But Dositheus expected students to read the beginnings of the sections on verbs and conjunctions before they had finished reading earlier sections of the grammar; that makes good sense, since both verbs and conjunctions are essential for reading any kind of Latin. A full analysis of the translation suggests that Dositheus' Latin course used the grammar in the following order: (1) introductory material, nouns, and the key points about verbs and conjunctions; (2) most of the information on pronouns, impersonal verbs and some other information about verbs, some information about adverbs and prepositions; (3) participles, interjections, and the remaining information on pronouns, adverbs, prepositions, and conjunctions.

The introductory material, which is all bilingual and therefore was used at the beginning of Dositheus' Latin course, is varied in nature. It includes some material that would obviously have been both new and useful for a Greek-speaking Latin student, such as a long discussion of the alphabet, but also some material that one might expect students previously trained in Greek literacy to know already: the different punctuation marks and their uses, an explanation of what the study of grammar is, etc. The inclusion of such material in the translated sections of the grammar strongly suggests that Dositheus could not rely on his students to know it already: he thought they might need to (re)learn it. Modern Latin teachers often feel that students arrive without knowledge of concepts of basic literacy that they should have learned in English classes, and Dositheus seems to have felt the same way.

Additional extracts from Dositheus can be found in passages 8.11–12.

3.1.1 Introduction to grammar

The extract below constitutes section 1, the beginning of Dositheus' work.[6] Like most ancient technical works it begins by delineating the scope of the subject about to be discussed, defining it, and dividing it into component parts. Note how different the ancient

---

[6] The text is taken from Bonnet (2005: 2–4), but the layout is reconstructed from the manuscripts of Dositheus. The original layout of Dositheus' grammar is debated, and Bonnet would not agree with this reconstruction; for the evidence in favor of it see Dickey (forthcoming a). The Stiftsbibliothek St. Gallen has kindly posted images of the best manuscript, St. Gall 902, at www.e-codices.unifr.ch/en/csg/0902; this passage can be found on p. 8.

boundaries of "grammar" are from our own: the ancient concept includes virtually all aspects of the study of language and literature, including ones that we would think of as literary criticism. The title is in Latin only.

1   **Incipit Grammatica Dosithei Magistri**

Ars	Grammar
grammatica	
est	is
5 scientia	the knowledge
emendati	of correct
sermonis	language
in loquendo	in speaking
et scribendo	and in writing,
10 poematumque	and (the knowledge) of poems,
ac lectionis	and of reading (it is)
prudens	the skilled
praeceptum.	training.
Grammaticus est	A grammarian is
15 qui uniuscuiusque	(one) who of every single
rei	thing
vim	the force
ac proprietatem	and the proper usage
potest	is able
20 explanare	to explain
loquela.	through discourse.
Artis	Of grammar
grammaticae	
officium	the goal
25 constat	consists of
partibus	four parts:
quattuor:	
lectione,	reading,
emendatione,	correcting,
30 enarratione,	commenting,
iudicio.	critical judgement.
Lectio est	Reading is
varia	varying pronunciation
cuiusque	of each

35	scripti	written text,
	pronuntiatio	
	serviens	respecting
	dignitati	the dignity
	personarum	of the characters
40	exprimensque	and expressing
	habitum	the state
	animi cuiusque.	of mind of each one.
	Emendatio est	Correction is
	recorrectio	the fixing
45	errorum,	of errors
	qui per scriptum	that arise through writing
	dictionemve	or (through) reading aloud.
	fiunt.	
	Enarratio est	Commenting is the explanation
50	obscurorum	of obscure
	sensuum	meanings
	quaestionumque	and of doubtful points.
	narratio.	
	Iudicium est	Critical judgement is
55	quo poemata	(the means) by which we judge and classify poems
	ceteraque	and other
	scripta	writings.
	perpendimus	
	et discernimus.	
60	Artis	Of grammar
	grammaticae	
	initia	the beginnings
	ab elementis	come from sounds,
	surgunt,	
65	elementa	sounds
	figurantur	are represented
	in litteras,	in letters,
	litterae	letters
	coguntur	are collected
70	in syllabas,	into syllables,
	syllabis	from syllables
	comprehenditur	is formed

	dictio,	the word,
	dictiones	words
75	coguntur	are collected
	in partes	into parts
	orationis,	of speech,
	oratio	speech
	in virtutes	into virtues
80	ac vitia	and flaws
	descendit.	is divided.

Figure 3 Beginning of Dositheus' grammar in the ninth-century manuscript St. Gall 902, p. 8. Printed by kind permission of the Abbey of St. Gall.

3.1.2 The case system

In section 18 of the grammar[7] Dositheus discusses the use of cases. Because his audience consisted of Greek speakers he wasted no time on the cases they already knew (nominative, genitive, dative, accusative, and vocative) and focused all his attention on the ablative, which from a Greek perspective was sometimes equivalent to a dative and sometimes to a genitive. Greek speakers' confusion about the ablative was probably not improved by dividing it into the ablative proper and the "seventh case" (really a subdivision of ablative uses), especially as that division did not match the division between uses in which the ablative was the equivalent of a Greek dative and uses in which it was the equivalent of a Greek genitive. Dositheus' discussion is not as clear as it might have been; part of the blame for this can be attributed to his source, which he follows closely for much of this passage,[8] but some words from the source have been omitted, making the discussion harder to follow. For the order of the cases see below, passage 3.3.

The layout is somewhat confusing because the right-hand column is not always complete, and the left-hand column sometimes contains phrases in Greek (or, in the version presented here, in English). These phrases belong in the Latin column because they are part of the original explanation Dositheus took from his source, not part of his translation. The Latin column of Dositheus' work could be read on its own, like the monolingual texts of the other Latin grammarians, and like those "monolingual" texts it sometimes contained Greek examples. The translation, by contrast, is not always complete and frequently cannot be read on its own.

1	Casus sunt VI:	There are 6 cases:
	nominativus	nominative,
	genetivus	genitive,
	dativus	dative,
5	accusativus	accusative,
	vocativus	vocative,
	ablativus.	ablative.
	adicitur	There is added
	a diligentioribus	by more careful people

---

[7] The text of this section is taken from Bonnet (2005: 35–8), but the layout is reconstructed from the manuscripts of Dositheus. The Stiftsbibliothek St Gallen has kindly posted images of the best manuscript, St. Gall 902, at www.e-codices.unifr.ch/en/csg/0902; this passage can be found on pp. 18–19.

[8] See *Anonymous Bobiensis* 3.16–4.21 De Nonno = Keil 1857–80: I.534.19–535.8; the *Anonymous Bobiensis* cannot itself be Dositheus' source, but it must be derived from that source and must have followed it more closely than Dositheus did.

10	etiam septimus casus.[9]	also a seventh case.
	semper	Always
	ablativus	the ablative
	uno modo	is used in a single way,
	profertur,	
15	cum a persona	when from a person
	aut a loco	or from a place
	aut a re	or from a thing
	ablatum quid	something taken away
	significetur,	is signified,
20	veluti	as in:
	ab Aenea stirpem	"from Aeneas Romulus traced his descent,"
	deducit	
	Romulus,	
	ab urbe	"from Rome
25	*in Africam redit,*	he returns to Africa,"
	a libris Ciceronis	"from Cicero's books
	intellectum est.	it was understood."
	septimus vero casus	But the seventh case
	modis IIII	in 4 ways
30	profertur.	is used.
	primo,	First,
	cum in persona	when in a person
	aut in loco	or in a place
	aut in re	or in/on a thing
35	intellegitur,	it is understood,
	veluti	as in
	in Scipione militaris	"in Scipio military
	virtus enituit,	virtue shone forth,"
	in monte Caucaso	"on Mount Caucasus
40	*poenas luit*	Prometheus paid the penalty,"
	Prometheus,	
	in statua Ciceronis	"on the statue of Cicero
	victoria	the victory
	coniuratorum	over the conspirators

[9] Dositheus' source had an extra sentence here, serving as a heading for what follows: *differentia ablativi et septimi casus.*

45	*inscribitur.*	is inscribed."
	et interpretatur	And such a construction is translated
	talis figura	
	per dativum:	with the dative:
	"in Scipio (dative),"	
50	"on the Caucasus (dative),"	
	"on the statue (dative)."	
	quae regula	Which rule is observed
	etiam in nominibus	even in nouns
	secundae	of the second
55	declinationis,	declension,
	quorum ablativus	whose ablative
	et dativus	and dative
	idem est,	is the same,
	observatur	
60	et in nominibus	and in nouns
	tertiae	of the third
	declinationis,	declension,
	quorum	whose
	item ablativus	ablative too
65	et dativus	and dative
	idem est,	is the same,
	veluti	as in:
	ab hac securi, ab hoc suavi.[10]	
	secundo,	Second,
70	cum ablativi	when ablatives
	copulati	joined together
	genetivo	are translated with a Greek genitive,
	interpretantur	
	Graeco,	
75	veluti	as in
	ducente dea elapsus est	"with the goddess leading him, Aeneas
	Aeneas,	escaped,"
	incusante Cicerone victus est	"with Cicero accusing him, Catiline was
	Catilina,	defeated,"

---

[10] I.e. these forms are ablatives because they come after *ab*, even though they look just like datives. Dositheus did not translate this line because it is the form of the Latin, rather than its meaning, that is at issue here.

	studente Sacerdote differentia inventa est.	"with Sacerdos[11] studying, *differentia* was discovered."
	tertio modo,	Thirdly,
	cum hanc figuram	when this Greek construction[12]
80	Graecam	
	"in the hope of being able,"	
	"from desire of robbery,"	
	"with a plan of conspiracy,"	
	Latine dixerimus	we say in Latin:
85	*spe posse,*	
	voluntate latrocinandi,	
	consilio insidiandi.[13]	
	quarto modo,	Fourthly,
	velut in illo:[14]	as in the following:
90	dicimus enim sic	For we say thus:
	nullo timore	"with no fear
	hostium	of the enemy
	castra irrupit,	he broke into the camp,"
	nulla spe	"with no hope.
95	*per vim potiundi*	of winning by force
	vallo fossaque	he encircles the walls with a fence and ditch,"
	moenia circumdat,	
	nullis custodibus	"with no guards
	palladium ereptum est,	the Palladium was stolen,"
100	*nullis insidiis*	"with no trickery
	palam victus est	the enemy was openly defeated."
	hostis.	
	ubique enim	For in all these
	deficit	the Latin phrase is defective

[11] Marius Plotius Sacerdos was a Latin grammarian who probably worked at the end of the third century AD; see Kaster (1988: 352–3).

[12] The following examples all consist of a noun in the dative followed by an articular infinitive in the genitive; it is the dative that interests Dositheus, and the infinitive is only there to provide a context so the reader can see how the dative functions. Dositheus' point is that this dative (of manner, in our terms) is equivalent to a Latin ablative.

[13] Dositheus did not translate these phrases into Greek because they are translations of Greek phrases already given (lines 82–4).

[14] There is a major omission here: Dositheus' source read *quarto cum, ut Asprus rettulit, Latinum eloquium in quodam verbo deficit, velut in illo* ὄντος οὔσης ὄντων οὐσῶν. In other words, the next set of phrases are what we might describe as the *me consule* construction, ablatives absolute with the participle of *esse* understood.

105	Latinus sermo,	
	scilicet ideo,	clearly because of the
	quoniam duo	fact that two
	ablativi	ablative
	nominales	nouns/adjectives
110	sunt copulati;	are joined;
	quodsi unus	because if one
	participialis sit,	should be participial,
	non deficit	the Latin phrase is not defective,
	Latinus sermo,	
115	sed plenus est,	but it is complete,
	ut supra	as above
	ducente dea elapsus est	
	et cetera	and the other things
	quae in secundo modo	that we explained in the second type.
120	exposuimus.	

3.2   Charisius' grammar

Flavius Sosipater Charisius, a fourth-century grammarian, produced a better Latin grammar than Dositheus', but without a translation. This work is far longer and more coherent than that of Dositheus and tells us a great deal about how ancient learners analysed the Latin language. For centuries it has been considered a key element in the Latin grammatical canon, but as far as I can tell there has never been an attempt to provide it with an English translation: scholars still believe that one ought to read Charisius in Latin.[15] Part of the reason for this belief is that Charisius' work is not difficult to read in Latin; he was clearly writing for beginners and made an effort to be clear.

Another extract from Charisius can be found in passage 9.3.

3.2.1 Introduction to the verb

This section of Charisius' grammar, from the start of the section on verbs,[16] restates concepts that should have been familiar to many students from their schooling in Greek.

---

[15]   As far as I know there is no French or German translation either, but there is a partial Spanish translation by Uría (2009).

[16]   Book 2.8 = Barwick (1964: 209.23–210.8) = Keil (1857–80: 1.164).

Much of the terminology may also be familiar to English speakers, as our own grammatical terminology is largely borrowed from Latin, but the following items of vocabulary may be helpful: *pars orationis* "part of speech," *tempus* "tense," *casus* "case," *accido* "be a characteristic of," *genus* "voice," *modus* "mood."[17] Although Charisius' analysis of Latin is mostly similar to ours, differences include the existence of five voices: active, passive, neuter (i.e. intransitive), common (i.e. passive in form but both active and passive in meaning), and deponent (i.e. passive in form but only active in meaning).

De verbo

Verbum est pars orationis administrationem rei significans cum tempore et persona numerisque carens casu. verbo accidunt qualitas genus figura numerus modus tempus persona coniugatio. Qualitas verborum aut finita est aut infinita. qualitas verborum finita est quae notat certum numerum, certum modum, certum tempus, certam personam, ut *lego, scribo*. infinita est quae nihil certum habet, ut *legere, scribere*. haec enim in omnibus numeris temporibus personis infinita sunt. ceterum *legisse, scripsisse* dicuntur quidem finita, sed tempore solo finita sunt. Verborum genera sunt quinque, activum, ut *lego, scribo*, passivum, ut *legor, scribor*, neutrum, ut *sedeo, curro*, commune, ut *adulor, criminor*, deponens, ut *luctor, convivor*. praeterea sunt et inpersonalia, ut *sedetur, itur, videtur*. non minus et illa inpersonalia dicuntur, ut *taedet, pudet, paenitet*.

3.2.2 Introduction to Latin conjugation

Charisius spends a long time on the theoretical classification of the verb, discussing a variety of different theories about topics such as how many voices Latin has. Eventually, however, he moves on to discuss conjugations (*ordines*).[18] In addition to the grammatical terminology mentioned above, readers may find the following useful: *correptus* "short," *productus* "long," *declinatio* "inflection," *instans* "present," *praeteritus* "past." The terms *appellatio* and *nomen* both refer to what we would call nouns, and *optativus*, *subiunctivus*, and *coniunctivus* all refer to what we would call the subjunctive: can you work out what distinction Charisius makes among these last three terms?

De ordinibus verborum

Ordines verborum sunt quattuor, qui verba dispertiunt. primi ordinis est verbum cuius secunda persona *-as* litteris terminatur, velut *amo amas*.

---

[17] Schad (2007) provides an excellent lexicon of Latin grammatical vocabulary.
[18] Book 2.9–10 = Barwick (1964: 215.18–217.13) = Keil (1857–80: I.168–9).

secundi ordinis est verbum cuius secunda persona *-es* terminatur, velut *teneo tenes*; tertii ordinis est verbum cuius secunda persona per *-is* correptam[19] terminatur, ut *ago agis*; quarti ordinis est verbum cuius secunda persona productis *-is* litteris terminatur, velut *munio munis*. itaque omnia verba quae eiusdem ordinis erunt similem etiam declinationem habent, et ideo satis est ex quoque ordine cuiusque verbi tam activi quam passivi declinationem per omnia tempora et modos exempli gratia perscribere. nam modi verborum sive qualitates sunt quinque, pronuntiativus seu finitivus, imperativus, optativus, subiunctivus seu coniunctivus, infinitivus. declinantur autem hoc modo.

Declinatio verbi ordinis primi

Verbum finitivum ordinis primi activum temporis instantis numeri singularis *amo amas amat* et pluraliter *amamus amatis amant*, praeteriti inperfecti *amabam amabas amabat*, perfecti *amavi*, plusquamperfecti *amaveram*, futuri *amabo*. imperativa instantis *ama amet*, futuri *amato tu, amato ille*. optativa instantis et praeteriti inperfecti *ut amarem*, perfecti *ut amaverim*, plusquamperfecti *ut amavissem*, futuri *ut amem*. subiunctiva instantis *cum amem*, praeteriti inperfecti *cum amarem*, praeteriti perfecti *cum amaverim*, plusquamperfecti *cum amavissem*, futuri *cum amavero*. infinita instantis temporis *amare*, praeteriti *amasse*, futuri *amatum ire, amaturum esse*. participia instantis *amans*, futuri *amaturus*. supina vel adverbia *amandi amando amandum*. passiva instantis temporis *amor amaris amatur*, pluraliter *amamur amamini amantur*, passiva inperfecti *amabar amabaris amabatur*, passiva perfecti *amatus sum, fui*, passiva plusquamperfecti *amatus eram, fueram*, passiva futuri *amabor*. passiva imperativa instantis *amare ametur*, futuri *amator*. optativa instantis et inperfecti *ut amarer*, perfecti *ut amatus sim, fuerim*, plusquamperfecti *ut amatus essem, fuissem*, futuri *ut amer*. subiunctiva instantis passiva *cum amer*, praeteriti inperfecti *cum amarer*, perfecti *cum amatus sim, fuerim*, plusquamperfecti *cum amatus essem, fuissem*, futuri *cum amatus ero, fuero*. passiva infinita instantis *amari*, praeteriti *amatum esse*, futuri *amatum iri*. participia praeteriti passivi *amatus*, futuri *amandus*. passiva inpersonalia *amatum amatu*. appellatio *amatio*; nomen *amator*; adverbium *amabiliter*. ergo in primo ordine, ita ut praedictum est, secundam personam per *-as* observabis finitam, ut *amo amas*, quae

---

[19] Here *correptam* agrees with *-is*, perhaps because of an understood *syllabam*; note the difference from the next clause, in which *productis* agrees with *-is* because of the presence of *litteris*.

a littera per totam declinationem media invenitur, futuri primam personam per *bo*, ut *amabo*, optativa *em*, coniunctiva *ro*.[20] imperativus modus *a* litteram habet subtracta *s*, ut *ama*; cui inpones *re* litteras et facies infinitivum, ut *amare*.

3.3   A set of noun paradigms

A set of sample declensions, laid out in tables very similar to those in modern grammars, survives on a leaf of parchment from Egypt dated to the fifth or sixth century AD (P.Louvre inv. E 7332).[21] That these paradigms were intended to be used by Greek speakers is indicated by the fact that each word is glossed in Greek before being declined; apart from these glosses and a Greek quire number the paradigms are presented entirely in Latin. As the format is rather different from our own it requires some explanation.

The cases are given in the traditional Latin order: nominative, genitive, dative, accusative, vocative, ablative. This order, which is still used in many European countries today but has been superseded in Britain by one based partly on the Sanskrit case-ordering principle of grouping similar endings together,[22] is effectively the Greek case order with the ablative tacked on at the end. (The Greek order itself may derive from a common order of case-forms in a sentence, i.e. NOM son of GEN gave to DAT the ACC, with the vocative added at the end.)

Despite the predictable order of presentation the writer took care to avoid any ambiguity by also specifying the gender, number, and case of each form. These are indicated primarily by the addition of forms of *hic* (or *o* in the vocative, since there is no vocative of *hic*); this practice was very common in Latin grammatical texts and must have been highly convenient compared to writing out the case-names. It derives from the Greek convention of using the definite article (or ὦ in the vocative) to indicate gender, number, and case. But the Greek article is more effective for this purpose than is Latin *hic*, as it has more distinct forms; *hic* has a significant number of ambiguous forms, such as *his* (found in all three genders of the dative and ablative plural) and *hoc* (found in the

---

[20] This somewhat unfortunate formulation refers to the ending of *amavero* (cf. above "subiunctiva instantis *cum amem*, praeteriti inperfecti *cum amarem*, praeteriti perfecti *cum amaverim*, plusquamperfecti *cum amavissem*, futuri *cum amavero*"); modern analysis of Latin grammar does not agree with Charisius on this point.

[21] Additional information on this text, which is number 2997 in the Mertens–Pack database (http://promethee. philo.ulg.ac.be/cedopal/indexsimple.asp) and number 6148 in the Leuven Database of Ancient Books (www. trismegistos.org/ldab/), can be found in Dickey, Ferri, and Scappaticcio (2013), Wessely (1886: 218–21), and Scappaticcio (forthcoming).

[22] The British order is nominative, vocative, accusative, genitive, dative, ablative; Allen and Brink (1980) provide a fascinating discussion of the history of both orders.

masculine and neuter ablative and the neuter nominative and accusative). To reduce such ambiguities the Latin grammarians normally used *ab* before ablative forms of *hic*; as *ab* is a preposition that always takes the ablative, its presence indicates that the following word must be ablative. Therefore *ab his animalibus* effectively means "ablative plural: *animalibus*," while *his animalibus* without the *ab* effectively means "dative plural: *animalibus*."

The paradigms are arranged by gender and termination; masculines probably came first and are not preserved on the surviving leaf, which contains three types of feminines (in *-io*, *-us*, and *-ix*) and four types of neuters (in *-or*, *-ma*, *-us*, and *-al*). For each type at least one paradigm is provided (though this example is not always complete in the plural); sometimes the beginning of a second paradigm is also given.[23]

5	**(Feminina) in *-io*: haec iussio**	
	"command"	
	huius	iussionis
	huic	iussioni
	hanc	iussionem
10	o	iussio
	ab hac	iussione
pl.	hae	iussiones
	harum	iussionum
	his	iussionibus
15	has	iussiones
	o	iussiones
	ab his	iussionibus
	(Feminina) in *-us*: haec palus	
	"marsh"	
20	huius	paludis
	huic	paludi
	hanc	paludem
	o	palus
	ab hac	palude
25 pl.	hae	paludes
	et cetera	

---

23 For a scholarly edition of this text see Dickey, Ferri, and Scappaticcio (2013); note that there are numerous spelling mistakes in the original (e.g. *pestor-* in most forms of *pectus*), which have been corrected in the version provided here.

(Feminina) in -*ix*: haec nutrix
                     "nurse"

		huius	nutricis
30		huic	nutrici
		hanc	nutricem
		o	nutrix
		ab hac	nutrice
	pl.	hae	nutrices
35		harum	nutricum

               et cetera

Haec meretrix
                  "prostitute"

	huius	meretricis
40	huic	meretrici

               et cetera

Neutralia in -*or*:
               hoc aequor "sea"

		huius	aequoris
45		huic	aequori
		hoc	aequor
		o	aequor
		ab hoc	aequore
	pl.	haec	aequora
50		horum	aequorum
		his	aequoribus
		haec	aequora
		o	aequora
		ab his	aequoribus

(Neutralia) in -*ma*: hoc poema
                   "poem"

		huius	poematis
		huic	poemati
		hoc	poema
60		o	poema
		ab hoc	poemate
	pl.	haec	poemata

		horum	poematum
		his	poematibus
65		haec	poemata
		o	poemata
		ab his	poematibus

(Neutralia) in -*us*: hoc sidus
"star"

		huius	sideris
70		huius	sideris
		huic	sideri
		hoc	sidus
		o	sidus
		ab hoc	sidere
75	pl.	haec	sidera
		horum	siderum
		his	sideribus
		haec	sidera
		o	sidera
80		ab his	sideribus

Hoc pectus "chest"

		huius	pectoris
		huius	pectoris
		huic	pectori
		hoc	pectus
85		o	pectus
		ab hoc	pectore
	pl.	haec	pectora
		horum	pectorum
		his	pectoribus
90		haec	pectora
		o	pectora
		ab his	pectoribus

(Neutralia) in -*al*: hoc vectigal
"revenue"

		huius	vectigalis
95		huius	vectigalis
		huic	vectigali
		hoc	vectigal
		o	vectigal
		ab hoc	vectigali

100	pl.	haec	vectigalia
		horum	vectigalium
		his	vectigalibus
		haec	vectigalia
		o	vectigalia
105		ab his	vectigalibus

Similiter hoc tribunal
"speaker's platform"

	huius	tribunalis
	huic	tribunali
110	hoc	tribunal
	o	tribunal
	et cetera	

Figure 4 Noun paradigms in P.Louvre inv. E 7332, recto. © Musée du Louvre, Paris/Documentation AE.

4 | Glossaries

Ancient learners used a variety of types of glossary. One of these was the alphabetically arranged dictionary, like those commonly used today; this format is attested from the second century AD for bilingual glossaries (and much earlier for Greek–Greek glossaries) but was never very popular in antiquity. Another type was the author-specific word list, a running list of the hard words occurring in a particular text with their definitions. Again this format is attested much earlier for Greek–Greek glossaries (particularly those to Homer and Hippocrates) than for Latin–Greek or Greek–Latin ones, but from the fourth century it gained popularity as a way of presenting Virgil vocabulary for students reading the *Aeneid*.

The most common type of glossary was the classified word-list; these works were arranged into sections (known as *capitula*, "little chapters") of words relating to different topics. Classified glossaries were primarily used not for finding the meanings of unfamiliar words (a function for which they are by nature not as well suited as alphabetical or text-order glossaries) but for systematic vocabulary building: students memorized the different sections one after another to improve their vocabulary knowledge.[1] Classified glossaries are attested from the first or second century AD, making them the earliest type of bilingual glossary known; they were also the earliest type of monolingual Greek glossary, going back at least to the Alexandrian scholar Aristophanes of Byzantium (*ca.* 257–*ca.* 180 BC).[2]

Most ancient glossaries contained only the words themselves, without any of the information on usage or inflection that is a standard feature of today's dictionaries. There are, however, some interesting exceptions to this principle, and some of those exceptions are very early: the earliest known papyrus fragment of a bilingual glossary, from the first century BC, contains a considerable amount of grammatical information.[3] It looks as though the earliest phase of production of Latin-learning materials may have tended to combine grammatical and lexical information, which later became separated as the field expanded and works became more specialized. The text in 4.4 below is one of the relatively early texts preserving the integrated format; the others come from the more developed tradition.

---

[1] See Debut (1983).

[2] For overviews of the history of Greek–Greek glossaries see Dickey (2007: 87–103, 2010b) and for Aristophanes in particular see Slater (1986).

[3] For this text (*BKT* IX.150, *M–P³* 2134.5, *LDAB* 6764) see Kramer (1983: no. 1); unfortunately it is too fragmentary to be reproduced here. The glossary's organizational principle, if any, is uncertain.

Glossaries transmitted via the manuscript tradition (the route taken by the vast majority of the surviving materials) are often highly corrupt, because they were copied repeatedly by people who did not know both (or, in some cases, either of) the languages involved and because it was more difficult for scribes to decipher words without a context. (When handwritten texts are copied scribes normally have to decipher words before they can copy them; the alternative, producing a drawing of an incomprehensible mass of characters, is both time-consuming and unhelpful to future readers, so both ancient and medieval scribes avoided it whenever they could.) When such corruption is added to the fact that ancient spelling was very flexible, the glossaries can be difficult to read today. In order to illustrate the way they appear in the sources, with its difficulties and its interest value, the first example below is reproduced without alteration from its source and notes are provided to explain the errors and non-standard features. Subsequent examples have been emended to remove corruptions and non-standard spellings.

Additional extracts from glossaries can be found in passages 7.3–4 and 8.14–16.

4.1   A glossary section for words beginning with H

Most alphabetical glossaries surviving today are alphabetized on the Greek, as the copies we have were usually made in the Middle Ages by Latin speakers interested in Greek.[4] The extract below is unusual in preserving the ancient alphabetization on the Latin despite having come to us via the medieval manuscript tradition. The alphabetization is surprisingly exact; in antiquity it was not usual to take every single letter of a word into account when determining its place in alphabetical order, as we do today. Rather "alphabetization" usually meant grouping words with similar beginnings together; depending on the number of words involved and therefore the level of exactness needed, words could be arranged by their first letters alone, their first two letters, their first three letters, etc.[5]

This glossary exhibits numerous features characteristic of ancient glossaries: the inclusion of words in inflected forms (rather than always in what we would think of as the citation form), of multi-word phrases, and of proper names; redundancy and inconsistency (resulting from the compilation of the glossary from a variety of sources),

---

[4]   A few alphabetical glossaries survive on papyrus; some of these are alphabetized on the Greek and some on the Latin, but unfortunately the examples of the latter category are all too fragmentary for inclusion here.

[5]   For the history of alphabetization see Daly (1967). It is possible that the full alphabetization of this glossary is not an original ancient feature, as one of the copyists who reproduced it could have improved the alphabetization. Nevertheless such later interference is unlikely because other obvious improvements to the glossary, such as the rationalization of duplicate entries, have not been made.

patchy coverage (the vast majority of Latin words beginning with *h* are not included in this section), misspellings, and errors.[6]

450.14	habet	he has
450.15	habita	notes[7]
	habitatio	dwelling
	haereditas[8]	inheritance
	haruspex	diviner using entrails
	hasta publica	public sale of confiscated property
450.20	herba	grass
	herbae	plants
	Herculus[9]	Hercules
	hereditas	inheritance
	heres	heir
450.25	heri	yesterday
	hernia	hernia
	hiatus	gap
	hibernatio[10]	wintering
	hic	this man
450.30	hic	here
	hilaris	cheerful
	hilarus	cheerful
	hittio[11]	I track
	holera	vegetables
450.35	homicidium	murder
	homo	human being
	honoratus	valued
	honorati	honorable men
	hora	hour

[6] The text and numbering of this extract follow Goetz's transcript (Goetz 1892: 450) of an edition made by Henricus Stephanus (Henri Estienne) on the basis of a manuscript now lost: *Glossaria duo e situ vetustatis eruta: ad utriusque linguae cognitionem et locupletionem perutilia* (Paris 1573).

[7] Although this is a surprising equation it is not simply a mistake; because *orationem habeo* could mean "make a speech" (see *OLD s.v. habeo* 20), the participle *habita* was sometimes equated with *dicta*, whence it is not an enormous step to ὑπομνήματα "notes" (see Goetz 1899: 510 *s.v. habitus* 1).

[8] This is the same word as *hereditas* in line 23, and the two entries have exactly the same Greek definition.

[9] Normally *Hercules* in Latin.

[10] This word is attested only here and in other glossary entries related to this one, but it has a very plausible Latin derivation (see *TLL s.v.*).

[11] This word is attested only here and in other glossary entries related to this one, but it must have been a real word as there is a related term *hittus* "sound made by dogs when tracking"; see *TLL s.vv. hittio* and *hittus*.

450.40	hordeum	barley
	hornum[12]	in this year, this year's[13]
	horria[14]	storehouse
	hortulanus	gardener
	hosnum[15]	wood
450.45	hospes	kind to visitors
	hospes	visitor
	hospis[16]	visitor
	hospitalis	hospitable
	hospitalis	host
450.50	hospitatur	he is a guest
	hospitium	hospitality
	hostiarius[17]	doorman
	humanus	humane
	humilis	humble

4.2   A glossary section on sacrifices

Classified glossaries survive both on papyrus and via the medieval manuscript tradition, where enormous glossaries with many different sections are preserved in the Hermeneumata Pseudodositheana. (The versions on papyrus often have the Latin transliterated; examples of such texts can be found in passages 7.3–4 and 8.15–16 below.) The Hermeneumata versions have the Latin in the Roman alphabet; their sections are arranged in a standard sequence that, roughly speaking, starts with the gods and divine matters and then moves to humans and associated topics, animals, and inanimate objects.[18] This section on sacrifices comes from the Hermeneumata Monacensia, where it is one of the earlier sections (preceded by sections on the names of gods, names of goddesses, weather and the sky, constellations, zodiac signs, and temples).[19]

---

[12] This must be the neuter or accusative of *hornus, -a, -um*.

[13] The Greek has two definitions with effectively the same meaning, τῆτες and ἐφετός.

[14] Given the definition this word should be *horreum*.

[15] This word occurs nowhere else and has no plausible etymology, so it is probably a corruption; given its definition here the most likely original reading is *ornum*, accusative of *ornus*, the name of a kind of ash tree (see *TLL* s.v. *hosnum*).

[16] In reality, of course, all three of these entries are the same term, which would now normally be spelled *hospes*.

[17] I.e. *ostiarius*; as the sound *h* ceased to be pronounced it became liable to addition by hypercorrection in places where it did not originally belong. This process began early and is satirized in Catullus 84.1–2: *Chommoda dicebat, si quando commoda vellet | dicere, et insidias Arrius hinsidias . . .*

[18] For a complete list of the glossary sections see Dickey (2012–15: I.249–61).

[19] The text is a corrected version of Goetz's transcript of one of the Monacensia version manuscripts (Munich, clm 13002), and the marginal numbers refer to the page and lines of that transcript (Goetz 1892: 171).

171.8	**De sacrificiis**	**On sacrifices**
	sacrificium	sacrifice
171.10	turibulum	incense-burner
	insignia	signs
	picturae	pictures
	cymbala	cymbals
	incendo	I burn (in sacrifice)
171.15	exta	entrails
	fistula	pipe
	tibiae	oboes
	cultores	worshippers
	purgamenta	rubbish
171.20	decoramenta	dedications
	sacerdos	priest
	aedituus	custodian of the temple
	divinus	seer
	somniorum iudex	interpreter of dreams
171.25	hariolus	soothsayer
	augur	bird-diviner
	victimator	calf-slaughterer
	hostia	sacrifice
	sanctum	holy sacrifice
171.30	sacrati	initiates
	ara	altar
	pontifex	magistrate in charge of religious matters
	oraculum	oracle
	immolatio	cattle-sacrifice

4.3   Glossary sections on entertainment

These four sections from the Hermeneumata Monacensia list the words for different types of popular entertainment in Rome, divided by the locations traditionally used

Complete photographs of the manuscript have kindly been posted online by the Bayerische Staatsbibliothek at http://mdz1.bib-bvb.de/~db/0003/bsb00036887/images/; this extract can be found on folio 214r (image 432). The translations given here are taken from the Greek of the original glossary and are therefore not always the definitions that we might choose for the Latin terms in question, but (in contrast to the next passage) none is actually wrong. My corrections to the text are usually minor, but note that *hariolus* at 171.25 is an emendation of the manuscript's *aliorum*, which is paired with an apparently meaningless *eubates* that may not be Greek at all but rather a corruption of *vates*; cf. Goetz (1899: 512 *s.v. hariolus*).

for the different entertainments; originally they were all part of a single section *De spectaculis*.[20]

172.29	**Quae in theatro**	**(Spectacles) that (happen) in the theater**
172.30	theatrum	theater
	ludi	games
	devotio	offering
	spectacula	spectacles
	auriga	charioteer
172.35	spectatores	spectators
	aulaeum	curtain
	scena	stage
	cantores	singers, oboe-players
	mimologi	mime-actors
172.40	mimi	mime-actors
	praeco	herald
	praestigiator	conjurer
	funambulus	rope-dancer
	calobatarius[21]	rope-dancer
172.45	pilarius	person who dances with balls
	Homeristae	performers of Homer
	cornicines	horn-players
	organarius	player of the hydraulic organ
	tubicen	trumpeter
172.50	comoedus	comic actor
	tragoedus	tragic actor
	citharoedus	cithara-player
	choraules	oboe-player accompanying dances
	mesochorus	chorus-leader
172.55	podarii	rattle-players[22]

[20] The text is a corrected version of Goetz's transcript of one of the Monacensia version manuscripts (Munich, clm 13002), and the marginal numbers refer to pages and lines of that transcript (Goetz 1892: 172–3). Complete photographs of the manuscript have kindly been posted online by the Bayerische Staatsbibliothek at http://mdz1.bib-bvb.de/~db/0003/bsb00036887/images/; this extract can be found on folios 214r–214v (images 432–3). The translations given here are taken from the Greek of the original glossary and are therefore not always the definitions that we might choose for the Latin terms in question; indeed some are simply wrong. Anomalous definitions have been flagged in the notes.

[21] This word occurs only here; see *TLL s.v.*

[22] This definition may be wrong; Lewis and Short define *podarius* as "one who performs mimes on the stage." See Goetz (1901: 100 *s.v. podarii*).

	pantomimus	dancer
	fabula	story
	personae	masks
	fimarium	little mask[23]
172.60	symphoniacus	musician
	Quae in stadio	**(Spectacles) that (happen) in the stadium**
	stadium	stadium
	praemium	honor, prize
	certamen	contest, competition
172.65	athletae	contestants
	cursores	runners
	luctatores	wrestlers
	pancratiastae	contestants in the pancration
173.1	pugiles	boxers
	comparatio	judging
	commissio	start of a contest
	corona	(victor's) crown
173.5	discobolus	discus-thrower
	palma	palm-wreath (as sign of victory)
	certamen	contest[24]
	Quae in amphitheatro	**(Spectacles) that (happen) in the amphitheater**
	amphitheatrum	amphitheater
173.10	munus	lavish display[25]
	famosum	famous
	editor	lavish giver[26]
	loca	places
	gradus	steps
173.15	vomitoria	exits

---

[23] See LSJ *s.v.* φιμάριον.

[24] This entry is redundant after the one on 172.64, but owing to corruption of the Greek that is not evident from the manuscript.

[25] The Latin word means "public show" (among other things); the translation reflects the fact that such shows were expensive.

[26] The Latin word means a person who produces a show; the translation reflects the expense of such productions.

	podium	emperor's balcony[27]
	suffragiae	voting equipment
	harena	sand
	portae	gates
173.20	harenarii	people who take risks[28]
	venatores	hunters
	colaphatores	bull-fighters[29]
	saltores	dancers
	pontarius	gladiator who fights on a bridge
173.25	noxae	beast-fighters[30]
	gladiatores	one-on-one fighters
	dictiarius	gladiator who fights with a net[31]
	secutor	pursuer[32]
	galea	helmet
173.30	crista	crest (on a helmet)
	scuta	shields
	fuscina	three-pronged spear
	provocatores	challengers (a kind of gladiator)
	galearii	soldiers' servants
173.35	messores	reapers (of men)
	lanistae	umpires[33]
	ferrea	iron weapons
	lancea	throwing-spear
	arborarius	tree-climber
173.40	decursio	running in full armor
	pugna	fight
	venabulum	hunting-spear
	venator	beast-fighter[34]
	damnaticii	condemned men

[27] The Greek translation, κύαθος, normally means "ladle," which is inappropriate to the context here; either κύαθος had a "balcony" meaning not otherwise attested, or the entry is corrupt.

[28] The Latin word means "gladiators."

[29] This whole entry is doubtful, and the Latin word is not attested elsewhere; see Goetz (1899: 293 *s.v. culpatores*).

[30] The Latin word means "criminals" (among other things); criminals could be sentenced to fight beasts in the arena.

[31] This type of fighter was normally called a *retiarius*.

[32] This was a type of gladiator who fought against the *retiarius*.

[33] The Latin word means "trainers of gladiators."

[34] This is not as redundant with line 21 as it may appear, since the two Latin entries have different translations.

173.45	**Quae in circo**	**(Spectacles) that (happen) in the circus**
	circus	racetrack
	circenses	contests in the Circus Maximus
	missus	a round
	victores	victors
173.50	carceres	starting-gates
	metae	turning-posts
	euripus	trench running around the circus
	canalis	water-conduit
	obeliscus	obelisk
173.55	quadrigae	quadrupeds[35]
	bigae	two-horsed chariots
	creta	white[36]
	iunctores	harnessers
	ianuae	doors
173.60	currus	chariot
	iugum	yoke
	temo	chariot-pole
	retinacula	reins[37]
	modioli	naves of wheels
173.65	canthus	iron tire for a wheel
174.1	vitus	rim
	axis	axle
	rota	wheel
	radii	spokes
174.5	lora	straps
	flagellum	whip
	pannus	piece of cloth
	prasinus	green[38]
	venetus	blue
174.10	roseus	scarlet
	albus	white
	singulatores	riding-horses

[35] The Latin word means "four-horse chariots."
[36] The Latin word means "chalk," which can be used to make a white mark.
[37] The Latin word means "tethers" or "halters."
[38] The colors are relevant here because they were the colors of the four "circus factions," for which see Cameron (1976).

	eques	cavalryman
	vexillarius	flag-bearer
174.15	cursus	race
	favisores	supporters (of a side or contestant)

4.4 A glossary of homonyms

A glossary of Latin words with multiple meanings is preserved in a papyrus of the third century AD (P.Sorb. inv. 2069 verso).[39] This text has a complex history: it seems to have started life as a purely Latin treatise on words with multiple meanings, which was then adapted for the use of Romans learning Greek by the addition of Greek translations of the different meanings. It was then readapted for the use of Greek speakers learning Latin by the addition of information on how to inflect the Latin words concerned. The normal format for entries (which is not always fully adhered to) begins with a Latin word and its multiple Greek translations (e.g. *ungula* "hoof" can be translated with ὁπλή, ὀνύχιον, or χηλή), followed by phrases illustrating the correct usage of each different translation (e.g. for *ungula* ὁπλή is used for a horse's hoof, ὀνύχιον for a pig's trotter, and χηλή for a cow's hoof), and concluding with an indication of how to inflect the Latin.

The inflectional information is given by reference to standard paradigm words: *alta* is used as a paradigm for the first declension, *altus* for the second declension masculine, *bellum* for the second declension neuter, *Cato* for most third-declension words, *calx* for third-declension words in *-x*, *altior* for third-declension words in *-r*, *accuso* for first-conjugation verbs, *foveo* for second-conjugation verbs, *ago* for third-conjugation verbs, and *rapio* for third-conjugation verbs in *-io*. Interestingly these paradigm words are always translated into Greek, even when the Greek translation does not belong to the same paradigm (for example *bellum* is translated by πόλεμος, which is masculine rather than neuter). This means that the Greek version of the text makes no sense on its own, for the inflectional information it provides often matches neither the Latin word nor the Greek translations of that word; it is not meaningful to say that *tectum* declines like πόλεμος, nor does δῶμα, ἐσταγασμένον, or στέγη (the three translations of *tectum* in the original) decline like πόλεμος. This fact tells us that the Greek translation was

---

[39] Additional information on this text, which is also known as P.Reinach 2069 and is number 3006 in the Mertens–Pack database (http://promethee.philo.ulg.ac.be/cedopal/indexsimple.asp) and number 5438 in the Leuven Database of Ancient Books (www.trismegistos.org/ldab/), can be found in Dickey (2010a), Dickey and Ferri (2010), Kramer (1983: no. 2), and Collart (1940). The papyrus is held at the Sorbonne in Paris, which has kindly made complete photographs available online at www.papyrologie.paris-sorbonne.fr/menu1/collections/pgrec/2Sorb2069.htm.

not intended to be read in isolation: it was a tool for deciphering the Latin, which was viewed as the primary text.

Inflections are also sometimes indicated by giving genitives of nouns or second- and third-person forms of verbs. Here too the words in question are translated into Greek even though the translation does not provide the morphological information that is the only reason for quoting the form in the first place; thus for example line 15 gives *turbinis* as the genitive of *turbo* and then translates *turbinis* into Greek. The authors of this work were evidently determined that no Latin word should remain untranslated; Greek words, on the other hand, are sometimes included without any equivalent in the Latin, for example "rarely" (γλωσσηματικῶς) in line 123, commenting on the "tire" meaning of *urus*. This policy is the opposite of that used by Dositheus, whose Greek translation was often incomplete but whose Latin was always complete.

The preserved portion of the glossary evidently comes from the end of a much longer text arranged in alphabetical order (alphabetization is by first letters only); we have the very end of the S section and most of the T and V sections. Some of the preserved material is very fragmentary, so only the relatively complete portions are presented here.[40]

7	T	T
8	Tibicen,	"Piper," "female piper";
8	tubicen;	"trumpeter," "female trumpeter";
9	horum duorum cetera	the other (cases) of these two (nouns)
9–10	ut *Cato* declinatur	are declined like "Cato,"
10	*e* recidente in *i*.	with the e changing to *i*.[41]
11	Tribus:	"Three (in the dative)," "tribe":[42]
11	"tribus generibus,"	"three kinds (in the dative),"
12	"tribus Collina."	"Colline tribe."
12	Turbo:	"Hurricane," "whipping-top," "whirling," "I disturb":
13	"turbo et vis venti,"	"hurricane and force of wind,"
13	"turbo buxeus,"	"whipping-top of boxwood,"
14	"turbo magicus,"	"magic wheel,"
14	"turbo composita";	"I disturb the peace";
15	turbinis;	(the genitive is) "of a hurricane";

[40] For scholarly editions see Dickey (2010a) and Dickey and Ferri (2010).

[41] I.e. they belong to the third declension and decline *tibicen, tibicinis*; cf. *Cato, Catonis*.

[42] I.e. *tribus* could be either the dative of *tres* "three" (strictly speaking it could also be the ablative of *tres*, but as there is no ablative in Greek that possibility cannot effectively be represented in the format of this glossary and so is ignored) or the nominative of *tribus* "tribe."

15	cetera ut *Cato* declinatur.	the other (forms) are declined like "Cato."
16	Trudo,	"I push," "I press",
16	trudis,	"you push," "you press,"
16	trudit;	"he pushes," "he presses";
17	cetera ut *ago.*	the other (forms of *trudo* are conjugated) like "I do."
	. . .	. . .
44	Tectum:	"House," "roofed," "roof":[43]
44–5	"tectum . . . ,"	" . . . house,"
45–6	"tectum est cubicellum,"	"the bedroom has been roofed,"
46–7	"tectum triclini aedificat";	"he builds the roof of the dining room";
47	cetera ut *bellum.*	the other (forms of *tectum* are declined) like "war."
48	Tendo:	"Stretch out," "go," "pitch a tent":
48	"tendo . . . ,"	"I stretch out . . . ,"
49	"tendo in forum,"	"I go to the forum,"
49–50	"tendo iuxta vallum";	"I pitch a tent near the defensive wall";
50	cetera ut *ago.*	the other (forms of *tendo* are conjugated) like "I do."
	. . .	. . .
60	Tactus.	"Touch," "touches," "having been touched."[44]
61	Tessera:	"Die"[45] and "pebble used in dice-playing";
61	et cetera ut *alta.*	and the other (forms of *tessera* are declined) like "high."
62	Tonsa:	"Having been cut" and rarely "oar";
62	cetera ut *alta.*	the other (forms of *tonsa* are declined) like "high."

---

[43] From our perspective the first and last of these three meanings are really the same word (*OLD* s.v. *tectum* 1 and 2) but the middle one is different (*OLD* s.v. *tectus*, perfect participle of *tego*).

[44] I.e. *tactus* "touch" (nominative singular of the noun), *tactūs* "touches" (nominative plural, to make the point that the noun belongs to the fourth declension), and *tactus* the perfect participle of *tango*.

[45] I.e. singular of "dice."

63	**V**	**V**
64	Voluptas:	"Pleasure," "enjoyment," "licentiousness," "luxuriousness";
64	cetera ut *Cato* . . .	the other (forms of *voluptas* are declined) like "Cato." . . .
65	"voluptatem capio";	"I take pleasure," "I live luxuriously," "I enjoy";
65–6	et cetera ut *rapio*.	and the other (forms of *capio* are conjugated) like "I seize."
	. . .	. . .
68–9	Vectura:	"Vehicle,"[46] "transportation," "passage-money";
69	et cetera ut *alta*.	and the other (forms of *vectura* are declined) like "high."
	. . .	. . .
79	Ventum:	"Wind (accusative)," "having come (neuter)":[47]
79	"ventum secundum,"	"favorable wind (accusative),"
80	"ventum est domum."	"there was an arrival home."
80	Ungula:	"Hoof," "trotter," "cloven hoof":
81	"ungula equi,"	"horse's hoof,"
81	"ungula porci,"	"pig's trotter,"
81–2	"ungula bovis";	"cow's cloven hoof";
82	et cetera ut *alta*.	and the other (forms of *ungula* are declined) like "high."
83	Ulciscor:	"I avenge" and "I punish":
83	"ulciscor hostis."	"I punish the enemy."
84	Ultrix:	"Vengeance," "avenger";
84	et cetera ut *calx*.	and the other (forms of *ultrix* are declined) like "limestone."

[46] For *uectura* meaning "vehicle" see Adams (2003b: 559).

[47] I.e. *ventum* can be the accusative of *ventus* "wind" or the perfect participle of *venio* "come"; the writer used the latter form only as an impersonal passive, so ambiguity arose only with the accusative of *ventus*.

85	Unde:	"Whence?" and "whence":
85	"unde homines fiunt";	"whence men arise";
86	in priore utramque syllabam	in the former (meaning) we accent each
87	acuimus,	syllable,[48]
87	in secundo secundam.	in the latter (meaning we accent) the second (syllable).[49]
	. . .	. . .
93	Verna:	"home-bred slave," "male foundling," "female foundling";
94	"verna meus,"	"my home-bred slave" or "my male foundling,"
94	"verna mea";	"my female foundling";
95	cetera ut *alta*.	the other (forms of *verna* are declined) like "high."
95	Vos:	"You (nominative plural)," "you (accusative plural)":
96	"vos priores venistis,"	"you (nominative plural) came earlier,"
96–7	"vos sic iussi";	"I ordered you (accusative plural) thus."
97–8	genetivi sic fit casus:	It becomes a genitive case (when translated into Greek) thus (i.e. in these phrases):
98	"audio vos,"	"I hear you (genitive)," "I hear you (accusative),"[50]
99	"contemno vos";	"I despise you (genitive)";[51]
99	dativi rursus sic:	but (it becomes) a dative thus:
100	"sequor vos,"	"I follow you (dative),"
100	"adiuvo vos."	"I help you (dative)."[52]
101	Uter:	"Which of two," "woman's uterus":
101	"uter uestrum,"	"which of you two,"

[48] The mismatch between the alignment of the two languages here is original.

[49] This intriguing statement about a pronunciation difference between interrogative and non-interrogative uses of *unde* ties in with some other evidence in ancient grammatical texts, though not in a very straightforward fashion; see Dickey (2010a: *ad loc.*) and Scappaticcio (2011).

[50] The point being made here is that since the verb ἀκούω usually takes the genitive, the Latin accusative *vos* normally needs to be changed to a genitive when *audio vos* is translated into Greek; this explanation has been made more complicated by admitting that in certain contexts ἀκούω actually takes an accusative and that therefore sometimes *vos* would be translated with an accusative even in this phrase.

[51] I.e. καταφρονέω takes the genitive.

[52] I.e. ἀκολουθέω "follow" and βοηθέω "help" take the dative.

102	"uter mulieris."	"uterus of a woman."[53]
102	Usus.	"Use," "having used."[54]
103	Vobis:	"You (dative plural)";[55]
103	in comparatione plurali	in comparison in the plural
104	hoc quoque Graece	in Greek this too
104–5	genetivus fit casus	becomes the genitive case
105	per omnia:	in all contexts:
105–6	ut "vobis acutior hic,"	as "this man (is) sharper than you,"
106	"vobis disertior,"	"more learned than you,"
107	"vobis prior."	"before you."
107–8	Vitio:	"I harm," "problem," "defect" (dative), but we say "defile" of a woman:
108	"vitio rem,"	"I spoil the business,"
108–9	"vitio hoc tenetur,"	"he is held in the grip of this problem,"
109	"vitio virginem";	"I defile the virgin,"
110	vitias;	"you harm," "you defile";
110	et cetera ut *accuso*.	and (you conjugate) the other (forms) like "I accuse."
111	Vero:	"True (dative)" or "but":
111	"vero amico,"	"true friend (dative),"
111–12	"hoc vero sciebam."	"but I knew this."
	. . .	. . .
115	Vertex:	"Top," "whirlpool":
116	"vertex capitis,"	"top of the head,"
116–17	"vertex fluminum";	"whirlpool of rivers";
117	cetera ut *calx*,	the other (forms of *vertex* are declined) like "limestone,"
117–18	masculine.	in the masculine.
118	idem significat	*Vortex* also means the same thing.
119	et *vortex*.	

[53] On this sense of *uter* see Adams (1982: 88).
[54] I.e. *usus* can be a fourth-declension noun meaning "use" or the perfect participle of *utor*.
[55] In fact *vobis* can be ablative as well as dative (cf. line 11 and note there), and it is the ablative of comparison that is discussed here.

128	Valetudo:	"Health" and "illness":
119	"valetudo bona,"	"good health,"
120	"valetudo incommoda";	"grave illness";
120–1	cetera ut *Cato* feminine,	the other (forms of *valetudo* are declined) like "Cato" in the feminine,
121–2	recidente *o* in *i*.	with the *o* changing to *i*.[56]
123	Urus:	"Tire on a wheel"[57] rarely, and a German ox;
124	cetera ut *altus*.	the other (forms of *urus* are declined) like "high."
124–5	Viator:	"Chief minister"[58] and "traveler";
125	cetera ut *altior*.	the other (forms of *viator* are declined) like "higher."
126	Vincit:	"He conquers" and rarely "he binds":[59]
127	"vincit prudentia,"	"he conquers by skill,"
127–8	"vincit manus."	"he binds the hands."
129	Valeo:	"I am healthy," "I am well," "I am strong":
129–30	"valeo tecum,"	"I am healthy along with you" and "I am well,"
130	"valeo studere";	"I am strong enough to study";
131	vales,	"you (sg.) are healthy," "you are strong," "you are well,"
131	valet,	"he is healthy," "he is strong," "he is well,"
132	valemus,	"we are healthy," "we are strong," "we are well,"
133	valetis,	"you (pl.) are healthy," "you are strong," "you are well,"
133–4	valent,	"they are healthy," "they are strong," "they are well,"
134	vale;	"be healthy!," "be strong!," "be well!/ goodbye";
135	et cetera sicut	and the other (forms of *valeo*)
135–6	*foveo* declinatur.	are conjugated like "I heat up."

[56] I.e. *valetudo, valetudinis*, third declension.
[57] For the equation see Goetz and Gundermann (1888: 338.27) and Kramer (1983: 39).
[58] Cf. Collart (1940: 74).
[59] I.e. *vincit* is usually from *vinco* "conquer" but ocasionally from *vincio* "bind."

5 | Prose composition

Many elementary Latin students spend a significant amount of time translating English sentences into Latin in order to practice different forms and constructions. It is striking that there is no evidence of such activity in antiquity; perhaps the evidence has been lost, but if ancient students had translated anything approaching as many sentences as modern ones do we would expect at least a few to survive. It is therefore tempting to conclude that ancient Latin learning aimed only at passive competence: students learned to read the language but not to write it.

Yet this can hardly be the right answer, since the purposes for which Greek speakers learned Latin required active competence: merchants negotiating with the Roman army needed to be able to speak Latin, and lawyers drawing up wills and other documents needed to be able to write it. How, then, was that competence achieved?

One possible answer to that question is provided by a papyrus of the third or fourth century AD containing a set of Greek fables translated into Latin by one or more learner(s).[1] These look strikingly like exercises in prose composition and raise the possibility that learners practiced translation into Latin only in paragraph-sized chunks, not with individual sentences. Although we tend to think of paragraphs as more difficult than sentences, the ancients may not have had the same view. Individual sentences of real Latin and Greek texts are notoriously difficult to understand out of context, and it may be that speakers of those languages simply considered the paragraph the smallest unit that it was practical to set for translation practice.

The translator of the extract below (Babrius, Fable 16, a misogynistic tale) can be recognized as an advanced Latin learner not from the spelling mistakes, which could have been made by a native speaker, nor from the use of the non-existent word *frestigiatur* (which is so strange that it cannot reliably be attributed to any particular source),[2] but from the participles. Latin has a limited set of participles: in the present tense all verbs

---

[1] *P.Amh.* II.26; this papyrus is number 172 in the Mertens–Pack database (http://promethee.philo.ulg.ac.be/cedopal/indexsimple.asp) and number 434 in the Leuven Database of Ancient Books (www.trismegistos.org/ldab/). For a detailed discussion of the Latin see Adams (2003a: 725–41). The text reproduced here is taken from Cavenaile (1958 no. 40: lines 1–8, 15–24); missing letters are supplied, but errors are not corrected in either language. Diacritics and punctuation are editorial.

[2] One possible explanation for it is that ἐνεδρεύσας "having lain in ambush" was misunderstood as ἐνεδρευθείς "having been deceived" and translated into Latin with *praestigiatus*, which was then corrupted to *frestigiatur*. Corruption after the initial translation is possible in this text, because there are other signs that it was transmitted after being translated.

have only active participles, and in the perfect tense, while most verbs have only passive participles, deponent verbs have only active ones. Greek, by contrast, has a full set of active, (middle), and passive participles in both the present and aorist (past) tenses; effectively this means that some Greek participles cannot be literally translated into Latin. The difficulty can be resolved by using a subordinate clause rather than a participle in Latin, by changing the tense, or by otherwise recasting the expression, but in order to take these steps one needs to be aware of the problem. The translator here seems not to have been aware, for he simply uses the perfect passive participle (e.g. *auditus* in line 11) to translate the Greek aorist active participle (e.g. ἀκούσας in line 3). Other interesting features include *tulitus* in line 17 and *quis* in line 18.

The Greek also contains errors; for example the last word of line 1 belongs at the start of line 2 in order to make the poem scan. One set of errors is particularly revealing: in line 6, where the papyrus has αὐτὸς δὲ πινῶν καὶ χανὼν λύκος ὄντος, the text of Babrius as transmitted elsewhere has αὐτὸς δὲ πεινῶν καὶ λύκος χανὼν ὄντως. This other version must be right, for the line in the papyrus neither scans (the meter is scazons, i.e. limping iambics) nor makes sense. The Latin translates the correct Greek rather than the Greek of the papyrus and must therefore have been made not from this copy of the Greek but from an earlier, less corrupt version. So this text has a transmission history (cf. Kramer 2007b): is it a fair copy made by a student to show his or her teacher, a teacher's collection of fair copies of the proses he liked to set, or an ancient example of student plagiarism?

```
1      ἄγροικος ἠπείλησε νηπίῳ τίτθη κλαίοντι·
       "σίγα, μή σε τῷ λύκῳ ῥίψω."
       λύκος δ' ἀκούσας τήν τε γραῦν ἀληθύειν
       νομίσας ἔμεινεν, ὡς ἕτοιμα δειπνήσων.
5      ἕως ὁ παῖς μὲν ἑσπέρας ἐκοιμήθη,
       αὐτὸς δὲ πινῶν καὶ χανὼν λύκος ὄντος
       ἀπῆλθε ψυχραῖς ἐλπίσιν ἐνεδρεύσας.
       λύκαινα δ' αὐτὸν ἡ σύνευνος ἠρώτα
       "πῶς οὐδὲν ἦλθες ἄρας, ὡς πρὶν εἰώθεις;"
10     κἀκεῖνος εἶπε "πῶς γάρ, ὃς γυναικὶ πιστεύω;"

       [2 lines of Latin missing]
       luppus autem auditus, anucellam vere dictum
       putatus, mansit quasi parata cenaret.
       dum puer quidem sero dormisset,
       ipse porro esuriens et luppus enectus vere
15     redivit frigiti spebus frestigiatur.
```

luppa enim eum coniugalis interrogabat,
"quomodo nihil tulitus venisti, sicut solebas?"
et ille dixit, "quomodo enim, quis mulieri credo?"

A country nurse threatened a crying baby, "Be quiet, lest I throw you to the wolf." And a wolf, hearing (this) and thinking that the old woman was telling the truth, waited, in order to dine on the ready meal. When the child was put to bed in the evening, the wolf himself, hungry and really exhausted, returned having lain in ambush for cold hopes. His wolf wife asked him, "How come you don't come bringing anything, as you used to?" And he said, "How could I, who trust(ed) a woman?"

6 | Alphabets

Most Greek-speaking Latin students began by learning the alphabet. The teacher wrote out the letters in alphabetical order, and students then copied them repeatedly to learn their shapes, while saying out loud either the equivalent Greek letter or the Latin letter-name in order to learn the sound that accompanied the shape; students also copied lines of verse to practice using the letters in a natural context.[1]

6.1 A learner's alphabet with line of verse

This exercise (*P.Oxy.* x.1315, from the fifth or sixth century AD) provided the alphabet in both capital and lower-case letters; although the two forms were not normally used in the same text the way they are today, students still needed to learn both since some texts used one and some the other. Someone (whether the student or the teacher is uncertain) has written the Greek equivalents over some of the Latin letters; note the mistakes. The alphabets were followed by a line of Virgil (*Aeneid* 4.129); both alphabets and verse are partly lost on the papyrus but have been restored here.[2]

α β κ δ ε φ γ η ι κ λ μ ν ο π
A B C D E F G H I K L M N O P Q R S T V X Y Z

α β κ δ ε φ κ η ι κ
a b c d e f g h i k l m n o p q r s t u x y z

OCEANVMINTEREASVRGENSAVRORARELIQVIT

6.2 A learner's alphabet with letter names

This version (on an ostrakon, i.e. a piece of broken pottery, from the first or second century) provided only the capital letters, which were accompanied by the letter-names

---

[1] See Feissel (2008), who refutes Clarysse and Rochette's (2005: 75) alternative explanation of how the alphabet was learned.

[2] Additional information on this text, which is number 3013 in the Mertens–Pack database (http://promethee. philo.ulg.ac.be/cedopal/indexsimple.asp) and number 4163 in the Leuven Database of Ancient Books (www. trismegistos.org/ldab/), can be found in Kramer (2001: no. 2).

of the Latin alphabet, written in Greek script.[3] Again the papyrus is broken and has been supplemented.[4]

α	βη	κη	δη	η	εφ	γη	ʽ	ι	κα	ιλ	μ	εν	ω	πη	κου	ρ	ες	τη	ου	ξη
A	B	C	D	E	F	G	H	I	K	L	M	N	O	P	Q	R	S	T	U	X	Y	Z

---

[3] In Latin script the names are usually *a, be, ce, de, e, ef, ge, ha, i, ka, el, em, en, o, pe, qu, er, es, te, u, ex*; see Allen (1978: 111–15). The last two letters, *y* and *z*, do not usually have names (as here) but were sometimes called *y graeca* and *zeta*.

[4] Additional information on this text, which is O.Max. inv. 356, *SB* xxviii.17105, number 3012.01 in the Mertens–Pack database (http://promethee.philo.ulg.ac.be/cedopal/indexsimple.asp), and number 10791 in the Leuven Database of Ancient Books (http://www.trismegistos.org/ldab/), can be found in Fournet (2003: 445) and Scappaticcio (forthcoming).

7 | Transliterated texts

A significant percentage of Latin learners did not learn the alphabet. Such learners must have been interested in oral proficiency rather than in the capacity to read or write, and it may well be that the majority of what they did is now lost to us because it was done orally and never written down. Some of these learners, however, have signaled their presence by producing transliterated Latin-learning texts, with the Latin in Greek script. Such texts are more common than the ones with the Latin in Roman script until the third century AD but become fairly rare after that century.

Additional transliterated texts, complete with the original Greek, can be found in passages 8.10, 8.13, and 8.15–16.

7.1 A transliterated colloquium

A papyrus of the fifth or sixth century AD (P.Berol. inv. 10582) contains a trilingual colloquium in Latin, Greek, and Coptic.[1] Originally this text would have resembled the colloquia in section 2.1, to which it is historically related, but it has been adapted for use by a very different group of Latin learners, apparently Coptic speakers. The section given here depicts the end of a dinner party; the beginning of the meal is unfortunately missing.

The transliteration reflects the pronunciation of both Latin and Greek in late antiquity: Latin *b* and *v*, originally pronounced like our *b* and *w* respectively, had both come to be pronounced more like our *v*, while Greek beta had come to have a similar sound; beta is therefore used to transcribe both *b* and *v*. The Latin vowel *u* continued to be pronounced like our *u*, while Greek upsilon had turned into a fronted vowel that sounded different (like modern French *u*); the digraph omicron upsilon is therefore used to transcribe *u*. The sound of *h* had been lost, though it might well not have been written in Greek anyway since breathings were often omitted in Greek papyri. The sound of *qu* is usually transcribed with kappa omicron, though there is some variation. The letters *i*

---

[1] Additional information on and scholarly editions of this text, which is number 3009 in the Mertens–Pack database (http://promethee.philo.ulg.ac.be/cedopal/indexsimple.asp) and number 6075 in the Leuven Database of Ancient Books (www.trismegistos.org/ldab/), can be found in Dickey (2015a), Kramer (1983: no. 15, 2010), and Schubart (1913). A photograph is available at http://ww2.smb.museum/berlpap/index.php/record/?result=0&Alle=10582; this passage begins near the top of the recto. In this version the Coptic and the more fragmentary sections have been omitted, but most errors in the Latin are left uncorrected.

and *e* are sometimes confused, as these sounds had merged in some circumstances.² In addition the transliteration contains outright mistakes that cannot derive from the way either Latin or Greek was pronounced, such as ακκεντιδε for *accendite* in 11 and εστ for *et* in 29. Another portion of this text can be found in passage 8.10.

4	"Σι ομνης	"If all
5	βιβεριντ,	have drunk,
	τεργε	wipe
	μενσαμ.	the table.
	αδπωνιτε	Put
	ιν μενδιουμ	amongst us
10	κανδελαβρας,	the candlesticks,
	ετ ακκεντιδε	and light
	λουκερνας.	the lamps.
	διλουκε.	Give us light!
	δατε νοβις	Give us
15	βελλαρια,	sweets (and)
	ουνγουεντουμ."	unguent."
	δικιτε	Say,
	ομνης	all of you,
	"φιλικιτερ."	"Good luck!"
20	"βενε νως	"You have entertained us well
	ακκιπιστι	
	ετ ρεγαλιτερ,	and royally,
	ουτ τιβι	as befits you."
	δεκετ."	
25	"νη κοιιδ	"Do you
	βουλτις	want
	ικ δορμιρε,	to sleep here,
	κουοδ σερω εστ;"	because it is late?"
	"εστ ιν οκ	"For this too
30	γρατιας	we are grateful."
	αβημος."	
	"ουτ ιουσσειστι."	"As you ordered."
	"κουοδ βως	"Whatever you
	βουλτις·	want:

35	εγω μεουμ φηκι."	I have done my (duty)."
	"ακκενδιτε	"Light
	λουκερνας	the lamps
39	ετ προσεκουαμινο	and accompany them home,
41	ομνης."	all of you!"

7.2   A transliterated list of verb conjugations

Learning Latin in transliteration did not mean avoiding grammar. Greek speakers were not frightened of the Latin noun and verb endings, since they had a similar system in their own language, and they sometimes wanted sets of paradigms even if they were not learning to read and write Latin. This list, from a papyrus of the third or fourth century AD (P.Strasb. inv. G 1175),[3] is surprising in several ways: it includes only the singulars of the verbs concerned, it starts with the third person rather than the first,[4] and it gives the first and second person even for the impersonal verb *pluit*, which exists only in the third person. It also has the Latin on the right and the Greek on the left, despite the fact that this text must have been used by Greek speakers to learn Latin, not by Latin speakers to learn Greek. Being earlier in date than the colloquium papyrus in 7.1, this text uses an older transliteration system in which Latin *v* is represented by omicron upsilon rather than by beta; *u* is also represented by omicron upsilon, and iota and epsilon iota are used interchangeably for *i* because they were pronounced identically in Greek. Another portion of this text is presented in passage 8.13 with the original Greek.

3	he greets	σαλουτατ
	you greet	σαλουτας
5	I greet	σαλουτω
	he rules	ρηγνατ
	you rule	ρηγνας
	I rule	ρηγνω
	he tortures	τορκετ
10	you torture	τορκες
	I torture	τορκεω

---

[3] Additional information on this text, which is number 2134.71 in the Mertens–Pack database (http://promethee. philo.ulg.ac.be/cedopal/indexsimple.asp) and number 9217 in the Leuven Database of Ancient Books (www. trismegistos.org/ldab/), can be found in Kramer (2001: no. 3), whose text is reproduced here, and Scappaticcio (forthcoming). It was once part of the same book as P.Strasb. inv. G 1173, quoted in sections 7.3 and 8.16.

[4] The order first person, second person, third person is adhered to almost without exception in other grammatical texts both Latin and Greek; the unusual order found here may be due to Semitic influence and if so might indicate that the papyrus was written by a speaker of Aramaic.

	he considers	κωγιτατ
	you consider	κωγιτας
	I consider	κωγιτω
15	he coughs	τουσσιτ
	you cough	τουσσις
	I cough	τουσσειω
	he dyes	τινγιτ
	you dye	τινγις
20	I dye	τινγω
	he harms	νοκετ
	you harm	νοκες
	I harm	νοκεω
	he thunders	τονατ
25	you thunder	τονας
	I thunder	τονω
	he sees	ουιδετ
	you see	ουιδες
	I see	ουιδεω
30	it rains	πλοουετ
	you rain	πλοουες
	I rain	πλοουω
	he sends	μιττιτ
	you send	μιττις
35	I send	μιττω
	he helps	αδιουτατ
	you help	αδιουτας
	I help	αδιουτω
	he sinks	μεργιτ
40	you sink	μεργις
	I sink	μεργω

7.3   A transliterated glossary of military terminology

Classified glossaries are common among transliterated materials. This papyrus from the third or fourth century AD (P. Strasb. inv. G 1173)[5] now contains two sections, the

[5] Additional information on this text, which is number 2134.61 in the Mertens–Pack database (http://promethee. philo.ulg.ac.be/cedopal/indexsimple.asp) and number 9218 in the Leuven Database of Ancient Books (www. trismegistos.org/ldab/), can be found in Kramer (2001: no. 6).

other of which can be found in passage 8.16; originally it contained more. Once again the Latin is on the right rather than the left, for this papyrus originally formed part of the same book as passage 7.2. Note the use of both iota and epsilon iota to represent *i*, the confusion between *e* and *i*, and the strange spelling error φρενεκτους for *praefectus*. The form λεγιων reflects the nominative not of *legio* but of λεγιών, the form *legio* assumed when borrowed into Greek.

24	**About soldiers**	**Δη μιλιτιβους**
25	warfare	μιλιτια
	camp	καστρα
	ditch	φοσσα
	leader	δουξ
	emperor	ιμπερατωρ
30	military tribune	τριβουνους μελιτουμ
	camp prefect	φρενεκτους καστρωρουμ
	commander	πρινκιψ
	commander's tent	ταβερνακουλα
	army	εξερκιτους
35	legion	λεγιων
	standard	σιγνα
	soldiers	μιλιτης
	footsoldiers	πεδεστρης
	cavalrymen	εκουειτης
40	standard-bearers	σιγνιφερει

7.4 A transliterated glossary of vegetable and fish names

This fragment of a papyrus from the first or second century AD (*P.Oxy.* XXIII.2660)[6] preserves two sections of a classified glossary, one on vegetables and one on fish. The words in this glossary would not be high on the priority list of any Latin learner today, and not just because Latin is no longer a spoken language used for buying and selling things: most of these words are ones that learners of a modern foreign language would also feel inclined to skip. The ancient attitude to such words was clearly different, for both vegetable names and fish names are common among surviving bilingual glossary

---

[6] Additional information on this text, which is number 2134.1 in the Mertens–Pack database (http://promethee. philo.ulg.ac.be/cedopal/indexsimple.asp) and number 4497 in the Leuven Database of Ancient Books (www. trismegistos.org/ldab/), can be found in Kramer (1983: no. 6). A photograph of the papyrus can been seen at www.papyrology.ox.ac.uk/POxy/.

materials; it is possible that this glossary and others like it were used by Greek speakers trying to sell food to the Roman army.

Note the Herculanean fish (which is known only from this text), the position of the Latin on the right, and the unusual spellings, including ρεια for *raia*. The word κυμα, exceptionally, has a Greek upsilon (not part of a diphthong) in a Latin transliteration: this spelling represents the Latin *cyma*, which uses *y* because the word is a Greek borrowing (cf. the word's occurrence in passage 2.1.21 above). The beginning of the first section is missing.

1	sorrel	λαπατιουμ
	spinach	βλιτουμ
	mustard	σιναπουμ
	salad	ακηταρια
5	lettuce	λακτουκα
	basil	ωκιμουμ
	endive	ιντουβους
	coriander	κοριανδρουμ
	sprout	κυμα
10	asparagus	ασπαραγους
	pennyroyal	πουλειουμ
	About fish	**Δη πισκιβους**
	pike	λουπους
	mullet	μουγιλ
15	Herculanean fish	ηρκουλανεους
	ray	ρεια
	mullets	μουλλει
	eel	ανγουιλλα
	conger eel	γονγερ
20	murena	μουρηνα
	cuttlefish	σηπια
	cuttlefish	λολλειγο
	crayfish	λουκουστα
	. . .	. . .
26	sprats	μηναι
	red fishes	ρουβριωνης
	mackerels	λακερτει
	dog-fishes	κατελλει

30	red fishes	ρουβελλιωνης
	grayling	ουμβρα
	pipefish	ακους
	oyster	οστρεα
	purple-fish	πουρπουρα
35	murexes	μουρικης
	little scallops	πεκτουνκουλει
	salted fish	σαλσαμεντουμ

8 | Texts with the original Greek

In this section a selection of ancient Latin-learning texts is presented with the Greek in its original language, rather than replaced by an English translation. To facilitate its comprehension by modern students, the Greek in this section is presented in a modern format, with word division, punctuation, etc.; see passage 9.2 for extracts with Greek in its original format.

8.1 A colloquium morning scene

For general background on the colloquia see section 2.1. This morning scene is related to the ones presented there but has a surprising difference: the child performs his ablutions meticulously but neglects to put on any clothes. Apparently he goes off to school naked from the knees up; this feature is probably due to the loss of a dressing scene at some stage of the transmission, unless *linteum*/ὡμόλινον, which ought to mean "linen towel," was intended to be a garment. Note the child's personal slave boy (common in the colloquia and probably also in real life, at least for rich children). The passage comes from the Colloquium Stephani; note the indirect command using an infinitive, a superfluous *ad*, and the non-standard use of cases with *in*.[1]

3a	Surrexi	Ἠγέρθην
	mane	πρωΐ
	expergefactus,	ἐξυπνισθείς,
	et vocavi	καὶ ἐκάλεσα
	puerum.	παῖδα.
3b	iussi aperire	ἐκέλευσα ἀνοῖξαι
	fenestram;	τὴν θυρίδα·
	aperuit cito.	ἤνοιξεν ταχέως.
3c	elevatus	ἐγερθεὶς
	assedi	ἐκάθισα
	supra spondam	ἐπὶ τοῦ ἐνηλάτου
	lecti.	τῆς κλίνης.
4a	poposci	ᾔτησα
	calciamenta	ὑποδήματα

---

[1] Additional information on this text and a scholarly edition of it can be found in Dickey (2012–15: I.219–45).

	et ocreas;	καὶ περικνημῖδας·
	erat enim frigus.	ἦν γὰρ ψῦχος.
4b	calciatus ergo	ὑποδεθεὶς οὖν
	accepi linteum.	ἔλαβον ὠμόλινον.
	porrectum est	ἐπεδόθη
	mundum.	καθαρόν.
5a	allata est aqua	προσηνέχθη ὕδωρ
	ad faciem	πρὸς τὴν ὄψιν
	in urceolum;	εἰς ὀρνόλην·
5b	cuius superfusu	ᾧ ἐπιχυθεὶς
	primum manus,	πρῶτον χεῖρας,
	deinde ad faciem	εἶτα κατὰ τὴν ὄψιν
	lavi;	ἐνιψάμην·
	et os clausi.	καὶ τὸ στόμα ἔκλεισα.
5c	dentes fricui	ὀδόντας ἔτριψα
	et gingivas.	καὶ οὖλα.
5d	exspui	ἐξέπτυσα
	inutilia	τὰ ἄχρηστα
	sicut superveniebant,	ὥς τινα ἐπήρχοντο,
	et emunxi me.	καὶ ἐξεμυξάμην.
5e	haec omnia	ταῦτα πάντα
	effusa sunt.	ἐξεχύθησαν.
6a	tersi manus,	ἐξέμαξα τὰς χεῖρας,
	deinde	ἔπειτα
	et brachia	καὶ τοὺς βραχίονας
	et faciem,	καὶ τὴν ὄψιν,
	ut mundus procedam.	ἵνα καθαρὸς προέλθω.
6b	sic enim	οὕτως γὰρ
	decet	πρέπει
	puerum ingenuum	παῖδα ἐλεύθερον
	discere.	μαθεῖν.

8.2 A colloquium school scene

The school scenes of the Colloquium Celtis are not very coherent because of the presence of large numbers of vocabulary alternatives and repetitions. The selections presented below are, therefore, extracts.[2] They contain a significant amount of

---

[2] Additional information on this text and a scholarly edition of it can be found in Dickey (2012–15: II.141–266).

technical terminology from the field of education, which can be tricky to translate today.

One of these technical terms is *reddo*/ἀποδίδωμι, which refers to producing one's assignment in whatever form it has been requested. In ancient schools that process usually entailed reciting something from memory to demonstrate that one had learned it, but it could also mean handing in a piece of written work or reading aloud a text that one had been preparing to read aloud. This last meaning is probably the one intended in this passage, to judge by the next clause.

Another is *ars*/τέχνη meaning "grammar" (i.e. standing for *ars grammatica*/τέχνη γραμματική); this usage is very common in certain contexts and gives rise to, among other things, the English term "artigrapher" for an author of a grammatical treatise. A third is *locus*/τόπος meaning "passage" in a literary work; one could do many different things with a passage, but here it is probably being read aloud, explained, and/or translated. Such work usually involved prior preparation of the passage by the student, perhaps leaving evidence like that now visible in the Sallust papyrus in passage 2.8.

The phase *partes orationis*/μέρη λόγου means "parts of speech"; the eight referred to here are probably nouns, pronouns, verbs, participles, adverbs, prepositions, conjunctions, and interjections. (Adjectives were often considered a type of noun in antiquity.) *Declinatio* means "inflection"; when referring to nouns this is equivalent to our "declension," but as verbs are at issue here (this is clearer in Greek than in Latin), the more specific term in this case would be "conjugation." The verbs in 35c mean that the students pronounce the passage with proper divisions (pauses in the right place), suspensions (i.e. they do not pause in the wrong places), and accentuation.

Note also the reference to Hermeneumata (*interpretamenta*), i.e. bilingual language-learning materials (glossaries and/or colloquia). They are being used by the youngest children, who have just learned the alphabet and are in the intermediate stage between reading letters and reading words, a stage in which ancient children read syllables.[3] The classified glossaries (for examples of which see passages 4.2–3, 7.3–4, and 8.14–16) are referred to with *capitula*/κεφάλαια. There is also a reference to Trojan war stories like those in passages 2.2 and 8.3 (although *lectio de Iliade* might mean an extract from the *Iliad*, Greek περὶ Ἰλιάδος makes clear that what is envisioned is not an extract but a reading about the *Iliad*, i.e. a paraphrase or summary). Note the post-Classical phrase *pro posse* and many post-Classical features in the Greek.

30b	edisco	ἐκμανθάνω
	scripta mea.	τὰ γραπτά μου.

---

[3] For ancient students learning to read via a progression from letters to syllables to words, rather than the immediate move from letters to words seen today, see Cribiore (1996: 47–8).

	si paratus sum,	εἰ ἑτοῖμός εἰμι,
	statim reddo;	εὐθὺς ἀποδίδωμι·
	sin autem,	εἰ δὲ μή,
	iterum lego.	πάλιν ἀναγινώσκω.
	…	…
32a	explanatur mihi	ἐξηγεῖταί μοι
	ignotus liber	ἄγνωστον βιβλίον
	aut ignota lectio.	ἢ ἀγνώστη ἀνάγνωσις.
33a	expositio traditur.	ἐξήγησις παραδίδοται.
	accipio locum,	λαμβάνω τόπον,
	et alii mecum	καὶ ἄλλοι μετ’ ἐμοῦ
	extemporalem,	σημερινόν,
33b	ceteri	οἱ λοιποὶ
	accuratum	ἀποφροντισμένον
	reddunt.	ἀποδιδοῦσι.
34a	minores	οἱ μικροὶ
	interpretamenta	ἑρμηνεύματα
	et syllabas,	καὶ συλλαβάς,
	sermonis declinationem,	τοῦ ῥήματος κλίσιν,
34b	artem omnem,	τέχνην ἄπασαν,
	sermonem	διάλεκτον
	exercent	διηγοῦνται
	apud subdoctorem:	παρὰ ὑποσοφιστῇ·
35a	casus nominum,	πτώσεις ὀνομάτων,
	genera nominum,	γένη ὀνομάτων,
	numeros,	ἀριθμούς,
	…	…
35b	litteras,	γράμματα,
	vocales	φωνήεντα
	et semivocales	καὶ ἡμίφωνα
	et mutas;	καὶ ἄφωνα·
35c	dividunt,	διαμερίζουσι,
	suspendunt,	συστέλλουσι,
	elevant.	ἐπαίρουσιν.
36a	deinde universa	εἶτα ἄπαντα
	pertranseunt,	διέρχονται,
	sed et capitula	τὰ δὲ κεφάλαια
	nominum,	ὀνομάτων,
36b	partes orationis	μέρη λόγου

	octo.	τὰ ὀκτώ.
	sic fit	οὕτως γίνεται
	silentium.	ἡ σιγεία.
37a	eunt priores	ἀπίουσιν πρωτόσχολοι
	ad magistrum;	πρὸς διδάσκαλον·
	legunt	ἀναγινώσκουσιν
	lectionem	ἀνάγνωσιν
	de Iliade,	περὶ Ἰλιάδος,
	aliam de Odyssia.	ἄλλην περὶ Ὀδυσσείας.
37b	accipiunt locum.	λαμβάνουσι τόπον.
	…	…
39a	tunc revertitur	τότε ἐπανέρχεται
	quisque,	ἕκαστος,
	in suo loco	ἐν τῷ ἰδίῳ τόπῳ
	considunt.	καθέζουσιν.
39b	quisque legit	ἕκαστος ἀναγινώσκει
	lectionem	ἀνάγνωσιν
	sibi subtraditam.	αὐτῷ δεδειγμένην.
	…	…
39c	in ordinem recitant	εἰς τάξιν ἀναγορεύουσιν
	quisque	ἕκαστος
	pro posse;	κατὰ τὴν δύναμιν·
39d	si quis bene	εἴ τις καλῶς
	recitavit,	ἀνηγόρευσεν,
	laudatur;	ἐπαινεῖται·
	si quis male,	εἴ τις κακῶς,
	coercetur.	δέρεται.
	…	…
40a	iubente praeceptore	κελεύοντος καθηγητοῦ
	surgunt minores	ἀνίστανται οἱ μικρότατοι
	ad syllabas,	πρὸς συλλαβάς,
40b	et nos recitamus	καὶ ἡμεῖς ἀνηγορεύκαμεν
	dictatum et versus	ἄμιλλαν καὶ στίχους
	ad subdoctorem;	πρὸς ὑποσοφιστήν·
40c	reddunt nomina	ἀποδιδοῦσιν ὀνόματα
	et interpretamenta,	καὶ ἑρμηνεύματα,
	scribunt lectionem.	γράφουσιν ἀνάγνωσιν.
41a	secunda classis	δευτέρα τάξις
	relegit.	ἐπαναγινώσκει.

	et ego in prima,	καὶ ἐγὼ ἐν τῇ πρώτῃ,
	ut sedimus,	ὡς ἐκαθίσαμεν,
41b	pertranseo	διέρχομαι
	commentarium meum	τὸ ὑπόμνημά μου
	et lexeis	καὶ λέξεις
	et artem.	καὶ τέχνην.

8.3   Stories about the Trojan War

Background to these stories can be found in the introduction to passage 2.2. The extracts given here cover books 14–16 of the *Iliad*; the numbers of the books are given only in Greek.[4] Note the use of words meaning 'one' as indefinite articles ('a'), of *Lyciae* where we would expect *ad Lyciam*, and of εἰς where we would expect ἐν, as well as non-standard sequence of tenses in Latin. Note also how the author handled idioms involving participles successfully by using very different constructions in the two languages (64.22 and 64.47); the contrast with the participle problems in passage 5 is striking.

Ξ

63.34	Nestor audiens	Νέστωρ ἀκούσας
63.35	clamorem et fugam	κραυγὴν καὶ φυγὴν
	Graecorum	τῶν Ἑλλήνων
	procedit et invenit	προέρχεται καὶ εὑρίσκει
	Diomedem in proelio	Διομήδην εἰς τὸν πόλεμον
	dimicantem.	πυκτεύοντα.
63.40	Neptunus autem et Iuno	Ποσειδῶν δὲ καὶ Ἥρα
	in adiutorium	εἰς βοήθειαν
	Graecis astabant.	τοῖς Ἕλλησιν παρεστήκεισαν.
	Somno enim Iuno	τῷ γὰρ Ὕπνῳ Ἥρα
	unam nympham	μίαν νύμφην
63.45	dare in coitum	δοῦναι εἰς συνουσίαν
	repromiserat Pasithean,	ὑπέσχετο Πασιθέην,
	ut Iovem	ἵνα τὸν Δία

---

[4] Additional information on this text can be found in Dickey (2012–15: 1.27–8). The text here is a slightly emended version of Flammini's scholarly edition (2004: 113–15), but the layout follows that of the Leiden manuscript, Vossianus Gr. Q. 7, and the numbering refers to Goetz's transcription of that manuscript (Goetz 1892: 63–5).

	in somnum mitteret	εἰς ὕπνον τρέψῃ
	a pugna.	ἀπὸ τοῦ πολέμου·
63.50	et tunc Aiax solus	καὶ τότε Αἴας μόνος
	Troianos fugavit.	τοὺς Τρῶας ἐφυγάδευσεν.

Ο

64.1	Cum vidisset Iuppiter	Ὅτε ἑώρακεν Ζεὺς
	deficientem animo	λιποψυχοῦντα Ἕκτορα
	Hectorem	
	ob ictum lapidis,	διὰ τὴν ὁρμὴν τοῦ λίθου,
	quem ei in pugna	ὃν αὐτῷ ἐν τῇ συμβολῇ
64.5	Aiax pepulerat,	Αἴας ἐνσεσείκει,
	iratus ergo Iunonem	ὀργισθεὶς οὖν τῇ Ἥρᾳ
	improperavit,	ὠνείδισεν,
	quod ab ea seductus esset	διότι ὑπ᾽ αὐτῆς ἐπλανήθη
	ut Hector occideretur.	ὅπως Ἕκτωρ σφαγῇ.
64.10	illa ergo dixit	ἐκείνη δὲ εἶπεν
	Neptunum non iussum	Ποσειδῶνα μὴ κεκελευσμένον
	adiutorem fuisse	βοηθὸν γεγονέναι
	Graecis,	τοῖς Ἕλλησιν,
	et tunc Iuppiter mittit	καὶ τότε ὁ Ζεὺς πέμπει
64.15	Irim ad Neptunum,	τὴν Ἶριν πρὸς Ποσειδῶνα,
	ut discederet	ἵνα ἀπονεύσῃ
	a pugna,	ἀπὸ τοῦ πολέμου,
	et Neptunus discessit	καὶ Ποσειδῶν ἀπένευσεν
	et Iuppiter Apollinem	καὶ Ζεὺς Ἀπόλλωνα
64.20	mittit adiutorem Hectori;	πέμπει βοηθὸν Ἕκτορι·
	et Patroclus	καὶ Πάτροκλος
	remisso Eurypylo	ἀφεὶς Εὐρύπυλον
	venit ad Achillem	ἦλθεν πρὸς τὸν Ἀχιλλέα
	et enarrat ei	καὶ διηγεῖται αὐτῷ
64.25	Hectoris et Aiacis	τὴν Ἕκτορος καὶ Αἴαντος
	pugnam.	μάχην.
	tunc ergo processit	τότε οὖν προεχώρησεν
	Hectori in victoriam,	Ἕκτορι ἐν τῇ νίκῃ,
	quod Protesilai	ὅτι ἡ Πρωτεσιλάου
64.30	navis incensa est,	ναῦς ἐνεπρήσθη,
	sed Aiax xii milites	ἀλλὰ Αἴας δώδεκα στρατιώτας
	fortissimos	τοὺς ἰσχυροτέρους
	Troianorum occidit.	τῶν Τρώων ἀπέκτεινεν.

Π

	Patroclus Menoetii	Πάτροκλος ὁ Μενοιτίου
64.35	venit ad Achillem	ἦλθεν πρὸς Ἀχιλλέα
	lacrimans	δακρύων
	Graecorum iniuriam	τῶν Ἑλλήνων ὕβριν
	et petiit ab eo	καὶ ᾐτήσατο παρ᾽ αὐτοῦ
	arma	τὰ ὅπλα,
64.40	et accepit cum exercitu.	καὶ ἔλαβεν μετὰ τοῦ στρατοῦ.
	ergo Patroclus armatus	ὁ δὲ Πάτροκλος ὁπλισθεὶς
	armis Achillis	τοῖς ὅπλοις τοῦ Ἀχιλλέως
	et visus Troianis	καὶ φανεὶς τοῖς Τρωσὶν
	timorem eis inmisit.	φόβον αὐτοῖς ἐνέβαλεν.
64.45	et tunc Sarpedo	καὶ τότε Σαρπήδων
	a Patroclo interficitur,	ὑπὸ Πατρόκλου ἀναιρεῖται,
	cuius corpus	οὗ τὸ πτῶμα
	Iovis iussu Lyciae	Διὸς κελεύσαντος εἰς Λυκίαν
65.1	allatum est.	ἀπηνέχθη.
	occidit et Cebrionem,	σφάζει δὲ καὶ Κεβριόνην
	aurigam Hectoris;	τὸν ἡνίοχον Ἕκτορος·
	postea autem et ipse	μεταξὺ δὲ καὶ αὐτὸς
65.5	interficitur ab Hectore;	ἀναιρεῖται ὑπὸ Ἕκτορος·
	primum autem exarmatur	πρῶτον δὲ ἐξοπλίζεται
	ab Apolline	ὑπὸ Ἀπόλλωνος
	et vulneratur	καὶ τραυματίζεται
	ab Euphorbo.	ὑπὸ Εὐφόρβου.

8.4 Aesop's fables

Background to these tales is given in the introduction to passage 2.3.[5] Note the non-standard use of agent constructions in *a velocitate* and ὑπὸ τῆς ὠκύτητος and of the preposition εἰς, but note also how the writer has managed to employ both μέν ... δέ

[5] Additional information on this text can be found in Dickey (2012–15: I.24–5); for general background on the Aesop corpus see Perry (1952). *De cervo* is number 1 in the Hermeneumata Leidensia, number 76 H. in Aesop, number 43 in Babrius, and number 1.12 in Phaedrus; *De patre familias* is number 4 in the Hermeneumata Leidensia but does not appear in the other collections (though Perry gives it as number 391). The text given here is a slightly emended version of that of Flammini (2004: 79–80, 82), but the layout follows that of the Leiden manuscript, Vossianus Gr. Q. 7, and the numbering follows Goetz's transcript of that manuscript (Goetz 1892: 40–2).

and τε … καί in Greek without losing parallelism with the Latin and has successfully handled the Greek participle problem by using subordinate clauses in Latin (40.13, 40.26).

40.6	**De cervo**	
	Cervus bonae magnitudinis	Ἔλαφος εὐμεγέθης
	aestivo tempore	ὥρᾳ θέρους
	siti deficiens	δίψῃ λειπόμενος
40.10	advenit	παραγίνεται
	ad quendam fontem	ἐπὶ πηγήν τινα
	limpidum et altum,	διαυγῆ καὶ βαθεῖαν,
	et cum bibisset	καὶ πιὼν
	quantum voluerat,	ὅσον ἤθελεν,
40.15	attendebat	προσεῖχεν
	ad corporis effigiem,	τῇ τοῦ σώματος ἰδέᾳ,
	et maxime quidem laudabat	καὶ μάλιστα μὲν ἐπήνει
	naturam cornuorum	τὴν φύσιν τῶν κεράτων
	excelsissimam	ἀνατεταμένων τε
40.20	in multo aere,	εἰς πολὺν ἀέρα,
	et quod ornamentum esset	καὶ ὡς κόσμος εἴη
	omni corpori;	παντὶ τῷ σώματι·
	culpabat autem	ἔψεγεν δὲ
	crurum	τὴν τῶν σκελῶν
40.25	exilitatem,	λεπτότητα,
	quasi non esset	ὡς οὐχ οἵων τε ὄντων
	ferre pondus.	αἴρειν τὸ βάρος.
	sed cum in his esset,	ἐν οἷς δὲ πρὸς τούτοις ἦν,
	latratus canum	ὑλακή τε κυνῶν
40.30	subito audiit	αἰφνιδίως ἀκούεται
	et venatores proximo.	καὶ κυνηγεταὶ πλησίον.
	at ille in fugam ibat,	ὁ δὲ πρὸς φυγὴν ὥρμα,
	et quamdiu quidem	καὶ μέχρις ὅπου
	per campos	διὰ πεδίων
40.35	faciebat cursum,	ἐποιεῖτο τὸν δρόμον,
	liberabatur	ἐσῴζετο
	a velocitate	ὑπὸ τῆς ὠκύτητος
	crurum;	τῶν σκελῶν·
	sed ubi in spissam	ἐπεὶ δὲ εἰς πυκνὴν

40.40	et condensam	καὶ δασεῖαν
	silvam incidit	ὕλην ἔπεσεν
	obligatis ei	ἐμπλακέντων αὐτῷ
	cornibus	τῶν κεράτων
	captus est,	ἑάλω,
40.45	modo perdiscens,	πείρᾳ μαθών,
	quod iniustus esset	ὅτι ἄρα ἄδικος ἦν
	suorum iudex,	τῶν ἰδίων κριτής,
	culpans quidem	ψέγων μὲν
	quae salvabant eum,	τὰ σῴζοντα αὐτόν,
40.50	laudans autem	ἐπαινῶν δὲ
	a quibus deceptus esset.	ὑφ' ὧν προδέδοται.
	…	…

41.53   **De patre familias**

	Nescio qui paterfamilias	Οἰκοδεσπότης τίς ποτε
41.55	navigans in mare	πλέων εἰς θάλασσαν
	laborabat in tempestate,	ἐκοπία ὑπὸ χειμῶνος
	et nautae	καὶ οἱ ναῦται
	imbecillius	ἀσθενέστερον
	ministrabant	ὑπηρέτουν
41.60	propter tempestatem.	διὰ τὸν χειμῶνα.
	quibus homo dixit,	οἷς ὁ ἄνθρωπος εἶπεν,
	"Vos," inquit,	"Ὑμεῖς," φησίν,
42.1	"nisi hanc navem	"εἰ μὴ τοῦτο τὸ πλοῖον
	celerius ducitis,	ταχύτερον ἄγετε,
	lapidibus vos deiciam."	λίθοις ὑμᾶς καταβαλῶ."
	tunc unus ex eis dixit,	τότε εἷς ἐξ αὐτῶν εἶπεν,
42.5	"Utinam enim	"Ὤφελον γὰρ
	in eo loco essemus,	ἐν ἐκείνῳ τῷ τόπῳ ἦμεν,
	ubi lapides	ὅπου λίθοι
	colligi possint!"	συλλεγῆναι δύνανται."
	huic ergo similia	τούτῳ οὖν ὁμοῖα
42.10	animas nostras[6]	τὰς ψυχὰς ἡμῶν
	baiulare debemus	βαστάζειν ὀφείλομεν
	leviores iacturas,	τὰς κουφοτέρας ζημίας,

---

[6] Take this line as an accusative of respect.

ut graviores	ἵνα τὰς βαρυτέρας
effugiamus.	ἐκφύγωμεν.

8.5 Judgements of Hadrian

Background to this text is given in the introduction to passage 2.4.[7] In this extract Hadrian, faced with an overly protective parent, gives him the reassurance he needs without upsetting the social order and does so in a way that strengthens the army. Note the reference here to conscription into the army; the *vitis* was a rod emblematic of a centurion, a type of army officer. Watch for *quis* used for *aliquis*, and for different constructions in the two languages brought about by the differences in their participle resources.

36.15	Interea autem	Ἐν τοσούτῳ δὲ
	interpellavit quis	ἐνέτυχέν τις
	Adriano dicens,	Ἀδριανῷ λέγων,
	"Filii mei, domine,	"Οἱ υἱοί μου, κύριε,
	militiae capti sunt."	ἐστρατολογήθησαν."
36.20	Adrianus dixit,	Ἀδριανὸς εἶπεν,
	"Feliciter!"	"Ἐπ᾽ ἀγαθῷ."
	respondit,	ἀπεκρίθη,
	"Sed inscientes sunt	"Ἀλλὰ ἰδιῶταί εἰσιν,
	et timeo	καὶ φοβοῦμαι
36.25	ne quid	μή τι
	extra ordinem	παρὰ τὸ καθῆκον
	faciant	ποιήσουσιν
	et miserum me	καὶ ἔρημόν με
	relinquant."	καταλίπωσιν."
36.30	Adrianus dixit,	Ἀδριανὸς εἶπεν,
	"Ne quid timeas;	"Μηδὲν εὐλαβοῦ·
	in pace enim	ἐν εἰρήνῃ γὰρ
	militant."	στρατεύονται."
	cui pater dixit,	ᾧ ὁ πατὴρ εἶπεν,
36.35	"Remitte ergo me,	"Ἐπίτρεψον οὖν μοι,
	domine imperator,	κύριε αὐτοκράτορ,

---

[7] Additional information on this text can be found in Dickey (2012–15: I.28) and Schiller (1971a, 1971b). The text given here is a slightly emended version of Flammini's scholarly edition (2004: 74–5), but the layout follows that of the Leiden manuscript, Vossianus Gr. Q. 7, and the numbering follows Goetz's transcript of that manuscript (Goetz 1892: 36).

	vel ministrum	κἂν ὑπηρέτην
	eorum esse,	αὐτῶν εἶναι,
	ut eos attendam."	ἵνα αὐτοὺς ἐπέχω."
36.40	Adrianus dixit,	Ἀδριανὸς εἶπεν,
	"Ne id faciant dii,	"Μὴ ποιήσειαν οἱ θεοί,
	ut te	ἵνα σε
	obsequentem	ὑπόδουλον
	filiis tuis	τοῖς τέκνοις σοῦ
36.45	faciam,	ποιήσω,
	sed vite accepta	ἀλλὰ κλῆμα λαβὼν
	centurio	ἑκατοντάρχης
	eorum esto."	αὐτῶν γενοῦ."

8.6 Treatise on manumission

Background to this text is given in the introduction to passage 2.5. The first extract quoted here discusses the restrictions on manumission by women, and the second discusses manumission by census (a type of manumission in which the freedman is enrolled in the census at the request of his former master).[8] A *tutor*/ἐπίτροπος was the husband, father, or other male who managed the property of most women; as one of the purposes of having such a guardian was to ensure that the woman did not impoverish herself (and her family) by unwise spending, a woman could not sell or give away property without her guardian's consent. Slaves formed part of a woman's property and their emancipation reduced its value, so a woman needed her guardian's consent to free them. The *ius (trium) liberorum* was a set of rights, including the right to manage their own property, accorded to women with three legitimate children; such rights could also be granted as an honor to women who did not have the required offspring. *Vindicta* was a type of manumission involving a ceremony at which the new freedman was touched with a rod (which was also known as *vindicta*). *Constitutio imperatoria* means an order from the emperor, and *administratio*/πολιτεία means "citizenship"; this last meaning is surprising in Latin as a whole but also occurs elsewhere in this text (cf. passage 2.5 above). The *lustrum* was a religious purification ceremony conducted by the censors; in theory it was carried out after the census, every five years, but in practice it could be omitted. The possibility of omission means that the juridical question raised here

---

[8] Additional information on this text can be found in Dickey (2012–15: I.28–30) and Honoré (1965). The text given here is a slightly emended version of Flammini's scholarly edition (2004: 100–3), but the layout follows that of the Leiden manuscript, Vossianus Gr. Q. 7, and the numbering follows Goetz's transcript of that manuscript (Goetz 1892: 53–5).

would have been a significant one. Note the indirect question with the indicative and the non-standard use of cases with *in*.

53.42	Mulier	Γυνὴ
	sine tutoris	χωρὶς ἐπιτρόπου
	auctoritate	αὐθεντίας
53.44a	manumittere non potest,	ἐλευθερῶσαι οὐ δύναται,
53.45	nisi ius	ἐκτὸς εἰ μὴ δίκαιον
	liberorum habeat;	τέκνων ἔχοι·
	tunc enim	τότε γὰρ
	ex vindicta	ἐκ προσαγωγῆς
	sine tutore	χωρὶς ἐπιτρόπου
53.50	potest manumittere.	δύναται ἐλευθερῶσαι.
	unde si	ὅθεν εἴ γε
	mulier	ἡ γυνὴ
	absens[9]	ἀποῦσα
	liberum esse[10]	ἐλεύθερον εἶναι
53.55	iubeat,	κελεύσῃ,
	quae ius	ἥτις δίκαιον
	liberorum	τέκνων
	non habeat,	μὴ ἔχοι,
	quaesitum est hoc,[11]	ἐζήτηται τοῦτο,
53.60	an, tutoris eius	εἰ, ἐπιτρόπου αὐτῆς
	auctoritatem	αὐθεντίαν
	praestantis	ἐπιχωροῦντος
	hoc tempore,[12]	τούτῳ τῷ χρόνῳ,
	sicut[13] epistula	ὡς ἐπιστολὴ
53.65	scribitur	γράφεται
	servo	δούλῳ
	a domina,	ὑπὸ τῆς δεσποίνης,
53.67a	is liber fieret.	οὗτος ἐλεύθερος γένοιτο.

[9] I.e. away from the slave so that she cannot speak to him directly; it is assumed that she has obtained the agreement of her guardian for the manumission, since if she had not done so the manumission would certainly be invalid and no other circumstances would be relevant.

[10] Understand here something along the lines of *aliquem servum* and δοῦλόν τινα.

[11] I.e. the following question has been a subject of debate between the jurists Julianus and Neratius Priscus.

[12] I.e. at this time of her guardian exercising his authority (when he agrees that the woman may free her slave).

[13] I.e. at the very moment when the letter is written (by the woman with her guardian's authority but without the knowledge of the slave).

	Iulianus	Ἰουλιανὸς
	negat;	ἀρνεῖται·
53.70	existimat enim	ὑπολαμβάνει γὰρ
	hoc tempore	τούτῳ τῷ χρόνῳ
	debere	ὀφείλειν
54.1	auctoritatem	αὐθεντίαν
	praestare,	παρέχεσθαι,
	quo peragitur	ἐν ᾧ ἀπαρτίζεται
	libertas;	ἡ ἐλευθερία·
54.5	tunc enim	τότε γὰρ
	peragi	ἀπαρτίζεσθαι
	intellegitur,	νοεῖται,
	cum servus	ὅτε ὁ δοῦλος
	agnoscet	ἐπιγνῷ
54.10	dominae	τῆς δεσποίνης
	voluntatem.[14]	τὴν θέλησιν.
	sed Neratius	ἀλλὰ Νηράτιος
	Priscus	Πρίσκος
	probat	δοκιμάζει
54.15	libertatem	ἐλευθερίαν
	servo	δούλῳ
	competere;[15]	συναιτεῖν·
	sufficere enim,	ἀρκεῖσθαι γάρ,
	quando epistola	ὁπότε ἡ ἐπιστολὴ
54.20	scribitur,	γράφεται,
	adhiberi[16]	παραλαμβάνεσθαι
	auctoritatem	αὐθεντίαν
	tutoris.	ἐπιτρόπου.
	cuius sententia[17]	οὗ ἡ γνώμη
54.25	et constitutione	καὶ διατάξει
	imperatoria	αὐτοκρατορικῇ
	confirmata est.	ἰσχυροπεποίηται.
	. . .	. . .

[14] I.e. the slave is not freed until he reads the letter; if it is not delivered, he is never freed.

[15] Taken in isolation the Latin might mean "Priscus agrees that freedom belongs to the slave," but given the Greek it is better to take "freedom" as the object rather than the subject of the infinitives, i.e. "Priscus thinks it right to confirm freedom to the slave."

[16] *Auctoritatem adhiberi* is accusative and infinitive after *sufficere*; *adhibeo* here means "apply."

[17] I.e. the opinion of Neratius Priscus just given.

55.42	Et qui in censum	Καὶ ὃς ἐν ἀποτιμήσει
	manumittitur,	ἐλευθεροῦται,
	si triginta annos habeat,[18]	εἰ τριάκοντα ἔτη ἔχοι,
55.45	administrationem	πολιτείαν
	Romanorum	Ῥωμαίων
	possidet.	κτᾶται.
	(census autem	(ἀποτίμησις δὲ
	in Roma	ἐπὶ Ῥώμης
55.50	agi solet;	ἄγεσθαι εἴωθεν·
	vel[19] census	ἡ ἀποτίμησις
	lustro conditur;	καθαρμῷ κτίζεται·
55.52a	est autem lustrum	ἐστὶν δὲ ὁ καθαρμὸς
55.52b	quinquiennale tempus,	πενταετηρικὸς χρόνος,
55.52c	quo Roma purgatur.)	ᾧ Ῥώμη καθαίρεται.)
55.52d	sed debet	ἀλλὰ ὀφείλει
55.52e	hic servus	οὗτος ὁ δοῦλος
55.52f	ex iure Quiritium	ἐκ δικαίου πολιτικοῦ
55.52g	manumittentis esse,	ἐλευθεροῦντος εἶναι,
55.52h	ut civis Romanus fiat.[20]	ἵνα πολίτης Ῥωμαίων γένηται.
	magna autem	μεγάλη μέντοι
	dissensio est	ἀμφισβήτησίς ἐστιν
55.55	inter peritos,[21]	ἐν τοῖς ἐμπείροις,
	utrum	πότερον
	hoc tempore	τούτῳ τῷ χρόνῳ
	vires	δυνάμεις
	accipiunt	λαμβάνουσιν
55.60	omnia,[22]	ἅπαντα,
	in quo census,	ἐν ᾧ ἡ ἀποτίμησις,
	aut in eo	ἢ ἐν ἐκείνῳ

[18] I.e. if the freedman is thirty years old or more.

[19] This word does not belong and should be ignored; although in general the Latin of this text is not simply a translation of the Greek, this is a mistranslation of the Greek article which, in an era when diacritics were not written, looked like ἤ "or."

[20] I.e. a freed slave only became a citizen if his master was a citizen and freed him using the right Roman legal procedures.

[21] *Peritos* refers to jurists, men skilled in Roman law.

[22] I.e. all the manumissions by census come into force.

	tempore,	τῷ χρόνῳ,
	in quo lustrum	ἐν ᾧ καθαρμὸς
55.65	conditur.	κτίζεται.
	sunt enim	εἰσὶν γὰρ
	qui existimant	οἱ ὑπολαμβάνοντες
	non alias	μὴ ἄλλως
	vires	δυνάμεις
56.1	accipere	λαμβάνειν
	quae aguntur	τὰ πρασσόμενα
	in censu,	ἐν τῇ ἀποτιμήσει,
	nisi	ἐὰν μὴ
56.5	haec dies	αὕτη ἡ ἡμέρα
	sequatur,	ἀκολουθήσῃ,
	qua lustrum	ὅτε ὁ καθαρμὸς
	conditur;	κτίζεται·
	existimant enim	ὑπολαμβάνουσιν γὰρ
56.10	censum descendere	ἀποτίμησιν καταβαίνειν
	ad diem	ἐπὶ τὴν ἡμέραν
	lustri,	τοῦ καθαρμοῦ,
	non lustrum	οὐχὶ τὸν καθαρμὸν
	decurrere	κατατρέχειν
56.15	ad diem	ἐπὶ τὴν ἡμέραν
	census. quod ideo	τῆς ἀποτιμήσεως. ὃ διὰ τοῦτο
	quaesitum est, quoniam omnia,	ἐζήτηται, ἐπειδὴ πάντα,
	quae in censum aguntur,	ἃ τῇ ἀποτιμήσει πράσσονται,
	lustro	τῷ καθαρμῷ
56.20	confirmantur.	ἰσχυροποιοῦνται.
	sed in urbem	ἀλλὰ ἐν τῇ πόλει
	Romanorum tantum	Ῥωμαίων μόνον
	censum agi	ἀποτίμησιν ἄγεσθαι
	notum est;	δεδήλωται·
56.25	in provincia autem	ἐν ταῖς ἐπαρχίαις
	magis professiones[23]	μᾶλλον ἀπογραφαῖς
	utuntur.	χρῶνται.

[23] The *professio* was a public register of people and property liable to taxation (we would expect it to be ablative here, as it is the object of *utuntur*); the implication is that manumission by census was not available outside Rome and was therefore irrelevant to this work's Greek-speaking audience.

8.7   Cicero's first Catilinarian oration

The first works of literary prose read by ancient Latin students seem to have been Cicero's Catilinarian orations, as several copies of these texts have been preserved in the bilingual format used by beginners. The bilingual format does not, however, work as well for Cicero as for the colloquia. The colloquia were bilingually composed, so their authors were able to avoid Latin constructions that might cause difficulties in Greek and to use word order suitable for both languages. In the case of Cicero a translator had to cope with a pre-existing Latin text that was not always easy to render into Greek.

The papyrus from which these extracts come (*P.Rain.Cent.* 163, from the fourth or fifth century AD) is fragmentary; although a large amount of text is preserved when all the fragments are considered together, the length of Cicero's sentences means that few intact sentences remain. The most complete ones are presented here: the first extract comes from section 16 of *In Catilinam* I, the second from sections 17 and 18, and the third from the end of section 19.[24]

22	nunc vero	νῦν δὲ
	quae tua est	ποία ἡ σή ἐστιν
	ista vita?	αὕτη ἡ ζωή;
25	sic enim	οὕτω γὰρ
	tecum	μετὰ σοῦ
	loquar,	λαλῶ,
	non ut odio	οὐχ ὡς μίσει
	permotus	κινηθεὶς
30	esse videar	εἶναι δοκῶ
	. . .	. . .
33	nunc te	νῦν σε
	patria,	ἡ πατρίς,
35	quae communis est	ἥτις κοινή ἐστιν
	parens	μήτηρ
	omnium	πάντων
	nostrum,	ἡμῶν,

[24] Additional information on this text, which is number 2922 in the Mertens–Pack database (http://promethee. philo.ulg.ac.be/cedopal/indexsimple.asp) and number 554 in the Leuven Database of Ancient Books (www. trismegistos.org/ldab/), can be found in Axer (1983) and Internullo (2011–12) no. 1. Here an emended version of Internullo's edition is presented, with the spelling corrected in both languages and with the Latin but not the Greek restored when not actually present on the papyrus. The reason for this discrepancy is that when the Latin is not preserved we know from other sources what it must have been, but when the Greek is lost (for more than a few letters at a time) any reconstruction is simply a modern exercise in prose composition.

	metuit	δέδοικε,
40	et iam diu	καὶ ἤδη πάλαι
41	nihil	οὐδέν . . .
41a	te iudicat	
41b	nisi	
41c	de parricidio	
41d	suo	
41e	cogitare:	
42	huius tu	. . .
	neque auctoritatem	οὔτε τὴν αὐθεντίαν
	verebere	εὐλαβῇ
45	nec	οὔτε
	iudicium	κριτήριον
	sequere	ἀκολουθεῖς
	neque vim	οὔτε τὴν δύναμιν
	pertimesces?	. . .
50	quae tecum,	ἥτις μετὰ σοῦ,
	Catilina,	Κατιλίνα,
	sic agit	οὕτω πράττει
	et quodam modo	καί τινι τρόπῳ
	tacita	σιωπῶσα
55	loquitur,	λαλεῖ,
	"nullum iam	"οὐδὲν λοιπόν
	aliquot	τισί ποτε
	annis	ἐνιαυτοῖς
	facinus	δράσμα
60	exstitit	ἀνεφάνη
	nisi per te . . ."	εἰ μὴ διὰ σοῦ . . ."
95	sed quam	ἀλλὰ πῶς
	longe	μακρὰν
	videtur	δοκεῖ
	a carcere	ἀπὸ φρουρᾶς
	atque a vinculis	καὶ ἀπὸ δεσμῶν
100	abesse	ἀπεῖναι
	debere,	ὀφείλειν,
	hic qui se	οὗτος ὅστις ἑαυτὸν
	ipse	αὐτὸς
	iam dignum	ἤδη ἄξιον

| 105 | custodia | φυλακῆς |
| | iudicaverit? | ἔκρινεν; |

8.8 Virgil's *Aeneid*

For background on this text see the introduction to passage 2.6. The first extract below, from a fourth-century papyrus,[25] covers lines 227–32 of book 1, the beginning of Venus' appeal to Jupiter on behalf of Aeneas. The second, from a papyrus of the fourth or fifth century,[26] contains lines 588–606 of the same book, Aeneas' first appearance before Dido.

227	Atque illum	
	talis	
	iactantem	. . .
	pectore	τῷ στήθει
	curas	φροντίδας
228	tristior	στυγνοτέρα
	et lacrimis	καὶ δακρύοις
	oculos	τοὺς ὀφθαλμοὺς
	suffusa	ὑποκεχυμένη
	nitentis	τοὺς λάμποντας
229	alloquitur	προσλαλεῖ
	Venus,	ἡ Ἀφροδίτη,
	"O qui res	"Ὠ ὅστις τὰ πράγματα
	hominumque	τῶν ἀνθρώπων τε
	deumque	καὶ τῶν θεῶν
230	aeternis	αἰωνίαις
	regis	εὐθύνεις
	imperiis	ἐπιταγαῖς
	et fulmine	καὶ κεραυνῷ

[25] *BKT* IX.39, which is number 4 in Scappaticcio (2013a), number 2939.1 in the Mertens–Pack database (http://promethee.philo.ulg.ac.be/cedopal/indexsimple.asp), and number 4149 in the Leuven Database of Ancient Books (www.trismegistos.org/ldab/). The text given here is based on that of Scappaticcio but with spelling in both languages corrected. For more information on this text and the Virgil papyri more generally see Scappaticcio (2013a), Fressura (2013), Gaebel (1970), and Rochette (1990).

[26] The Ambrosian palimpsest, which is number 8 in Scappaticcio (2013a), number 2943 in the Mertens–Pack database (http://promethee.philo.ulg.ac.be/cedopal/indexsimple.asp), and number 4156 in the Leuven Database of Ancient Books (www.trismegistos.org/ldab/). The text given here is based on that of Scappaticcio but with spelling in both languages corrected. For more information on this text see Kramer (1996) and Scappaticcio (2009, 2013a).

	terres,	πτοεῖς,
231	quid meus	τί ὁ ἐμὸς
	Aeneas	Αἰνείας
	in te	εἴς σε
	committere	ἁμαρτῆσαι
	tantum,	τοσοῦτον,
232	quid Troes	τί οἱ Τρῶες
	potuere	ἐδυνήθησαν
	. . .	. . .
588	restitit Aeneas	ἀπέστη ὁ Αἰνείας
	claraque in luce	καὶ ἐν καθαρῷ τῷ φωτὶ
	refulsit	ἀντέλαμψεν
589	os umerosque	τὸ πρόσωπον καὶ τοὺς ὤμους
	deo similis;	θεῷ ὅμοιος·
	namque ipsa decoram	καὶ γὰρ αὐτὴ εὐπρεπῆ
590	caesariem nato	τὴν κόμην τῷ παιδὶ
	genetrix lumenque	ἡ γεννήτειρα καὶ φῶς
	iuventae	τῆς νεότητος
591	purpureum et laetos	πορφύρεον καὶ ἱλαρὰς
	oculis	τοῖς ὀφθαλμοῖς
	adflarat honores:	προσπεπνεύκει τιμάς·
592	quale manus addunt	ὁποῖον χεῖρες προστιθέασιν
	ebori decus	ἐλεφαντίνῳ ὀστέῳ κόσμον
	aut ubi flavo	ἢ ὁπηνίκα ξανθῷ
593	argentum	ἄργυρος
	Pariusve lapis	ἢ Πάριος λίθος
	circumdatur auro.	. . .
594	tum sic reginam	τότε οὕτως τὴν βασίλισσαν
	adloquitur	προσφθέγγεται
	cunctisque repente	σύμπασίν τε αἰφνιδίως
595	improvisus ait:	ἄποπτός φησιν·
	"Coram, quem	"Ἐνώπιον ὃν
	quaeritis, adsum	ζητεῖτε πάρειμι
596	Troius Aeneas,	ὁ Τρωϊκὸς Αἰνείας,
	Libycis ereptus	τῶν Λιβυκῶν ἐξαρπασθεὶς
	ab undis.	ἀπὸ τῶν κλυδώνων.
597	o sola infandos	ὦ μόνη τοὺς ἀθεμίτους
	Troiae miserata	τῆς Τροίας οἰκτείρασα

	labores,	καμάτους,
598	quae nos,	ἥτις ἡμᾶς,
	reliquias Danaum,	τὰ λείψανα τῶν Ἑλλήνων,
	terraeque marisque	τῆς τε γῆς καὶ τῆς θαλάσσης
599	omnibus exhaustos	πάσαις ἐξαντληθέντας
	iam casibus,	ἤδη συμφοραῖς,
	omnium egenos,	πάντων ἐνδεεῖς,
600	urbe, domo	τῇ πόλει, τῷ οἴκῳ
	socias – grates	ἑταιροποιεῖς – χάριτας
	persolvere dignas	διευλυτῆσαι ἀξίας
601	non opis est nostrae,	οὐ τῆς περιουσίας ἐστὶν τῆς ἡμετέρας,
	Dido, nec quicquid	ὦ Διδώ, οὔτε ὅ τι δήποτε
	ubique est	καὶ ὅπου δήποτέ ἐστιν
602	gentis Dardaniae,	τοῦ ἔθνους τῆς Τροίας,
	magnum quae sparsa	τὸν μέγαν ἥτις διέσπαρται
	per orbem.	ἀνὰ τὸν κύκλον.
603	di tibi, si qua	οἱ θεοί σοι, εἴ τινα
	pios respectant	τοὺς εὐσεβεῖς ἐφορῶσιν
	numina, si quid	θεῖα, εἴ τι
604	usquam iustitiae est,	…
	et mens sibi	καὶ διάνοια ἑαυτῇ
	conscia recti	συνειδυῖα τοῦ ὀρθοῦ
605	praemia digna	ἔπαθλα ἄξια
	ferant. quae te tam	κομίσειαν. ποῖαί σε οὕτως
	laeta tulerunt	ἱλαραὶ ἤνεγκαν
606	saecula? qui	γενεαί; τίνες
	tanti talem	τοσοῦτοι τοιαύτην
	genuere parentes?"	ἐγέννησαν γονεῖς;"

8.9 Model letters

Background to this text is given in the introduction to passage 2.7. Two extracts from the same papyrus seen there are are quoted here, first three letters offering consolation on the receipt of a smaller inheritance than the addressees had expected (i.e. commiseration with disappointed legacy-hunters) and then a letter of congratulation for a new freedman.[27] In places the Greek is evidently a literal translation of the Latin.

[27] The papyrus is *P.Bon.* 5. Additional information on this text, which is number 2117 in the Mertens–Pack database (http://promethee.philo.ulg.ac.be/cedopal/indexsimple.asp) and number 5498 in the Leuven

26   **De minimis legatis**
        suasoriae[28]
        Συνβουλευτικαὶ περὶ ἐλαχίστων
        καταλελειμμένων

30   Licinnium amicum tibi   Λικίννιον φίλον σου
            verum   γνήσιον
            obitum compertus sum,   τεθνηκότα ἔμαθον,
            quem parum memorem   ὃν ὀλίγον ἐμνημονευκότα
            obsequi tui fuisse.   τῆς σῆς ὑπεικίας[29] γεγονέναι.
35   doleo quidem,   λυποῦμαι μέν,
            sed hortor te   ἀλλὰ παρορμῶ σε
            ut fortiter feras;   εὐσταθῶς ἐνεγκεῖν·
            tabulas enim   διαθήκας γὰρ ἐσχάτων
                supremorum
            homines quidem faciunt,   ἄνθρωποι μὲν ποιοῦσιν,
40   sed ordinant fata.   διατάσσουσιν δὲ μοῖραι.
        Quod aliter   Ὅπερ ἄλλως
            quam meruisse te   ἢ ἠξιῶσθαί σε
            scimus   οἴδαμεν[30]
            remuneratus es[31]   ἀντεδωρήθης
45   a Publio amico tuo,   ἀπὸ Πουβλίου τοῦ φίλου σου,
            quem defunctum   ὃν τεθνηκότα
            narrant litterae,   λέγουσιν τὰ γράμματα,
            nihil ex moribus tuis   μηδὲν οὖν ἐκ τῶν σῶν ἠθῶν
            mutet.   ἀλλαξέτω.
50   parum[32] ingrata   οὕτως ἀχάριστος ἀπόφασις[33]
                sententia

[ ] Database of Ancient Books (www.trismegistos.org/ldab/), can be found in Kramer (1983: no. 16), whose text is reproduced here in a slightly emended version. A photograph of the complete papyrus can be found at http://amshistorica.unibo.it/247; the extracts quoted here come from columns III–V and XIII–XIV.

[28] Understand *litterae* here, and ἐπιστολαί in the Greek.

[29] This seems to be an otherwise unattested noun on the stem of ὑπείκω "yield"; it must mean something like "obligingness."

[30] This is the normal late Greek form for Classical ἴσμεν.

[31] The papyrus has *remuneratus non es* and οὐκ ἀντεδωρήθης, but this must be a mistake.

[32] This may be corrupt, as *parum* neither makes sense nor matches Greek οὕτως; perhaps the text originally read *parum grata sententia*, but in that case the Greek is even more puzzling than it currently seems.

[33] The Greek does not make sense here; probably the translator took this line of Latin as a nominative when in fact it is ablative (after *inaequales*: we are all unequal to, i.e. not up to bearing with equanimity, such ingratitude).

	omnes enim homines	πάντες γὰρ ἄνθρωποι
	inaequales sumus.	ἄνισοί ἐσμεν.
	Parum grate[34] in merita tua	Ὠλιγωρηκέναι τὴν σὴν παροχὴν
	in supremis suis	ἐν τοῖς ἐσχάτοις αὐτοῦ
55	Licinnium amicum	Λικίννιον τὸν φίλον
	quondam communem	ποτὲ κοινὸν
	mirarer quidem,	ἐθαύμαζον ἄν,
	nisi putarem	εἰ μὴ συνελογιζόμην
	tam prosperas res	τὰ κρείττονα
60	quam adversas –	ἢ τὰ φαῦλα –
	quaecumque mortalibus	ἅτινα θνητοῖς
	adscriptae sunt –	προσγέγραπται –
	non esse	μὴ εἶναι
64	in tua potestate.	ἐν τῇ σῇ ἐξουσίᾳ.
	…	…

169	**Gratulatoriae[35] libertatis acceptae**	
170	**Συνχαριστικαὶ ἐλευθερίας δεδομένης**	
	Libertati quidem	Τῇ μὲν ἐλευθερίᾳ
	omnes favemus,	πάντες σπουδάζομεν,
	meritissimo autem tibi	ἀξιωτάτῳ δὲ σοὶ
	contigisse scimus.	γεγενῆσθαι οἴδαμεν.
175	ego certe	εἰς τάδε ἐγὼ
	peculiariter gaudeo,	καθ' ἰδίαν χαίρω,
	quod eam	ἐπειδὰν[36] αὐτὴν
	tam iudicio domini tui	καὶ τῇ κρίσει τοῦ κυρίου σου
	quam meritis tuis	καὶ τῇ παροχῇ σου
180	consecutus es.	ἔτυχες.
	…	…
188	hic enim demum	αὕτη γὰρ οὕτως
	beatus est	εὔμοιρός ἐστιν
190	titulus[37]	στήλη
	ut illud	ἵνα[38] κεῖνος

---

[34] Understand *fuisse* here.   [35] Understand *litterae* here, and ἐπιστολαί in the Greek.

[36] In late Greek ἐπειδή and ἐπειδάν are interchangeable.

[37] Probably a notice proclaiming the freedman's new status.

[38] In Classical Greek we would expect ὥστε here, but in late Greek the use of ἵνα in result (consecutive) clauses is common.

	libertatis ornamentum	τῆς ἐλευθερίας κόσμος
	constet inter omnes	συνεστηκέναι πᾶσιν δηλωθῇ
	non datam tibi	μὴ δεδομένην σοι
195	sed redditam.[39]	ἀλλὰ ἀποδεδομένην.

8.10 A transliterated colloquium

This extract is a continuation of the one given in passage 7.1; see the introduction to that passage for information on the text.[40] Although the heading at the start of this extract suggests that the following material should all be a phrasebook section on daily conversation, only lines 45–54 really fall into that category; from line 55 onwards the text seems to form a coherent dialogue about messengers and letters. Note the extended use of "brother" to friends and acquaintances as well as the rare deliberative indicative construction in lines 45–6. A few spelling errors have been corrected to make the passage intelligible, but others remain.

42	**Σερμω**	**Ὁμιλία**
43	**κωτιδιανους**	**καθημερινή**
45–6	"Κοιδ φακιμους,	"Τί ποιοῦμεν,
47	φρατερ;	ἀδελφέ;
48	λιβεντερ τη	ἡδέως σε
50	βιδεω."	ὁρῶ."
	"Ετ εγω δη,	"Κἀγὼ σέ,
	δομινε."	δέσποτα."
	(ετ νως	(καὶ ἡμεῖς
	βως.)[41]	ὑμᾶς.)
55	"Νεσκιω[42]	"Οὐκ οἶδα

[39] Grammatically *datam* and *redditam* should agree with *ornamentum*, but they really refer to the freedom and therefore take its gender; the same occurs in the Greek.

[40] The papyrus is P.Berol. inv. 10582; additional information on and scholarly editions of this text, which is number 3009 in the Mertens–Pack database (http://promethee.philo.ulg.ac.be/cedopal/indexsimple.asp) and number 6075 in the Leuven Database of Ancient Books (www.trismegistos.org/ldab), can be found in Dickey (2015a), Kramer (1983: no. 15, 2010), and Schubart (1913). A photograph is available at http://ww2.smb. museum/berlpap/index.php/record/?result-=0&Alle=10582; this passage begins in the middle of the second column on the recto. In this version the Coptic and the more fragmentary sections have been omitted.

[41] This is an alternative to the previous response, in case a plural version is needed.

[42] There are two possible meanings for the Latin here (bearing in mind that indirect questions in late Latin often have their verbs in the indicative), and only one for the Greek; do you think the Greek meaning is the better of the two that the Latin could have?

	κοις	τίς
	οστιουμ	τὴν θύραν
	πωλσατ·	κρούει·
	εξειτο	ἔξελθε
60	κιτω φορας	ταχέως ἔξω
62	ετ δισκε	καὶ μάθε
64	κοις εστ,	τίς ἐστιν,
	αυτ κοιεμ	ἢ τίνα
66	πετιτ."	ἀναζητεῖ."
68	"Αβ Αυρηλιω	"Ἀπ' Αὐρηλίου
	βηνιτ·	ἦλθεν·
70	νουντιουμ	φάσιν
	τουλιτ."	ἤνεγκεν."
	"Κλαμα	"Κάλεσον
	ιλλουμ ικ.	αὐτὸν ἐνταῦθα.
	κοιιδ εστ,	τί ἐστιν,
75	πουερ;	παῖ;
	κοιδ	τί
	νουντιας;	ἀναγγέλλεις;
	ομνια	πάντα
	βενε;"	καλῶς;"
80	"Μαξιμους	"Μάξιμός
	τη βουλτ	σε βούλεται
	σαλουταρε."	ἀσπάσασθαι."
	"Ουβι εστ;"	"Ποῦ ἐστιν;"
	"Φορας	"Ἔξω
85	στατ."	ἵσταται."
	"Βενιατ	"Ἐλθάτω
	ιντρο.	ἔνδον.
	βενε	καλῶς
	βενιστι."	ἦλθας."
90	"Σαλουταντ	"Ἀσπάζονταί
92	τη ινφαντης,	σε τὰ βρέφη,
94	ετ παρεντης	καὶ οἱ γονεῖς
95	ιστορουμ.	αὐτῶν.
	μισηρουντ	ἔπεμψάν
	τιβι αυτεμ	σοι δὲ
	ανκ	ταύτην
	επιστουλαμ	τὴν ἐπιστολὴν

100	περ πουερουμ	διὰ τοῦ παιδὸς
102	σιγναταμ·	ἐσφραγισμένην·
103	Ἐτ βαλδε	Ἰκαὶ πάνυ
104–5	κονστηρνατους σουμ,	ἐλυπήθην,
	φρατερ,	ἀδελφέ,
	κουοδ	ὅτι
	μουλτω	πολλῷ
	τεμπορε	τῷ χρόνῳ
110	λιττερας	γράμματα
	α τη	ἀπό σου
	νον ακκιπι.	οὐκ ἔλαβον.
113	ποστ μουλτουμ	μετὰ πολὺν
115	εργο	τοιγάρτοι
	τεμπους	χρόνον
	μιττε μιι	ἀπόστειλόν μοι
	επιστουλαμ,	ἐπιστολήν,
119	ουτ ιλαριους[43]	ἵνα ἱλαρὸς
121	φιαμ.	γενηθῶ.
122	σαλουτα	ἄσπασαι
123	ομνις τουως.'"	πάντας τοὺς σούς.'"

8.11 Dositheus' explanation of accents

This extract from the Latin grammar of Dositheus constitutes the start of section 2 of the work and so follows immediately on the passage quoted above in 3.1.1; see the introduction to that passage for background information.[44] This is only the beginning of Dositheus' treatment of accents; after this extract he discusses the possible accents of monosyllables and disyllables, points out that Greek words borrowed into Latin retain their Greek accents if considered foreign enough to be written in Greek script, and describes the shape of each accent. Among "accents" Dositheus includes all diacritic signs (Greek προσῳδία often means simply "diacritic"): not only the ones marking stress and/or pitch (i.e. "accents" as the term is now applied to ancient Greek and Latin) but also breathings, macrons, and short marks.

---

[43] This appears to be a blend of *hilaris* and *hilarus*.

[44] The text of this section is taken from Bonnet (2005: 4–5), but the layout is reconstructed from the manuscripts of Dositheus. The Stiftsbibliothek St Gallen has kindly posted images of the best manuscript, St. Gall 902, at www.e-codices.unifr.ch/en/csg/0902; this passage begins on p. 8.

1	**De accentibus**	**Περὶ προσῳδιῶν**
	Accentus	Προσῳδία
	est	ἐστὶν
	uniuscuiusque	μιᾶς ἑκατέρας
5	syllabae	συλλαβῆς
	proprius	ἴδιος
	sonus,	ἦχος,
	quem Graeci	ὃν ἐν τῇ Ἑλληνικῇ
	προσῳδίαν	
10	dicunt.	λέγουσιν.[45]
	accentus	προσῳδία
	quasi accantus.[46]	παρὰ τὸ προσᾴδεσθαι.
	accentus	προσῳδίαι
	in Graeca	ἐν τῇ Ἑλληνικῇ
15	lingua	γλώττῃ
	sunt VII,	εἰσὶν ἑπτά,[47]
	in Latina	ἐν τῇ Ῥωμαϊκῇ
	V:	πέντε·
	/ acutus,	ὀξεῖα,
20	\ gravis,	βαρεῖα,
	∧ circumflexus,	περισπωμένη,
	‾ longus,	μακρά,
	˘ brevis.	βραχεῖα.
	in omni parte	ἐν παντὶ μέρει
25	orationis[48]	λόγου
	Latinae,	Ῥωμαϊκοῦ,
	item	ὁμοίως
	ut Graecae,	ὥσπερ τοῦ Ἑλληνικοῦ,
	aut acutum	ἢ ὀξεῖαν

---

[45] The Greek column does not make sense unless one borrows προσῳδίαν from the Latin column; this type of omission is part of the evidence that the Greek was not intended to be used on its own.

[46] This is an etymology of "accent," which works in both languages because the Latin term is calqued on the Greek: *accentus* comes from *ad* + *cantus*, just as προσῳδία comes from πρός + the root of ᾠδή, ἀείδω.

[47] Dositheus may originally have had the Greek numeral for 7 here, ζ, but if so it was replaced with the word "seven" once the text started to be used by people unfamiliar with the Greek numeral system. The two extra προσῳδίαι in Greek are the rough and smooth breathings.

[48] Although the phrases *pars orationis* and μέρος λόγου often mean "part of speech" (in the sense of nouns, verbs, prepositions, etc.), they can also mean "word."

30	aut circumflexum	ἢ περισπωμένην
	accentum	προσῳδίαν
	poni	τίθεσθαι
	necesse est,	ἀναγκαῖόν ἐστιν,
	nec amplius	οὐ πλεῖον δὲ
35	quam unum,	ἢ μίαν,
	vel hunc	ἢ ταύτην
	vel illum.⁴⁹	ἢ ἐκείνην.
	nam gravis	ἡ γὰρ βαρεῖα
	ponitur	τίθεται
40	in pluribus.⁵⁰	ἐπὶ πλειόνων.
	acutus	ἡ ὀξεῖα
	cum	ὁπότε
	apud Graecos	παρὰ τοῖς Ἑλληνικοῖς
	tria loca teneat,	τρεῖς τόπους ἔχει,
45	ultimam	τὴν τελευταίαν
	et paenultimam	καὶ τὴν παρατέλευτον
	et ei	καὶ τὴν ταύτῃ
	proximam	ἔγγιστα
	syllabam,	συλλαβήν,
50	apud nos⁵¹	παρ' ἡμῖν
	duobus tantum	δύο μόνον
	locis	τόποις
	poni	τίθεσθαι
	potest:	δύναται,
55	in paenultima,	ἐν τῇ παρατελεύτῳ συλλαβῇ
	ut *praelegisti*,	ὡς τὸ προανέγνως,⁵²
	aut in ea	ἢ ἐπὶ ταύτης,

⁴⁹ I.e. either circumflex or acute. Most modern scholars do not think that Latin had circumflex accents, but the ancient grammarians normally state that it did; the reasons for such statements are the subject of much lively debate.

⁵⁰ Since the ancients used the grave accent to indicate any unaccented syllable (a usage very different from, though not unrelated to, its modern meaning), by this Dositheus means that although each word has exactly one accented syllable, it can have any number of unaccented syllables.

⁵¹ Note Dositheus' identification with Latin speakers; this stance is interesting in view of his completely Greek name.

⁵² The translation of the example into Greek is unexpected from our perspective, as the meaning of *praelegisti* is not relevant for the argument, but this type of translation was common in antiquity: see passage 4.4. Note the different solution to the same situation in line 60, where the Greek is omitted.

	quae	ἥτις
	a fine sit tertia,	τρίτη ἀπὸ τέλους ἐστίν
60	ut *praelegimus.*	
	circumflexus,	ἡ περισπωμένη,
	si pars	ἐὰν τὸ μέρος
	orationis	τοῦ λογοῦ
	trium	τριῶν
65	aut amplius	ἢ πλειόνων
	fuerit	ἔσται
	syllabarum,	συλλαβῶν,
	non ponitur,	οὐ τίθεται,
	nisi	εἰ μὴ
70	paenultimum	τὸν παρατέλευτον
	locum	τόπον
	poterit	δυνήσεται
	invenire,	εὑρεῖν,
	ut *turbare.*	ὡς τὸ[53]

8.12 Dositheus' explanation of the alphabet

This extract, sections 7 and 8 of Dositheus' grammar, is the start of a lengthy description of the letters of the alphabet and their different properties.[54]

1	**De litteris**	**Περὶ γραμμάτων**
	Littera est	Γράμμα ἐστὶν
	elementum	στοιχεῖον
	vocis	φωνῆς
5	articulatae.	ἐνάρθρου.
	elementum est	στοιχεῖόν ἐστιν
	unius cuiusque	ἑνὸς ἑκάστου
	rei initium,	πράγματος ἀρχή,
	a quo sumitur	παρ' οὗ λαμβάνεται

---

[53] The peculiar ending of the passage in Greek arises because the reader is expected to take *turbare* from the Latin column.

[54] The text of this passage is taken from Bonnet (2005: 12–16), but the layout is reconstructed from the manuscripts of Dositheus. The Stiftsbibliothek St. Gallen has kindly posted images of the best manuscript, St. Gall 902, at www.e-codices.unifr.ch/en/csg/0902; this passage begins on p. 11.

10	incrementum,	τὸ ἐπαύξημα
	et in quod resolvitur.	καὶ εἰς ὃ ἀναλύεται.
	accidunt[55]	συμβαίνει
	uni cuique litterae	ἑκάστῳ γράμματι
	nomen,	ὄνομα,
15	figura,	σχῆμα,
	potestas.	δύναμις.
	nomen est	ὄνομά ἐστιν
	quo appellatur,	ᾧ προσαγορεύεται,
	figura	σχῆμα
20	qua notatur,	ᾧ σημειοῦται,
	potestas	δύναμις
	qua valet.	ᾗ ἰσχύει.
	litterarum sunt	τῶν γραμμάτων εἰσὶν
	aliae vocales,	τὰ μὲν φωνήεντα,
25	aliae consonantes.	τὰ δὲ σύμφωνα.
	vocales sunt	φωνήεντά ἐστιν[56]
	quae per se	ἃ καθ᾽ ἑαυτὰ
	proferuntur	ἐκφωνεῖται
	et per se	καὶ καθ᾽ ἑαυτὰ
30	syllabam	συλλαβὴν
	facere possunt.	ποιῆσαι δύναται.
	sunt autem	ἔστιν δὲ
	numero	τὸν ἀριθμὸν
	v:	πέντε·
35	*a, e, i, o, u.*	α, ε, η, ι, ο, ω, ου.[57]
	ex his duae,	ἐκ τούτων δύο
	i et *u,*	
	transeunt	μετέρχονται
	in consonantium	εἰς τὴν τῶν συμφώνων
40	potestatem,	δύναμιν,
	cum aut ipsae	ὁπότε ἢ αὐτὰ
	inter se	εἰς ἄλληλα
	geminantur	ζεύγνυται

55 I.e. the "accidents" (properties) of letters are names, shapes, and sounds.

56 In the usual Greek of Dositheus' day neuter plural subjects normally took plural rather than singular verbs, as in line 23 above, but from this point Dositheus remembers the classical rule that the verb should be singular.

57 Note the equation between *u* and ου: Latin had no sound equivalent to fourth-century Greek υ.

	aut cum aliis	ἢ μετὰ ἄλλων
45	vocalibus	φωνήεσσιν[58]
	iunguntur,	ζεύγνυται,
	veluti	οἷον
	Iuno, vates.[59]	
	consonantium	τῶν συμφώνων
50	species est	τὸ εἶδός ἐστιν
	duplex:	διπλοῦν·
	sunt enim	ἔστιν γὰρ
	aliae semivocales,[60]	ἃ μὲν ἡμίφωνα,
	aliae mutae.	ἃ δὲ ἄφωνα.
55	semivocales sunt	ἡμίφωνά ἐστιν,
	quae per se quidem	ἃ καθ' ἑαυτὰ μὲν
	proferuntur,	ἐκφωνεῖται,
	sed per se	ἀλλὰ καθ' ἑαυτὰ
	syllabam	συλλαβὴν
60	facere	ποιῆσαι
	non possunt.	οὐ δύναται.
	sunt	ἔστιν
	autem numero	δὲ τὸν ἀριθμὸν
	VII:	ἑπτά·
65	*f, l, m, n, r, s, x.*	ἐκ τούτων διπλοῦν
	ex his duplex	
	est *x:*	ἐστιν τὸ *x·*
	constat enim	συνέστηκεν γὰρ
	aut ex *g* et *s,*	ἢ ἐκ τοῦ *g* καὶ *s,*
70	ut *rex, regis,*	ὡς τὸ *rex,*
	aut ex *c* et *s,*	ἢ ἐκ τοῦ *c* καὶ *s,*
	ut	ὡς τὸ
	pix, picis.	
	ideoque littera	διὰ τοῦτο γράμμα

[58] This word has become dative in an attempt to agree with *vocalibus,* though it ought really to be genitive like ἄλλων.

[59] Roman spelling made no distinction between the vowel *u* and the consonant *v,* so this word would have been spelled *uates* for the original readers.

[60] As the following definition makes clear, *semivocales* is not at all the same as the English term "semivowels," which refers to *y* and *w* (i.e. Latin consonantal *i* and *v*); it is equivalent to English "continuants."

75	negatur.[61]	ἀρνεῖται.
	mutae sunt	ἄφωνά ἐστιν,
	quae nec per se	ἃ οὔτε καθ' ἑαυτὰ
	proferri possunt	ἐκφωνεῖσθαι δύναται
	nec	οὔτε
80	syllabam	συλλαβὴν
	facere.	ποιῆσαι.
	sunt autem	ἔστιν δὲ
	numero VIIII:	τὸν ἀριθμὸν ἐννέα·
	b, c, d, g, h, k, p, q, t.	
85	ex his	ἐκ τούτων
	supervacuae quibusdam	περισσά τισιν
	videntur	δοκιμάζεται
	k et q,	τὸ k καὶ τὸ q,
	quod c littera	ὅτι τὸ c γράμμα
90	harum locum	τὸν τούτων τόπον
	possit implere.	δύναται ἀναπληρῶσαι.
	h quoque	καὶ τὸ h
	aspirationis	τῆς δασείας
	nota,	σημεῖον,
95	non littera	οὐχὶ γράμμα
	existimatur.[62]	ὑπολαμβάνεται.
	y et z	τὸ υ δὲ καὶ τὸ ζ
	propter Graeca	διὰ τὰ Ἑλληνικὰ
	nomina	ὀνόματα
100	admittimus.	προσβάλλομεν.
	A littera vocalis,	A γράμμα φωνῆεν,
	quae quidem	ὅπερ μὲν οὖν
	per se	καθ' ἑαυτὸ
	facit	ποιεῖ
105	syllabam	συλλαβὴν
	brevem	βραχεῖαν
	et longam	καὶ μακρὰν

---

[61] I.e. some people deny that *x* is a letter at all.

[62] This seems a very Greek perspective on the Latin alphabet, but it must be remembered that in Dositheus' day *h* had probably been lost in pronunciation from both languages; the Latin *h* was therefore as redundant as the Greek breathings.

	itemque	ὁμοίως δὲ
	conexa	συνεζευγμένον
110	cum aliis	μετὰ ἄλλων
	tam praeposita	καὶ προστασσόμενον
	quam media	καὶ μέσον
	finiensque,	καὶ ἐπὶ τέλους,
	ut *Ahala*;[63]	ὡς τὸ
115	nota etiam	καὶ σημεῖον
	praenominis,	χρηματισμοῦ,
	cum *Aulum*	ὁπότε Αὖλον
	sola	μόνον
	significat.	σημαίνει.
120	*E* littera vocalis	Ε γράμμα φωνῆεν
	per se nominata	καθ᾽ ἑαυτὸ ὀνομασθὲν
	itemque	ὁμοίως τε
	cum aliis	μετὰ ἄλλων
	iuncta	ζευχθὲν
125	et breves	καὶ βραχείας
	facit	ποιεῖ
	syllabas	συλλαβὰς
	et longas.[64]	καὶ μακράς.
	I littera vocalis	Ι γράμμα φωνῆεν
130	interdum	ἔσθ᾽ ὅτε
	transiens	μετερχόμενον
	in consonantium	εἰς τὴν τῶν συμφώνων
	potestatem	δύναμιν
	per se	καθ᾽ ἑαυτὸ
135	nec minus	οὐδὲν ἔλαττον
	aliis	καὶ μετὰ ἄλλων
	sociata	ἐζευγμένον
	tam breves	καὶ βραχείας
	facit	ποιεῖ

[63] The point that *a* can appear anywhere in a word seems an obvious one, but it makes more sense in light of Dositheus' subsequent discussion of the consonants, where he often points out that a particular consonant can appear only in certain positions in a word. Such knowledge was useful in reading texts without word division.

[64] The fact that *e* could be either long or short bothered Greek speakers, who were used to having different letters for long and short *e* (sounds that by Dositheus' day were distinguished qualitatively more than quantitatively).

140	syllabas	συλλαβὰς
	quam longas.	καὶ μακράς.
	nota numeri,	σημεῖον ἀριθμοῦ
	cum *unum*	ὁπότε ἕνα
	significat.	σημαίνει.
145	*O* littera vocalis	Ο γράμμα φωνῆεν
	tam corripitur	καὶ συστέλλεται
	quam producitur	καὶ ἐκτείνεται
	et singularis	καὶ μόνον
	et cum aliis	καὶ μετὰ ἄλλων
150	copulata.	ζευγνύμενον.
	V littera vocalis,	V γράμμα φωνῆεν,
	non numquam	ἔσθ᾽ ὅτε
	transiens	μετερχόμενον
	in consonantium	εἰς τὴν τῶν συμφώνων
155	potestatem,	δύναμιν,
	corripitur	συστέλλεται
	produciturque	καὶ ἐκτείνεται
	et sola	καὶ μόνον
	et cum aliis	καὶ μετὰ ἄλλων
160	coniuncta;	συνεζευγμένον·
	nota numeri,	σημεῖον ἀριθμοῦ
	cum v	ὁπότε πέντε
	significat.	σημαίνει.

8.13 A transliterated list of verb conjugations

The text here is a continuation of that in passage 7.2;[65] see the introduction to that passage for background information. Note the use of both iota and epsilon iota for *i*, the occasional use of alpha iota (which in Roman-period Greek was pronounced like epsilon) for *e*, and some outright errors in spelling (for example the alternation between ο and ω in the stem of *nōvi*, the missing ε in *exerceo*, the superfluous final ς in βόσκεις, and the superfluous final ι in γογγύζωι). The first verb is the one normally spelled *quirito*.

---

[65] P.Strasb. inv. G 1175. Additional information on this text, which is number 2134.71 in the Mertens–Pack database (http://promethee.philo.ulg.ac.be/cedopal/indexsimple.asp) and number 9217 in the Leuven Database of Ancient Books (www.trismegistos.org/ldab/), can be found in Kramer (2001: no. 3), whose text is reproduced here in a slightly emended version, and Scappaticcio (forthcoming).

42	βοᾷ	κουριτατ
	βοᾷς	κουριτας
	βοῶ	κουριτω
45	βόσκεται	ουεσκιτουρ
	βόσκεις	ουεσκερις
	βόσκομαι	ουεσκορ
	βαστάζει	πορτατ
	βαστάζεις	πορτας
50	βαστάζω	πορτω
	γυμνάζει	εξερκετ
	γυμνάζεις	εξερκες
	γυμνάζω	εξερκω
	γεμίζει	ιμπλετ
55	γεμίζεις	ιμπλες
	γεμίζω	ιμπλεω
	γογγύζει	μορμορατ
	γογγύζεις	μορμορας
	γογγύζωι	μορμορω
60	γινώσκει	νοουιτ
	γινώσκεις	νοουις
	γινώσκω	νωουι
	γαμεῖ	νουβιτ
	γαμεῖς	νουβις
65	γαμῶ	νουβω
	γελᾷ	ρειδιτ
	γελᾷς	ρειδες
	γελῶ	ρειδω
	γλύφει	σκουλπιτ
70	γλύφεις	σκουλπις
	γλύφω	σκουλπεω
	γηράσκει	σενησκιτ
	γηράσκεις	σενησκις
	γηράσκω	σενησκω
75	γεννᾶται	νασκιτουρ
	γεννᾶσαι	νασκαιρης
	γεννῶμαι	νασκορ
	γνάπτι	πολιτ
	γνάπτις	πολις

80	γνάπτω	πολιω
	γράφει	σκριβιτ
	γράφεις	σκριβις

8.14 A glossary section on family relationships

The extract below comes from the Hermeneumata Leidensia, where it is section 35 of the classified glossary. It covers a field much wider than genetic kinship, extending to all members of a Roman household with a few extra words included for good measure (such as "enemy," which is included because it is the opposite of "friend"). Although as it appears in manuscripts this glossary was employed for learning Greek rather than Latin, it is clear that the Greek terms were originally intended as definitions of the Latin, not the other way around, owing to the Greek periphrases used for the Latin terms for "aunt" and "uncle."[66]

28.24	**De cognatione**	**Περὶ συγγενείας**
28.25	cognatio	συγγένεια
	parentes	γονεῖς
	liberi	τέκνα
	pater	πατήρ
	mater	μήτηρ
28.30	frater	ἀδελφός
	soror	ἀδελφή
	filius	υἱός
	filia	θυγάτηρ
	amita	πατρὸς ἀδελφή
28.35	matertera	μητρὸς ἀδελφή
28.35a	avia	τήθη
	avus	πάππος
	nutrix	τροφός
	nutritor	τροφεύς
	socer	πενθερός
28.40	gener	γαμβρός
	privignus	πρόγονος

[66] The text is that of Flammini (2004: 62–4), but the numbering follows Goetz's transcript of the Leiden manuscript, Vossianus Gr. Q. 7 (Goetz 1892: 28–9).

	amicus	φίλος
	amica	φίλη
	inimicus	ἐχθρός
28.45	noverca	μητρυιά
	alumnus	θρεπτός
	consobrinus	ἀνεψιός
	patruus	πατρὸς ἀδελφός
	neptis	θυγατριδοῦς
28.50	adoptivus	υἱοποίητος[67]
	conlactaneus	σύντροφος
	vidua	χήρα
	sterilis	στεῖρα
	patricius	αὐτόχθων[68]
28.55	pupillus	ὀρφανός
	dominus	κύριος
	domina	κυρία
	ingenuus	εὐγενής
	liber	ἐλεύθερος
29.1	servus	δοῦλος
	ancilla	δούλη
	virgo	παρθένος
	concubina	παλλακή
29.5	spurius	νόθος
	adfinis	ἀγχιστεύς
	gemini	δίδυμοι
	cliens	πρόσφυξ

8.15 A transliterated glossary of goddesses

This extract from a classified glossary found on a papyrus of the second or third century AD gives the names of traditional and less traditional goddesses.[69]

[67] These terms refer to an adopted son.
[68] The Latin means "noble" and the Greek "native," i.e. having a very long pedigree in the country, which can be grounds for nobility.
[69] P. Mich. inv. 2458, which is number 2685.1 in the Mertens–Pack database (http://promethee.philo.ulg.ac.be/cedopal/indexsimple.asp), and number 5062 in the Leuven Database of Ancient Books (www.trismegistos.org/ldab/). A photograph is available at www.papyri.info/apis/michigan.apis.1596. For more information on this text see Kramer (1983: no. 12) and Priest (1977).

	Θεαων ονοματα	Δεαρουμ νωμινα
12		
	υγιεια	σαλους
	γη μητηρ	τερρα ματερ
15	ηρα	ιουνων
	ηρα βασιλισσα	ιουνων ρηγινα
	ειλειθυια	ιουνων λουκινα
	αρτεμις	διανα
	λητω	λατωνα
20	αφροδειτη	ουενους
	νεμεσις	ουλτριξ
	δημητηρ	κερης
	φερσεφονη	πρωσερπινα
	εστια	ουεστα
25	τυχη	φορτουνα
	σεμελη	λειβερα
	εισις	εισις
	μητηρ μεγαλη	ματερ μαγνα

8.16 A transliterated glossary of spices

The text here comes from the same papyrus as passage 7.3; see the introduction to that passage for background information. Although the heading suggests that the words in this section should be any type of item that can be sold, the list that follows consists largely of spices and other expensive substances. The Greek is left uncorrected and without diacritics to give a sense of the difficulty of the original. Note the following potentially unfamiliar items: λίβανος "frankincense" (an aromatic resin burned as an offering to gods), σμύρνα "myrrh" (an aromatic resin used for embalming corpses, making scented oil, and burning as incense), στυπτηρία "alum" (a chemical compound used in dyeing and medicine), ἰξός "birdlime" (a sticky substance, made from mistletoe berries, smeared on branches to catch perching birds), θεῖον "sulphur," ῥητίνη "pine resin" (the equation of this term with *pix* "pitch" is probably a mistake, as normally the Latin for "pine resin" is *resina* and the Greek for "pitch" is πίσσα), ἄσφαλτον "bitumen" (a kind of tar), κίσηρις "pumice stone," κηκίς "oak gall" (a type of growth on oak trees used to make ink), λευκαία "Spanish broom" (a plant used for making ropes, nets, etc.), ὀπός "silphium juice" (a rare and highly prized condiment).

	περι φορτιων	δη μερκιβους
4		
5	φορτιον	μερς
	λιβανος	τους

	ζμυρνα	μουρρα
	αρωματα	οδωρης
	στυπτηρια	αλουμεν
10	γη λευκη	κρητα
	ιξος	ουισκους
	θειον	σουλπουρ
	ρετεινη	πιξ
	ασφαλτον	βιτουμεν
15	κισηριν	πουμεξ
	κηκιδες	γαλλαι
	οθονια	λεντιαμεν
	λευκεα	σπαρτουμ
	οπος	λασερ
20	πιπεριν	πιπερ

9 | Texts without word division

Reading one's native language without word division, punctuation, or capitalization is largely a matter of practice; it takes only a brief period to reach a level at which one is reasonably comfortable as long as all the words in the passage are familiar. For example:

JINGLEBELLSJINGLEBELLS
JINGLEALLTHEWAY
OHWHATFUNITISTORIDE
INAONEHORSEOPENSLEIGH

The task is somewhat more difficult when the passage contains unusual words or archaic language, but even then such reading is more feasible than we might expect, particularly when the text is not wholly unfamiliar to the reader. For example:[1]

TOBEORNOTTOBETHATISTHEQUESTION
WHETHERTISNOBLERINTHEMINDTOSUFFER
THESLINGSANDARROWSOFOUTRAGEOUSFORTUNE
ORTOTAKEARMSAGAINSTASEAOFTROUBLES
ANDBYOPPOSINGENDTHEMTODIETOSLEEP
NOMOREANDBYASLEEPTOSAYWEEND
THEHEARTACHEANDTHETHOUSANDNATURALSHOCKS
THATFLESHISHEIRTOTISACONSUMMATION
DEVOUTLYTOBEWISHEDTODIETOSLEEP
TOSLEEPPERCHANCETODREAMAYTHERESTHERUB
FORINTHATSLEEPOFDEATHWHATDREAMSMAYCOME
WHENWEHAVESHUFFLEDOFFTHISMORTALCOIL
MUSTGIVEUSPAUSETHERESTHERESPECT
THATMAKESCALAMITYOFSOLONGLIFE
FORWHOWOULDBEARTHEWHIPSANDSCORNSOFTIME
THOPPRESSORSWRONGTHEPROUDMANSCONTUMELY
THEPANGSOFDISPRIZEDLOVETHELAWSDELAY
THEINSOLENCEOFOFFICEANDTHESPURNS
THATPATIENTMERITOFTHUNWORTHYTAKES
WHENHEHIMSELFMIGHTHISQUIETUSMAKE

---

[1] Shakespeare, *Hamlet* Act 3 scene 1.

WITHABAREBODKINWHOWOULDTHESEFARDELSBEAR
TOGRUNTANDSWEATUNDERAWEARYLIFE
BUTTHATTHEDREADOFSOMETHINGAFTERDEATH
THEUNDISCOVEREDCOUNTRYFROMWHOSEBOURN
NOTRAVELLERRETURNSPUZZLESTHEWILL
ANDMAKESUSRATHERBEARTHOSEILLSWEHAVE
THANFLYTOOTHERSTHATWEKNOWNOTOF

In a foreign language, even one the reader knows well, use of this format poses significantly more difficulty. It becomes almost impossible to use a dictionary when one does not know where the individual words begin and end, and without a dictionary most language learners are helpless. For example:[2]

VTBELLISIGNVMLAVRENTITVRNVSABARCE
EXTVLITETRAVCOSTREPVERVNTCORNVACANTV
VTQVEACRISCONCVSSITEQVOSVTQVEIMPVLITARMA
EXTEMPLOTVRBATIANIMISIMVLOMNETVMVLTV
CONIVRATTREPIDOLATIVMSAEVITQVEIVVENTVS
EFFERADVCTORESPRIMIMESSAPVSETVFENS
CONTEMPTORQVEDEVMMEZENTIVSVNDIQVECOGVNT
AVXILIAETLATOSVASTANTCVLTORIBVSAGROS
MITTITVRETMAGNIVENVLVSDIOMEDISADVRBEM
QVIPETATAVXILIVMETLATIOCONSISTERETEVCROS
ADVECTVMAENEANCLASSIVICTOSQVEPENATIS
INFERREETFATISREGEMSEDICEREPOSCI
EDOCEATMVLTASQVEVIROSEADIVNGEREGENTIS
DARDANIOETLATELATIOINCREBESCERENOMEN
QVIDSTRVATHISCOEPTISQVEMSIFORTVNASEQVATVR
EVENTVMPVGNAECVPIATMANIFESTIVSIPSI
QVAMTVRNOREGIAVTREGIAPPARERELATINO

It was this situation that led the ancients to give their beginning students running translations.[3] Below are some examples of ancient Latin-learning materials in this original format.

---

[2] Virgil, *Aeneid* 8.1–17.
[3] Sometimes word divisions (in the form of dots, not spaces) were also provided for beginners; see Dickey (forthcoming b).

9.1   The preface to the "Genealogy of Hyginus"

Hyginus was the author of a mythographical work that has survived in Latin with the title *Fabulae*; his date is disputed but may be as early as the Augustan period. A drastically abridged version of this work, in bilingual form, is attached to the Hermeneumata Leidensia with the title "Genealogy of Hyginus." The extract below constitutes the preface to this abridged version.[4] The clause at the start is a dating formula referring to AD 207; the illustrations referred to have, alas, been lost, along with the stories listed in the table of contents with which the preface ends.

56.30	MAXIMOETAPRO	(When) Maximus and Aper
	CONSVLIBVS	(were) consuls,
	TERTIOIDSEPTEMBRES	on the third day before the Ides of September,
	HYGINIGENEALOGIAM	the Genealogy of Hyginus,
	OMNIBVSNOTAMDESCRIPSI	which is known to all, I transcribed;
56.35	INQVAERVNT	in which (work) will be
	PLVRESHISTORIAE	rather many stories
	INTERPRETATAE	translated
	INHOCLIBRO	in this book.
	DEORVMENIMETDEARVM	For the gods' and goddess'
56.40	NOMINAINSECVNDO	names in the second (book)
	EXPLICVIMVS	we explained,
	SEDINHOC	but in this (book)
	ERVNTEORVMENARRATIONES	will be their tales,
	LICETNONOMNES	even if not all (the tales),
56.45	EORVMTAMEN	at least the ones
	QVORVMINTERIMPOSSVM	that I can manage in the time.
	PICTVRAEIGITVR	So the illustrations
	HVIVSLABORIS	of this work
	MVLTISLOCIS	in many places
56.50	DANTTESTIMONIVM	give evidence,
	NAMETGRAMMATICI	for grammarians too
	ARTISEIVS	of that art (i.e. of illustration)
	NONSOLVMLAVDANT	not only praise
	INGENIVM	the value,

---

[4] Additional information on this text can be found in Dickey (2012–15: I.27, 37–9), Cameron (2004: 317–18), Boriaud (1997), and Flammini (1990: 24–6). The text quoted here is a slightly emended version of Flammini's scholarly edition (2004: 104), but the layout is that of the Leiden manuscript, Vossianus Gr. Q. 7, and the numbering gives the page and line references to Goetz's transcription of that manuscript (Goetz 1892: 56–7).

56.55	SEDETVTVNTVR	but they also use (it).
	FABVLAEQVOQVE	Also the stories
	PANTOMIMORVM	of the pantomimes
	INDEACCIPIVNTLAVDEM	receive praise from this (visual element),
	ETTESTANTVR	and testify
57.1	INSALTATIONE	in dance
	VERAESSEQVAESCRIPTASVNT	that what is written is true.
	VTVEROFACILIVSINVENIAS	So that you may more easily find
57.3a	VNIVSCVIVSQVEENARRATIONEM	the story of each (deity),
	EXSVBIECTISRECOGNOSCES	you will recognize (it) from the (list) below:
57.5	PRIMVMERGOOMNIVM	so first of all
	MVSARVMVIIIINOMINA	the names of the 9 muses
	ETARTESETFILIOS	and their arts and their sons,
	ETCVMQVIBVSCONCVBVERINT	and who they slept with,
	ETDEORVMXIINOMINA	and the names of the 12 gods,
57.10	ETSEPTEMZODIACI	and (the names) of the seven (days) of the zodiac,
	ETSIGNORVMXII	and (the names) of the 12 signs (of the zodiac).
	DEPROMETHEO	About Prometheus,
	DEVENEREETMARTE	about Venus and Mars,
	DEMINERVAETNEPTVNO	about Minerva and Neptune ...

9.2   Stories about the Trojan War

For background on these texts see the introduction to passage 2.2. The extracts given here cover books 17–18 (with English translation in modern format), 19–20 (with the original Greek in its original format), and 21–2 (with English translation using the ancient format).[5] Note the non-standard indirect statement and indirect command constructions, and the way that *autem* can mean both "and" and "but."

		BOOK 17
65.10	CORPOREIACENTE	As the body lay there
	PATROCLI	of Patroclus
	MENELAVSTEGEBAT	Menelaus defended (it),
	QVEMVVLNERATEVPHORBVS	(Menelaus) whom Euphorbus wounded;
	POSTEAAVTEM	but later

---

[5] Additional information on this material can be found in Dickey (2012–15: 1.27–8). The text given here is a slightly emended version of the scholarly edition of Flammini (2004: 110–11), but the layout follows that of the Leiden manuscript, Vossianus Gr. Q. 7, and the numbering refers to Goetz's transcription of that manuscript (Goetz 1892: 65–9).

65.15	ABEOINTERFICITVR	(Euphorbus) was killed by him (Menelaus).
	HECTORAVTEM	But Hector,
	APOLLINEHORTANTE	with Apollo encouraging him,
	INDEFENSIONEM	in defense
	OCCISI	of the slain man
65.20	INSILVITINPVGNAM	leapt into battle,
	ETIMPETVMEIVS	and his attack
	AIAXEXCEPIT	Ajax withstood,
	ETMENELAVM	and Menelaus
	APERICVLOLIBERAVIT	he (Ajax) freed from danger.
65.25	ETHECTORACHILLIS	And Hector in Achilles'
	ARMISGLORIABATVR	arms exulted,
	CVIGLAVCVSIMPROPERAVIT	(Hector) whom Glaucus reproached
	SARPEDONEMIACENTEM	with the death of Sarpedon.
	PVGNANTIBVSAVTEM	And when they were fighting
65.30	CIRCACORPVS	around the body
	PATROCLI	of Patroclus,
	AENEASPRIMORES	Aeneas killed (some) foremost men of the
	GRAECORVMINTERFECIT	Greeks;
	IVNXITSE	he joined himself
65.35	CVMHECTORE	with Hector
	CONTRAAVTOMEDONTEM	against Automedon,
	QVICVSTODIEBAT	who was guarding
	ACHILLISEQVOS	the horses of Achilles,
	INQVIBVS	by which
65.40	VECTATVSFVERATPATROCLVS	Patroclus had been carried.
	AVTOMEDONTEMERGO	So the two Ajaxes saved Automedon;
	DVOAIACESCONSERVAVERVNT	
	MENELAVSAVTEM	and Menelaus
	AMINERVAVRSVS	urged[6] on by Athena
65.45	VIRILITERSTETIT	stood bravely.
	POSTEAERGO	So afterwards
	TONITRANTECAELO	when the heavens thunder
	SVADETTELAMON	Telamon advises
	AIACEMDISCEDERE	Ajax to leave,

[6] *Ursus* is here used as the past participle of *urgeo*.

65.50	MENELAVSAVTEM	and Menelaus
	MITTITADACHILLEM	sends to Achilles
	ANTILOCHVM	Antilochus
	NVNTIANTEMPATROCLIMORTEM	reporting the death of Patroclus.

BOOK 18

	NVNTIATANTILOCHVS	Antilochus reports
66.1	ACHILLEIPATROCLI	to Achilles Patroclus'
	MORTEM	death,
	ETILLEAVDIENS	and he hearing (it),
	CVMMATRESVA	with his mother
66.5	THETIDEMVLTA	Thetis, greatly
	LACRIMAVIT	he wept;
66.7	ETTVNCIRIS	and then Iris,
68.20	AIVNONEMISSA	sent by Hera,
	ADACHILLEMVENIT	came to Achilles.
	POLYDAMASAVTEM	And Polydamas
	DIXITVTSE	said that (the Trojans)
	INTRAMVROSCONSERVARENT	should protect themselves inside the walls,
68.25	SEDHECTOR	but Hector
	CONTRARIASAPIEBAT	knew better.
	ETACHILLESCORPVS	And Achilles buried the body of Patroclus.
	PATROCLISEPELIVIT	
	ETTHETISPETIIT	And Thetis asked
68.30	AVVLCANO	Hephaestus
	VTACHILLIARMAFACERET	to make arms for Achilles;
	VVLCANVSAVTEM	and Hephaestus
	CELERITERFACIENS	making (them) quickly
	ATTVLITTHETIDI	brought (them) to Thetis,
68.35	ETILLAFILIVMARMAVIT	and she armed her son
	ETANIMOSIOREM	and she sent him off to battle bolder.
	ADPVGNAMDIMISIT	

T[7]

VLIXESDAT	ΟΔΥΣΣΕΥΣΔΙΔΩΣΙΝ
CONSILIVM	ΓΝωΜΗΝ

---

[7] The difference between ancient and modern formats is greater for Greek than for Latin, for in addition to word division and the capital/lower case distinction shared with Latin, ancient Greek as written today includes accents, breathings, and iotas subscript. In the Classical period accent and breathing marks had not yet been invented, and the iotas that are now subscript were written as full letters (iota adscript), since they were

68.40	VTEXEVNTES	ΟΠΩΣΕΞΙΟΝΤΕΣ
	ADPVGNAM	ΕΙΣΤΟΝΠΟΛΕΜΟΝ
	ANTEPRANDERET	ΠΡΟΤΕΡΟΝΑΡΙΣΤΗΣΩΣΙΝ
	DEINDESVADETAGAMEMNONEM	ΕΠΕΙΤΑΠΕΙΘΕΙΑΓΑΜΕΜΝΟΝΑ,
	VTQVAEPOLLICITVSERATMVNERA	ΙΝΑΑΥΠΕΣΧΕΤΟΔΩΡΑ
68.45	MITTERETACHILLI	ΠΕΜΨΗΑΧΙΛΛΕΙ
	QVIBVSADLATISACCEPTA[8]	ΩΝΕΝΕΧΘΕΝΤΩΝΛΑΒΟΝΤΕΣ
	MIRMIDONES	ΟΙΜΥΡΜΙΔΟΝΕΣ
	CIRCANAVES	ΠΑΡΑΤΑΙΣΝΑΥΣΙΝ
	EXPOSVERVNT	ΔΙΕΘΗΚΑΝ
68.50	ETBRISEISCVMVENISSET	ΚΑΙΒΡΙΣΗΙΣΠΑΡΟΥΣΑ
	PATROCLVM	ΠΑΤΡΟΚΛΟΝ
	MVLTVMMAERVIT	ΠΟΛΛΑΩΔΥΡΑΤΟ
	ETTVNCIVNO	ΚΑΙΤΟΤΕΗΡΑ
	FECITVNVMEXEQVIS	ΠΟΙΕΙΕΝΑΤΩΝΙΠΠΩΝ
68.55	XANTHVM	ΤΟΝΞΑΝΘΟΝ
	DICEREHVMANAVOCE	ΕΙΠΕΙΝΑΝΘΡΩΠΙΝΗΦΩΝΗ
69.1	ACHILLI	ΤΩΑΧΙΛΛΕΙ
	QVONIAMETIPSE	ΕΠΕΙΔΗΚΑΙΑΥΤΟΣ
	MORITVRVSEST	ΤΕΘΝΗΞΕΤΑΙ
	ETPRAEDIXIT	ΚΑΙΠΡΟΕΙΠΕΝ
69.5	ACHILLIS	ΤΟΝΑΧΙΛΛΕΩΣ
	CITATAMMORTEM	ΤΑΧΥΝΘΑΝΑΤΟΝ
69.7	ETACHILLES	ΚΑΙΑΧΙΛΛΕΥΣ
66.8	FORTIANIMOTVLIT	ΑΝΔΡΕΙΑΨΥΧΗΗΝΕΙ˙ΚΕΝ
	QVODPROVENERIT	ΤΟΕΠΕΛΕΥΣΟΜΕΝΟΝ

Υ

66.10	CVMCOEPISSETACHILLES	ΟΤΕΗΡΞΑΤΟΑΧΙΛΛΕΥΣ
	EXIREADPVGNAM	ΕΞΕΡΧΕΣΘΑΙΕΙΣΠΟΛΕΜΟΝ
	IVPPITEROMNIBVSDEIS	ΖΕΥΣΠΑΣΙΝΘΕΟΙΣ

pronounced as full letters. By the time Greek speakers had started to learn Latin these iotas had ceased to be pronounced and therefore were generally not written; accent and breathing marks had been invented but were not normally used. The modern customs of applying accents and breathings regularly, writing the unpronounced iotas as subscripts, and leaving spaces between words all date to the introduction of minuscule script (a gradual development centered around the ninth century).

[8] The two languages have different constructions here; the Latin means "when these had been brought the Myrmidons displayed the accepted gifts" and the Greek "when these had been brought the Myrmidons having accepted (them) displayed (them)." This situation may have arisen because the Greek aorist active participle was what the writer really wanted but had no equivalent in Latin. There was a better solution in both languages; what is it?

	PERMISIT	ΕΠΕΤΡΕΨΕΝ
	VTQVISQVISVOLVERIT	ΩΣΑΝΤΙΣΤΙΝΙΘΕΛΗ
66.15	IVVAREFAVEAT[9]	ΒΟΗΘΕΙΝΒΟΗΘΕΙΤω
	INQVIBVSFAVEBANT	ΕΝΟΙΣΕΒΟΗΘΟΥΝ
	QVIDEMGRAECIS	ΤΟΙΣΜΕΝΕΛΛΗΣΙΝ
	IVNOETMINERVA	ΗΡΑΚΑΙΑΘΗΝΑ
	NEPTVNVSETMERCVRIVS	ΠΟΣΕΙΔωΝΚΑΙΕΡΜΗΣ
66.20	ETVVLCANVS	ΚΑΙΗΦΑΙΣΤΟΣ
	TROIANISAVTEM	ΤΡωΣΙΝΔΕ
	MARSETAPOLLO	ΜΑΡΣΚΑΙΑΠΟΛΛωΝ[10]
	LATONAETDIANA	ΛΗΤωΚΑΙΑΡΤΕΜΙΣ
	VENVSETXANTHVSFLVVIVS	ΑΦΡΟΔΙΤΗΚΑΙΞΑΝΘΟΣΠΟΤΑΜΟΣ
66.25	TVNCERGOAPOLLO	ΤΟΤΕΟΥΝΑΠΟΛΛωΝ
	TRANSFIGVRATVS	ΜΕΤΑΜΟΡΦωΘΕΙΣ
	INLYCAONEMSVADETAENEAM	ΕΙΣΛΥΚΑΟΝΑΠΕΙΘΕΙΑΙΝΕΙΑΝ
	VTADVERSVS	ΙΝΑΚΑΤΕΝΑΝΤΙ
	ACHILLEMPVGNARET	ΑΧΙΛΛΕωΣΠΥΚΤΕΥΣΗ
66.30	ETILLESVASVS	ΚΑΚΕΙΝΟΣΠΕΙΣΘΕΙΣ
	PVGNAVIT	ΕΠΥΚΤΕΥΣΕΝ
	ETPERICLITANTEM	ΚΑΙΚΙΝΔΥΝΕΥΟΝΤΑ
	EVMOCCIDI	ΑΥΤΟΝΣΦΑΓΗΝΑΙ
	ABACHILLE	ΥΠΟΑΧΙΛΛΕωΣ
66.35	RAPVITNEPTVNVS	ΗΡΠΑΣΕΝΠΟΣΕΙΔωΝ
	ETHECTOREM	ΚΑΙΕΚΤΟΡΑ
	CVMVIDISSETAPOLLO	ΩΣΕΙΔΕΝΑΠΟΛΛωΝ
	IMPAREMESSE[11]	ΑΝΙΣΟΝΟΝΤΑ
	NVBECOOPERTVM	ΝΕΦΕΛΗΠΕΡΙΒΑΛωΝ
66.40	DEPROELIOEXIVIT	ΕΚΤΟΥΠΟΛΕΜΟΥΕΡΥΣΑΤΟ
	ETTVNCACHILLES	ΚΑΙΤΟΤΕΑΧΙΛΛΕΥΣ
	COMPLVRESTROIANORVM	ΠΛΕΙΣΤΟΥΣΤωΝΤΡωωΝ
	INTERFECIT	ΕΦΟΝΕΥΣΕΝ
		BOOK 21
	INTEREAACHILLES	MEANWHILEACHILLES
66.45	DVODECIMIVVENES	TWELVEYOUNGMEN

[9] The constructions in the two languages are not entirely parallel in lines 14 and 15.
[10] We would expect Ἄρης rather than Μάρς in Greek.
[11] I.e. about to lose the fight he was engaged in.

	CAPTIVOS	CAPTIVES
	MITTITADNAVES	SENDSTOTHESHIP
	QVOSINCIPIEBATSACRIFICARE	WHOMHEWASBEGINNINGTOSACRIFICE
	PATROCLIMANIBVS	TOTHESHADESOFPATROCLUS
66.50	ETINTERFECIT	ANDHEKILLED
	LYCAONEM	LYCAON
	QVEMPRIVSCAPTVM	WHOMWHENHECAPTUREDHIMBEFORE
	VENDIDITINLEMNVM	HEHADSOLDTOLEMNOS
	ETASTEROPAEVM	ANDASTEROPAEUS
66.55	INTERFECIT	HEKILLED
	ETPAEONEM	ANDPAEON
	DVCES	RULERS
	INQVIBVSIRATVS	ANGRYBECAUSEOFWHOM
	SCAMANDRVSFLVVIVS	THERIVERSCAMANDER
67.1	ACHILLI	(ANGRYAT)ACHILLES
	PROPTERQVODVNDASEIVS	BECAUSEHE(ACHILLES)HISWATERS
	SANGVINAVIT	FILLEDWITHBLOOD
	IVNGENSERGOSE	SOJOININGHIMSELF
67.5	CVMSIMVNTE	WITHSIMOEIS
	CONCVRRIT	HERANTOGETHER
	VTACHILLEMSVFFOCARET	INORDERTODROWNACHILLES
	QVOSIVNO	BUTHERATHROUGHHEPHAESTUSBURNEDTHEM
	PERVVLCANVMCOMBVSSIT	
67.10	ETACHILLEMLIBERAVIT	ANDFREEDACHILLES
	DEIAVTEM	ANDTHEGODS
	ALTERALTERIDIMICAVERVNT	FOUGHTONEAGAINSTANOTHER
	INTERSE	AMONGTHEMSELVES
	INQVIBVSMARTEMMINERVA	AMONGWHOMATHENAFLATTENEDARESWITHASTONE
67.15	SAXOPROSTRAVIT	
	ETVENEREMEXPALMAVIT,	ANDSLAPPEDAPHRODITE
	NEPTVNVSAVTEMETAPOLLO	BUTPOSEIDONANDAPOLLO
	CVMCONSENSV	BYAGREEMENT
	DISCESSERVNT	DEPARTED
67.20	DIANAMAVTEMIVNOSAGITTA VVLNERAT	ANDHERAWOUNDSARTEMISWITHANARROW
	LATONAAVTEMETMERCVRIVS	ANDLETOANDHERMES
	HOSTILITER	ASENEMIES
	PVGNAVERVNT	FOUGHT

67.25	AGENORAAVTEM	ANDAPOLLOFREEDAGENOR
	ANTENORISFILIVM	SONOFANTENOR
	PERICLITANTEMOCCIDI	WHORISKEDBEINGKILLED
	ABACHILLE	BYACHILLES
	APOLLOLIBERAVIT	
67.30	POSTEAAVTEMDEI	BUTAFTERWARDSTHEGODS
	SVISLOCIS	TOTHEIROWNPLACES
	REDIERVNT	RETURNED

BOOK 22

	ETHECTOREMEXEVNTEM	ANDHECTORWHOISGOINGOUT
	INPVGNAM	TOBATTLE
67.35	CONTRAACHILLEM	AGAINSTACHILLES
	ROGATPRIAMVS	PRIAMASKS
	ETHECVBA	ANDHECUBA
	VTIINTRETINTRAPORTAS	TOCOMEINSIDETHEGATES
	ETNONSVASERVNTEVM	ANDTHEYDIDNOTPERSUADEHIM
67.40	ETACHILLES	ANDACHILLES
	INTERPONENTESEAPOLLINE	WITHAPOLLOPUTTINGHIMSELFINBETWEEN
	PERSEQVITVREVMETMALEDICIT	PURSUESHIM(HECTOR)ANDCURSES(HIM)
	ETMINERVAAVTEM	BUTATHENAALSO
	TRANSFIGVRATA	TRANSFORMED
67.45	INDEIFOBVM	INTODEIPHOBUS
	FALLITHECTOREM	DECEIVESHECTOR
	ETIVGVLATVRABACHILLE	ANDHEISMURDEREDBYACHILLES
	ETLIGATVSCVRROTRAHITVR	ANDTIEDTOHISCHARIOTHEISDRAGGED
	TERCIRCAMVROS	THREETIMESAROUNDTHEWALLS
67.50	ETHECVBACVMPRIAMO	ANDHECUBAWITHPRIAM
	ETTROIANIS	ANDTHETROJANS
	DIVTIVSEVMDEPLANXERVNT	BEWAILEDHIMFORALONGTIME

9.3   Charisius on the participle

This extract comes from the beginning of Charisius' explanation of participles.[12] Note that when a prose text is written in the ancient monolingual format line breaks often occur in the middle of a word.

---

[12]   Book 2.12 = Barwick (1964: 230.1–18) = Keil (1857–80: I.178–9).

DE PARTICIPIO
PARTICIPIVMESTPARSORATIONISCVMTEMPOREETCASVSINE
PERSONAACTIVEVELPASSIVEALIQVIDSIGNIFICANSVTLIMANS
LEGENSINPARTICIPIISEADEMPLERVMQVEOMNIAOBSERVABI
MVSQVAEINAPPELLATIONIBVSVERBISQVE
PARTICIPIORVMALIAADPRAETERITVMTEMPVSREFERVNTVR
VTLIMATVSSCRIPTVSALIAADINSTANSVTLIMANSSCRIBENSA
LIAADFVTVRVMVTLIMATVRVSSCRIPTVRVSPRAETERITITEM
PORISQVAEDAMSVNTACTIVATANTVMMODOQVAEDAMPASSI
VAQVAEDAMNEVTRAACTIVALVCTATVSSECVTVSPASSIVAFV
GATVSABLATVSNEVTRANATVSORTVSNEQVEENIMVTDVCIT
FVGATFACITDVCTVSFVGATVSEANDEMETIAMINNATVSETOR
TVSFORMAMVERBORVMPOSSVMVSEXPRIMERESVNTALIATA
MACTIVAQVAMPASSIVAVADATVSCRIMINATVSTAMENIMEGIS
SEQVIDQVAMPASSVMESSESIGNIFICANTITAQVEINSTANTIFV
TVROQVEFIVNTACTIVAVTVADANSCRIMINANSVADATVRVS
CRIMINATVRVSPARTICIPIAQVAEVMEXEVNTFIVNTETIAMVER
BAINFINITIVAVTSCRIPTVMLECTVM

10 | Overview of the ancient Latin-learning materials

The lists below contain, to the best of my knowledge, all ancient Latin-learning materials that have been published to date; there are also numerous unpublished papyri. Although this list contains less information on each text than the similar list in Dickey (2012–15: I.7–10), it contains more texts and more recent editions, as a number of documents have been published or re-edited since that earlier list was finalized.

Under "Where to find it" is given not a complete list of editions, let alone a complete bibliography, but rather the name or number by which the text is most commonly known (often an *editio princeps*, though as a publication this is often seriously out of date), one or two references to usable editions, and the numbers in the Mertens–Pack database (http://promethee.philo.ulg.ac.be/cedopal/indexsimple.asp) and Leuven Database of Ancient Books (www.trismegistos.org/ldab/), either of which can be consulted for further bibliography. Although Cavenaile (1958) is not explicitly mentioned except when it has the best text of a papyrus, that work provides texts of many of the papyri and is worth consulting if one cannot obtain another edition. Similarly McNamee (2007) provides texts of the annotations found on annotated papyri (i.e. the monolingual Latin texts with glosses and/or notes in Greek); sometimes her edition supersedes a previous text of the annotations. Scappaticcio (forthcoming) will provide re-editions and detailed discussion of the alphabets and grammatical texts found on papyri.

The designation "transliterated" indicates that the Latin is transliterated into Greek script; bilingual texts with the Greek in Latin script also exist but have not been included here since they were probably designed for Latin speakers learning Greek rather than Greek speakers learning Latin. Also excluded are Latin papyri, even alphabets or grammatical treatises, that do not contain clear evidence of use by speakers of Greek (or another language); these could have been used by monolingual Latin speakers and so are not necessarily evidence of foreign-language learning.

10.1 Papyri

This section includes all texts that survive as original ancient documents; some are on parchment, wood, or ostraca rather than papyrus. Papyrological publications (italicized) and collections (not italicized) are indicated by a standard set of abbreviations, for which a complete key can be found in the *Checklist of editions of Greek, Latin, Demotic, and Coptic Papyri, Ostraca, and Tablets*, available online at www.papyri.info/docs/checklist.

Century	Material	Where to find it
I BC	Greek–Latin glossary/paradigms (transliterated)	*BKT* IX.150 = Kramer 1983: no. 1 (*M–P*³ 2134.5, *LDAB* 6764)
I–II AD	Latin alphabet with transliterated letter names	O.Max. inv. M356 = *SB* XXVIII.17105 = Fournet 2003: 445 (*M–P*³ 3012.01, *LDAB* 10791)
I–II AD	Greek–Latin classified glossary (transliterated)	*P.Oxy.* XXXIII.2660 = Kramer 1983: no. 6 (*M–P*³ 2134.1, *LDAB* 4497)
I–II AD	Latin–Greek classified glossary (transliterated)	*P.Oxy.* XLVI.3315 = Kramer 1983: no. 8 (*M–P*³ 3004.2, *LDAB* 4498)
I–II AD	Greek–Latin classified glossary (transliterated)	*P.Oxy.* LXXVIII.5162 (*LDAB* 171907)
I–II AD	Greek–Latin classified glossary (transliterated)	*P.Oxy.* LXXVIII.5163 (*LDAB* 171908)
II AD	Latin–Greek classified glossary (transliterated)	*P.Lund* I.5 = Kramer 1983: no. 9 (*M–P*³ 3004, *LDAB* 4741)
II AD	Greek–Latin alphabetical glossary (transliterated)	*P.Oxy.* XLIX.3452 = Kramer 2001: no. 7 (*M–P*³ 2134.7, *LDAB* 4812)
II–III AD	Greek–Latin classified glossary (transliterated)	P.Mich. inv. 2458 = Kramer 1983: no. 12 (*M–P*³ 2685.1, *LDAB* 5062)
II–III AD	Aesop with Latin translation	*P.Yale* II.104 + *P.Mich.* VII.457 (*M–P*³ 2917, *LDAB* 134)
III AD	Latin–Greek alphabetical glossary	P.Sorb. inv. 2069 = Dickey and Ferri 2010 (*M–P*³ 3006, *LDAB* 5438)
III AD	Latin–Greek alphabetical glossary	*P.Sorb.* I.8 = Kramer 1983: no. 3 (*M–P*³3008, *LDAB* 5439)
III AD	Greek–Latin classified glossary (transliterated)	*P.Oxy.* XXXIII.2660a = Kramer 1983: no. 7 (*M–P*³ 2134.2, *LDAB* 5382)
III AD	Greek–Latin classified glossary (transliterated)	*P.Laur.* IV.147 = *SB* XIV.12137 = Kramer 1983: no. 5 (*M–P*³ 2134.3, *LDAB* 4675)
III–IV AD	Latin–Greek classified glossary	P.Vindob. inv. L 27 = Kramer 2001: no. 4 (*M–P*³ 3004.21, *LDAB* 5755)
III–IV AD	Greek–Latin classified glossary (transliterated)	P.Strasb. inv. G 1173 = Kramer 2001: no. 6 (*M–P*³ 2134.61, *LDAB* 9218)
III–IV AD	Babrius with Latin translation	*P.Amh.* II.26 = Cavenaile 1958: no. 40 = Kramer 2007a: no. 10 (*M–P*³ 172, *LDAB* 434)
III–IV AD	Latin–Greek model letters	*P.Bon.* 5 = Kramer 1983: no. 16 (*M–P*³ 2117, *LDAB* 5498)
III–IV AD	Greek–Latin conjugation table (transliterated)	P.Strasb. inv. G 1175 = Kramer 2001: no. 3 (*M–P*³ 2134.71, *LDAB* 9217)
III–IV AD	Greek–Latin conjugation table	*P.Oxy.* LXXVIII.5161 (*LDAB* 171906)

(cont.)

Century	Material	Where to find it
IV AD	Latin–Greek classified glossary	Kramer 1983: no. 10 (*M–P³* 3007, *LDAB* 5631)
IV AD	Latin–Greek classified glossary (transliterated)	*P.Fay.* 135v descr. = Kramer 1983: no. 11 (*M–P³* 2013.1, *LDAB* 7680)
IV AD	Latin–Greek glossary (transliterated)	*P.Lond.* II.481 = Dickey 2012–15: II section 4.3 (*M–P³* 3005, *LDAB* 5678)
IV AD	Latin–Greek glossary/colloquium	P.Berol. inv. 21860 = Dickey 2012–15: II section 4.2 (*M–P³* 3004.02, *LDAB* 8897)
IV AD	Aesop with Latin translation	*PSI* VII.848 = Kramer 2001: no. 10 (*M–P³* 52, *LDAB* 138)
IV AD	Virgil with Greek translation	*P.Ryl.* III.478 + P.Cairo inv. 85644 + *P.Mil.* I.1 = Scappaticcio 2013a: no. 5 (*M–P³* 2940, *LDAB* 4146)
IV AD	Virgil with Greek translation	*BKT* IX.39 = Scappaticcio 2013a: no. 4 (*M–P³* 2939.1, *LDAB* 4149)
IV AD	Terence with Greek glosses	*P.Oxy.* XXIV.2401 (*M–P³* 2934, *LDAB* 3982)
IV AD	Seneca's *Medea* with Greek notes	Markus and Schwendner 1997 (*M–P³* 2933.01, *LDAB* 3907)
IV AD	Latin grammatical notes	*P.Bodl.* I.2 = Scappaticcio 2013b (*M–P³* 2997.2, *LDAB* 6142)
IV–V AD	Latin alphabets with transliterated letter names	P.Ant. inv. 1 fr. 1 = Kramer 2001: no. 1 (*M–P³* 3012, *LDAB* 5832)
IV–V AD	Fragment of Colloquium Harleianum	*P.Prag.* II.118 = Dickey and Ferri 2012 (*M–P³* 3004.22, *LDAB* 6007)
IV–V AD	Cicero with Greek translation	*P.Rain.Cent.* 163 = Internullo 2011–12: no. 1 (*M–P³* 2922, *LDAB* 554)
IV–V AD	Virgil with Greek translation	Ambrosian Palimpsest = Scappaticcio 2013a: no. 8 (*M–P³* 2943, *LDAB* 4156)
IV–V AD	Virgil with Greek translation	*P.Fouad* 5 = Scappaticcio 2013a: no. 15 (*M–P³* 2948, *LDAB* 4154)
IV–V AD	Virgil glossary	*PSI* VII.756 = Scappaticcio 2013a: no. 13 (*M–P³* 2946, *LDAB* 4155)
IV–V AD	Terence with Greek glosses	P.Vindob. inv. L 103 = Danese 1989 (*M–P³* 2933.1, *LDAB* 3983)
IV–V AD	Sallust with Greek glosses	*PSI* I.110 = Funari 2008 (*M–P³* 2932, *LDAB* 3877)
IV–V AD	Ulpian (jurist) with Greek notes	*PSI* XIV.1449 (*M–P³* 2960, *LDAB* 4131)
IV–V AD	Grammatical exercise?	*P.Rain.Unterricht* 181 (*M–P³* 3015.21, *LDAB* 5861)
IV–V AD	Conjugation exercise	P.Vindob. inv. L 156 = *ChLA* XLV.1357 (*M–P³* 2167.02)
IV–VI AD	Gaius (jurist) with Greek notes	*PSI* XI.1182 (*M–P³* 2953, *LDAB* 1068)

Century	Material	Where to find it
V AD	Latin transcription of Greek alphabet	Feissel 2008 (*M–P³* 2704.06, *LDAB* 9949)
V AD	Greek–Latin classified glossary	P.Vindob. inv. L 150 = Kramer 2001: no. 5 (*M–P³* 2134.6, *LDAB* 6053)
V AD	Cicero with Greek translation	*P.Ryl.* I.61 = Internullo 2011–12: no. II (*M–P³* 2923, *LDAB* 4135)
V AD	Cicero with Greek translation	P.Vindob. inv. L 127 = Internullo 2011–12: no. III (*M–P³* 2923.1, *LDAB* 559)
V AD	Cicero with Greek translation	*PSI Congr.* XXI 2 = Internullo 2011–12: no. IV (*M–P³* 2921.01, *LDAB* 556)
V AD	Cicero with Greek notes	*P.Ryl.* III.477 (*M–P³* 2919, *LDAB* 558)
V AD	Virgil with Greek translation	Husselman 1957 = Scappaticcio 2013a: no. 33 (*M–P³* 2936, *LDAB* 4159)
V AD	Virgil with Greek translation	*P.Oxy.* L.3553 = Scappaticcio 2013a: no. 9 (*M–P³* 2943.1, *LDAB* 4160)
V AD	Virgil with Greek translation	P.Vindob. inv. L 24 = Scappaticcio 2013a: no. 20 (*M–P³* 2951, *LDAB* 4161)
V AD	Virgil with accents and macrons	*PSI* I.21 = Scappaticcio 2013a: no. 17 (*M–P³* 2949, *LDAB* 4158)
V AD	Legal text with Greek notes	*P.Ant.* III.153 (*M–P³* 2979.2, *LDAB* 6326)
V AD	Legal definitions and maxims	*PSI* XIII.1348 (*M–P³* 2982, *LDAB* 5796)
V–VI AD	Latin alphabets with Greek aids	*P.Oxy.* X.1315 descr. = Kramer 2001: no. 2 (*M–P³* 3013, *LDAB* 4163)
V–VI AD	Latin–Greek–Coptic colloquium	P.Berol. inv. 10582 = Dickey 2015a (*M–P³* 3009, *LDAB* 6075)
V–VI AD	Virgil glossary	*P.Oxy.* VIII.1099 = Scappaticcio 2013a: no. 19 (*M–P³* 2950, *LDAB* 4162)
V–VI AD	Juvenal with Greek notes	Roberts 1935 (*M–P³* 2925, *LDAB* 2559)
V–VI AD	Declension table with Greek glosses	Dickey, Ferri, and Scappaticcio 2013 (*M–P³* 2997, *LDAB* 6148)
V–VI AD	Greek commentary on legal texts	Fragmenta Sinaitica = Dareste 1880 (*M–P³* 2958, *LDAB* 3526)
V–VI AD	Grammatical exercise	*PSI* XIII.1309 = Scappaticcio 2013c: 46–50 (*M–P³* 3016, *LDAB* 6095)
VI AD	Latin–Greek/Greek–Latin alphabetical glossary	Fragmenta Helmstadiensia + Folium Wallraffianum = Kramer 1983: no. 4 (*M–P³* 2134.4, *LDAB* 6279)
VI AD	Virgil with Latin translation, Virgil glossary	*P.Ness.* II.1 (also called *P.Colt* 1) = Scappaticcio 2013a: no. 6 (*M–P³* 2939, *LDAB* 4166)

(cont.)

Century	Material	Where to find it
VI AD	Virgil with Latin translation	P.Vindob. inv. L 62 = Scappaticcio 2013a: no. 11 (*M–P³* 2944.1, *LDAB* 6194)
VI AD	Virgil with macrons	*P.Ness.* II.2 = Scappaticcio 2013a: no. 12 (*M–P³* 2945, *LDAB* 4164)
VI AD	Legal work with Greek notes	*P.Ant.* III.152 = Amelotti and Migliardi Zingale 1985: no. 4 (*M–P³* 2979.1, *LDAB* 6136)
VI AD	Greek index to Justinian's *Digest*	*PSI* I.55 (*M–P³* 2965, *LDAB* 2553)
VI AD	Justinian's *Digest* with Greek glosses	P.Sorb. inv. 2173 = de Ricci 1912 (*M–P³* 2966.1)
VI AD	Justinian's *Codex* with Greek glosses	*PSI* XIII.1347 = Amelotti and Migliardi Zingale 1985: no. 3 (*M–P³* 2970, *LDAB* 6272)
VI AD	Justinian's *Codex* with Greek glosses	P.Sorb. inv. 2219 + 2173 = Amelotti and Migliardi Zingale 1985: no. 2 (*M–P³* 2971, *LDAB* 2555)
VI AD	Index to Justinian's *Codex*	*P.Oxy.* XV.1814 = Amelotti and Migliardi Zingale 1985: no. 1 (*M–P³* 2969, *LDAB* 6324)
VI–VII AD	Justinian's *Digest* with Greek notes	P.Heid. inv. L 4 = Cavenaile 1958: no. 87 (*M–P³* 2966, *LDAB* 2557)

10.2 Texts surviving via the medieval manuscript tradition

Century	Material	Where to find it
various	Hermeneumata Pseudodositheana	Dickey 2012–15 + Goetz 1892, cf. Dionisotti 1982a
various	ps.-Philoxenus' Latin–Greek glossary	Goetz and Gundermann 1888: 1–212
various	ps.-Cyrillus' Greek–Latin glossary	Goetz and Gundermann 1888: 213–483
various	Idiomata (grammatical glossaries)	Goetz and Gundermann 1888: 487–597
IV AD	Charisius' grammar	Barwick 1964 = Keil 1857–80: I.1–296
IV AD	Dositheus' grammar	Bonnet 2005 = Keil 1857–80: VII.376–436
IV–V AD	Diomedes' grammar	Keil 1857–80: I.299–529
V AD	*Anonymus Bobiensis* grammar	De Nonno 1982 = Keil 1857–80: I.533–65; cf. Dionisotti 1984: 203–5
V AD	Cledonius' grammatical work	Keil 1857–80: V.9–79
V–VI AD	*Fragmentum Bobiense de nomine et pronomine*	Passalacqua 1984: 3–19 = Keil 1857–80: V.555–66; cf. Dionisotti 1984: 207–8
V–VI AD	*De verbo*	Passalacqua 1984: 21–60 = Keil 1857–80: V.634–54; cf. Dionisotti 1984: 206–7
VI AD	Priscian's grammar	Keil 1857–80: vols. II and III
VI AD	Eutyches' treatise on the verb	Keil 1857–80: V.447–89

Bibliography

Abbreviations of papyrological publications follow the *Checklist of Editions of Greek, Latin, Demotic, and Coptic Papyri, Ostraca, and Tablets*, online at: http://www.papyri.info/docs/ checklist. Other abbreviations include:

LSJ   *Greek–English Lexicon*, ed. H. G. Liddell, R. Scott, and H. S. Jones, 9th edn (Oxford 1940)

OLD   *Oxford Latin Dictionary*, ed. P. G. W. Glare (Oxford 1968–82)

TLL   *Thesaurus Linguae Latinae* (Leipzig 1900–)

Adams, J. N. (1982) *The Latin Sexual Vocabulary*. London.
    (2003a) *Bilingualism and the Latin Language*. Cambridge.
    (2003b) "The New Vindolanda Writing-Tablets," *Classical Quarterly* 53: 530–75.
Allen, W. S. (1978) *Vox Latina: A Guide to the Pronunciation of Classical Latin*, 2nd edn. Cambridge.
Allen, W. S., and Brink, C. O. (1980) "The Old Order and the New: A Case History," *Lingua* 50: 61–100.
Amelotti, M., and Migliardi Zingale, L. (1985) *Le costituzioni giustinianee nei papiri e nelle epigrafi*, 2nd edn. Milan.
Axer, J. (1983) "Reedition of the Viennese Fragments of Cicero, In Catilinam I," in *Festschrift zum 100-jährigen Bestehen der Papyrussammlung der Österreichischen Nationalbibliothek, Papyrus Erzherzog Rainer*. Vienna: 468–82.
Barwick, K. (1964) *Flavii Sosipatri Charisii Artis Grammaticae Libri v*. Leipzig.
Berschin, W. (1988) *Greek Letters and the Latin Middle Ages: From Jerome to Nicholas of Cusa*, revised edition translated by J. C. Frakes. Washington, DC.
Bischoff, B. (1951) "Das griechische Element in der abendländischen Bildung des Mittelalters," *Byzantinische Zeitschrift* 44: 27–55; reprinted in Bischoff (1967): 246–75.
    (1967) *Mittelalterliche Studien* II. Stuttgart.
Bloomer, W. M. (2011) *The School of Rome: Latin Studies and the Origins of Liberal Education*. Berkeley.
Bonner, S. F. (1977) *Education in Ancient Rome: From the Elder Cato to the Younger Pliny*. London.
Bonnet, G. (2005) *Dosithée: Grammaire latine*. Paris.
Boriaud, J.-Y. (1997) *Hygin: Fables*. Paris.
Cameron, A. (1976) *Circus Factions: Blues and Greens at Rome and Byzantium*. Oxford.
    (2004) *Greek Mythography in the Roman World*. New York.
Cavenaile, R. (1958) *Corpus Papyrorum Latinarum*. Wiesbaden.
Clackson, J., and Horrocks, G. (2007) *The Blackwell History of the Latin Language*. Malden, MA.

Clarysse, W., and Rochette, B. (2005) "Un Alphabet grec en charactères latins," *Archiv für Papyrusforschung* 51: 67–75.

Collart, P. (1940) "Glossaire latin–grec inédit sur un papyrus d'Oxyrhynchos," in *Mélanges de philologie, de littérature et d'histoire anciennes offerts à A. Ernout*. Paris: 61–74.

Cribiore, R. (1996) *Writing, Teachers, and Students in Graeco-Roman Egypt*. Atlanta.

(2001) *Gymnastics of the Mind: Greek Education in Hellenistic and Roman Egypt*. Princeton.

Cuvigny, H. (2003) *La route de Myos Hormos: l'armée romaine dans le désert oriental d'Égypte*. Cairo.

Daly, L. W. (1967) *Contributions to a History of Alphabetization in Antiquity and the Middle Ages*. Brussels.

Danese, R. M. (1989) "Revisione del PVindob L 103 (Terenzio)," *Studi Classici e Orientali* 39: 133–57.

Dareste, R. (1880) "Fragments inédits de droit romain," *Bulletin de Correspondance Hellénique* 4: 449–60.

Debut, J. (1983) "De l'usage des listes de mots comme fondement de la pédagogie dans l'antiquité," *Revue des Études Anciennes* 85: 261–74.

De Nonno, M. (1982) *La grammatica dell'Anonymus Bobiensis*. Rome.

Derda, T., Markiewicz, T., and Wipszycka, E. (eds) (2007) *Alexandria: Auditoria of Kom el-Dikka and Late Antique Education*. Warsaw.

De Ricci, S. (1912) "Deux Nouveaux Papyrus juridiques," in *Études d'histoire juridique offertes à Paul Frédéric Girard* I. Paris: 273–82.

Dickey, E. (2007) *Ancient Greek Scholarship*. New York.

(2010a) "The Creation of Latin Teaching Materials in Antiquity: A Re-Interpretation of P.Sorb. inv. 2069," *Zeitschrift für Papyrologie und Epigraphik* 175: 188–208.

(2010b) "Greek Dictionaries Ancient and Modern," in C. Stray (ed.), *Classical Dictionaries: Past, Present, and Future*. London: 5–24.

(2012–15) *The Colloquia of the Hermeneumata Pseudodositheana*. Cambridge.

(2015a) "How Coptic Speakers Learned Latin? A Reconsideration of P.Berol. inv. 10582," *Zeitschrift für Papyrologie und Epigraphik* 193: 65–77.

(2015b) "Columnar Translation: an Ancient Interpretive Tool that the Romans gave the Greeks," *Classical Quarterly* 65: 807–21.

(forthcoming a) "The Authorship of the Greek Version of Dositheus' Grammar and What It Tells us about the Grammar's Original Use," in R. Ferri and A. Zago (eds.), *The Latin of the Grammarians: Reflections about Language in the Roman World*. Turnhout.

(forthcoming b) "Word Division in Bilingual Texts," in G. Nocchi Macedo and M. C. Scappaticcio (eds.), *Signes dans les textes, textes sur les signes* (Papyrologica Leodiensia 6). Liège.

Dickey, E., and Ferri, R. (2010) "A New Edition of the Latin–Greek Glossary on P.Sorb. inv. 2069 (verso)," *Zeitschrift für Papyrologie und Epigraphik* 175: 177–87.

(2012) "A New Edition of the *Colloquium Harleianum* Fragment in P.Prag. 2.118," *Zeitschrift für Papyrologie und Epigraphik* 180: 127–32.

Dickey, E., Ferri, R., and Scappaticcio, M. C. (2013) "The Origins of Grammatical Tables: A Reconsideration of P.Louvre inv. E 7332," *Zeitschrift für Papyrologie und Epigraphik* 187: 173–89.

Dionisotti, A. C. (1982a) "From Ausonius' Schooldays? A Schoolbook and its Relatives," *Journal of Roman Studies* 72: 83–125.

(1982b) "On Bede, Grammars, and Greek," *Revue Bénédictine* 92: 111–41.

(1984) "Latin Grammar for Greeks and Goths," *Journal of Roman Studies* 74: 202–8.

Fagan, G. G. (1999) *Bathing in Public in the Roman World*. Ann Arbor.

Feissel, D. (2008) "Deux Modèles de cursive latine dans l'ordre alphabétique grec," in F. A. J. Hoogendijk and B. P. Muhs (eds.), *Sixty-Five Papyrological Texts Presented to Klaas A. Worp on the Occasion of his 65th Birthday*. Leiden: 53–64.

Flammini, G. (1990) "Prolegomeni alla recensio plenior degli Hermenumata pseudodositheana," *Giornale Italiano di Filologia* 42: 3–43.

(2004) *Hermeneumata Pseudodositheana Leidensia*. Munich.

Fournet, J.-L. (2003) "Langues, écritures et culture dans les *praesidia*," in Cuvigny (2003): 427–500.

Fressura, M. (2013) "Tipologie del glossario virgiliano," in M.-H. Marganne and B. Rochette (eds.), *Bilinguisme et digraphisme dans le monde gréco-romain: l'apport des papyrus latins*. Liège: 71–116.

Funari, R. (2008) "2 Sallustius 2 F: *Catil*. 10, 4–5; 11, 6–7," in *Corpus dei papiri storici greci e latini, parte B.1.2: Caius Sallustius Crispus*. Pisa: 51–62.

Gaebel, R. E. (1970) "The Greek Word-Lists to Vergil and Cicero," *Bulletin of the John Rylands Library* 52: 284–325.

Goetz, G. (1892) *Hermeneumata Pseudodositheana* (vol. III of *Corpus Glossariorum Latinorum*). Leipzig.

(1899) *Thesaurus Glossarum Emendatarum: Pars Prior* (vol. VI of *Corpus Glossariorum Latinorum*). Leipzig.

(1901) *Thesaurus Glossarum Emendatarum: Pars Posterior* (vol. VII of *Corpus Glossariorum Latinorum*). Leipzig.

Goetz, G., and Gundermann, G. (1888) *Glossae Latinograecae et Graecolatinae* (vol. II of *Corpus Glossariorum Latinorum*). Leipzig.

Herren, M. W. (ed.) (1988) *The Sacred Nectar of the Greeks: The Study of Greek in the West in the Early Middle Ages*. London.

Honoré, A. M. (1965) "The Fragmentum Dositheanum," *Revue Internationale des Droits de l'Antiquité* 3rd ser. 12: 301–23.

Husselman, E. M. (1957) "A Palimpsest Fragment from Egypt," in *Studi in onore di Aristide Calderini e Roberto Paribeni* II. Milan: 453–9.

Internullo, D. (2011–12) "Cicerone latinogreco: corpus dei papiri bilingui delle Catilinarie di Cicerone," *Papyrologica Lupiensia* 20–1: 25–150.

Joyal, M., McDougall, I., and Yardley, J. C. (2009) *Greek and Roman Education: A Sourcebook*. New York.

Kaczynski, B. M. (1988) *Greek in the Carolingian Age: The St. Gall Manuscripts.* Cambridge, MA.

Kaster, R. (1988) *Guardians of Language: The Grammarian and Society in Late Antiquity.* Berkeley.

Keil, H. (1857–80) *Grammatici Latini.* Leipzig.

Kramer, J. (1983) *Glossaria Bilinguia in Papyris et Membranis Reperta.* Bonn.

    (1996) "Der lateinisch–griechische Vergilpalimpsest aus Mailand," *Zeitschrift für Papyrologie und Epigraphik* 111: 1–20.

    (2001) *Glossaria Bilinguia Altera.* Munich.

    (2007a) *Vulgärlateinische Alltagsdokumente auf Papyri, Ostraka, Täfelchen und Inschriften.* Berlin.

    (2007b) "P.Amh. II 26, 25: *bulpeculam imfortunam*," *Archiv für Papyrusforschung* 53: 45–52.

    (2010) "Neuedition des lateinisch–griechisch–koptischen Gesprächsbuchs von Berlin (P.Berol. inv. 10582, LDAB 6075)," in H. Knuf, C. Leitz, and D. von Recklinghausen (eds.), *Honi soit qui mal y pense: Studien zum pharaonischen, griechisch–römischen und spätantiken Ägypten zu Ehren von Heinz-Josef Thissen.* Leuven: 557–66.

Markus, D., and Schwendner, G. W. (1997) "Seneca's *Medea* in Egypt (663–704)," *Zeitschrift für Papyrologie und Epigraphik* 117: 73–80.

McNamee, K. (2007) *Annotations in Greek and Latin Texts from Egypt.* New Haven.

Morgan, T. (1998) *Literate Education in the Hellenistic and Roman Worlds.* Cambridge.

Passalacqua, M. (1984) *Tre testi grammaticali Bobbiesi (GL V 555–566; 634–654; IV 207–216 Keil).* Rome.

Perry, B. E. (1952) *Aesopica.* Urbana.

Priest, N. E. (1977) "A List of Gods," *Zeitschrift für Papyrologie und Epigraphik* 27: 193–200.

Roberts, C. H. (1935) "The Antinoë Fragment of Juvenal," *Journal of Egyptian Archaeology* 21: 199–209.

Rochette, B. (1990) "Les traductions grecques de l'*Énéide* sur papyrus: une contribution à l'étude du bilinguisme gréco-romain au Bas-Empire," *Les Études Classiques* 58: 333–46.

    (1997) *Le latin dans le monde grec: recherches sur la diffusion de la langue et des lettres latines dans les provinces hellénophones de l'empire romain.* Brussels.

Rössl, J. (1974) "Studien zur Frühgeschichte und Historiographie Zwettls im 12. Jahrhundert" (diss. Vienna).

Russell, D. A. (2001) *Quintilian: The Orator's Education.* Cambridge, MA.

Scappaticcio, M. C. (2009) "Appunti per una riedizione dei frammenti del Palinsesto Virgiliano dell'Ambrosiana," *Archiv für Papyrusforschung* 55: 96–120.

    (2011) "Sull' *unde* del *PSorb.* inv. 2069 (lin. 84–87): il modello di un *de accentibus*?," *Maia* 63: 552–65.

    (2013a) *Papyri Vergilianae: l'apporto della papirologia alla storia della tradizione virgiliana (I–VI d.C.).* Liège.

(2013b) "La *scriptio inferior* latina del *P.Bodl.* I 2 (inv. Gr. bibl. d. 2): lemmi e flessioni parziali in forma tabulare, tra lessico giuridico e *Artes grammaticae*," *Archiv für Papyrusforschung* 59: 326–46.

(2013c) "Un dibattito processuale bilingue, il *De trinitate* di Faustino Luciferiano, il salmo 52, e un'*exercitatio scribendi* latina: il *PSI* XIII 1309, un felice riciclo dalla Ossirinco della tarda antichità," *Analecta Papyrologica* 25: 23–52.

(forthcoming): *Artes grammaticae in frammenti: i testi grammaticali latini e bilingui greco-latini su papiro: edizione commentata.* Berlin.

Schad, S. (2007) *A Lexicon of Latin Grammatical Terminology.* Pisa.

Schiller, A. A. (1971a) "Vindication of a Repudiated Text: *Sententiae et Epistolae Hadriani*," in *La critica del testo: atti del Secondo congresso internazionale della Società italiana di storia del diritto.* Florence: 717–27.

(1971b) "*Alimenta* in the *Sententiae Hadriani*," in *Studi in onore di Giuseppe Grosso* IV. Turin: 399–415.

Schubart, W. (1913) "Ein lateinisch–griechisch–koptisches Gesprächsbuch," *Klio* 13: 27–38.

Slater, W. J. (1986) *Aristophanis Byzantii Fragmenta.* Berlin.

Thomas, J. D. (2007) "Latin Texts and Roman Citizens," in A. K. Bowman, R. A. Coles, N. Gonis, D. Obbink, and P. J. Parsons (eds.), *Oxyrhynchus: A City and its Texts.* London: 231–43.

Uría, J. (2009) *Arte gramática: libro 1.* Madrid.

Wessely, K. (1886) "Bericht über griechische Papyri in Paris und London," *Wiener Studien* 8: 175–230.